CHORA
Managing Editor: Alberto Pérez-Gómez

CHORA, the Greek word for "space," is the title of a new collection of books devoted to exploring the potential of architecture beyond conventional aesthetic and technological reductions. In a world where unabated scientism and irrelevant nihilism are prevalent, where the supposed alternatives to the rationalist and functionalist building practices of modernity are often no more than empty formalism and extrapolation of deconstructivist positions into architecture, CHORA offers a forum for pondering other possibilities. Is it possible to affirm the specificity of architecture vis-à-vis both technological building and the mass media, while avoiding futile turns into nostalgia? Can we recognize the truth present in our architectural tradition and the hope revealed in our presence as embodied human beings, while rejecting the dangerous delusions of absolute, transparent truth and logocentric power?

Architecture is at a crossroads. If its role as a stage for the perpetuation of human culture is not recognized and redefined, its demise will be inevitable. The work of the architect – a work of imagination – cannot be simply a dominating gaze, a solipsistic play of mirrors, or a manifestation of the will to power. It may yet be something different – something that must be explored and that may, as reconciliatory action, point to a referent *other* than itself. In a world where the media establish new paradigms of communication approaching the ephemeral nature of embodied perception and the primary orality of language, architecture may indeed be able to carry intersubjective values, convey meaning through metaphor, and embody a cultural order beyond tyranny or anarchy.

CHORA will offer a space to meditate on the possibility of such an architecture, capable of both respecting cultural differences and acknowledging the globalization of technological culture. Interdisciplinary by definition, and reflecting a variety of cultural concerns, its essays will operate from *within* the discipline of architecture. Generated by personal questions of pressing concern for architecture and our culture, these radical explorations of form and content may suggest alternatives for a more significant practice. While the main philosophical framework for CHORA stems from phenomenology and hermeneutic ontology, the architectural pursuits in this collection could be placed generally in the broad context of European philosophy, which demands a fundamental redefinition of thought and action, and a substantial rethinking of traditionally accepted values.

I INTERVALS IN THE PHILOSOPHY OF ARCHITECTURE (1994)
Edited by Alberto Pérez-Gómez and Stephen Parcell

Chora 1: Intervals in the Philosophy

of Architecture

Chora

VOLUME ONE

Intervals in the Philosophy
of Architecture

Edited by Alberto Pérez-Gómez
and Stephen Parcell

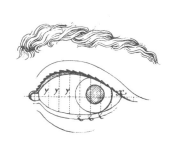

Published for
the History and Theory of
Architecture Graduate Program,
McGill University
by
McGill-Queen's University Press
Montreal & Kingston
London   Buffalo

CHORA is a publication of the History and Theory of Architecture graduate program at McGill University, Montreal, Canada

MANAGING EDITOR

Alberto Pérez-Gómez

EDITORS

Alberto Pérez-Gómez, *McGill University*
Stephen Parcell, *Technical University of Nova Scotia*

ADVISORY BOARD

Annmarie Adams, *McGill University*
Ricardo L. Castro, *McGill University*
Derek Drummond, *McGill University*
Marco Frascari, *University of Pennsylvania*
Arthur Kroker, *Concordia University*
Donald Kunze, *Pennsylvania State University*
Phyllis Lambert, *Canadian Centre for Architecture*
David Leatherbarrow, *University of Pennsylvania*
David Michael Levin, *Northwestern University*
Katsuhiko Muramoto, *Pennsylvania State University*
Juhani Pallasmaa, *University of Helsinki*
Stephen Parcell, *Technical University of Nova Scotia*
Louise Pelletier, *McGill University*

SECRETARIAL ASSISTANCE

Susie Spurdens

EDITORIAL ASSISTANCE

Michel Forand

Legal deposit third quarter 1994
Bibliothèque nationale du Québec

Printed on acid-free paper in Canada

Canadian Cataloguing in Publication Data

Chora : intervals in the philosophy of architecture
   1994–
   Annual.
   ISSN 1198-449X
   1. Architecture – Philosophy – Periodicals. I. McGill University.
   History and Theory of Architecture Graduate Program.
   NA1.C46   720'.1   C94-900762-5

Typeset in Sabon 11/13 by Caractéra production graphique inc.,
Quebec City.

Contents

Chora: The Space of Architectural Representation

Alberto Pérez-Gómez

Chora

WHAT DOES ARCHITECTURE REPRESENT within the context of every-day life? Given its techno-political context, is it even conceivable that this well-proven instrument of power may represent something other than male, egocentric will or repressive political or economic forces? Could it be that despite its common origin with instrumental and technological forms of representation, it may nonetheless allow for participatory human action and an affirmation of life-towards-death through symbolization as "presencing" through the constructed work, rather than manifest the very denial of man's capacity to recognize existential meaning in privileged artifacts such as works of art? Could it then embody values of a different order than those rooted in fashion, formal experimentation, or publicity and be cast in forms other than the seductive gloss characterizing all mechanisms of cultural domination today?

As we near the end of the millennium, the time may have come for us to attempt to differentiate between architecture and building in terms other than those of eighteenth-century aesthetics – to reach beyond the exhausted philosophical distinction between the good and the beautiful and to articulate the specific status of architecture as embodying wisdom while remaining in the context of a thoroughly utilitarian, constructed world – our technological world. If this distinction can be made, it is crucial, for the survival of a civilization whose worth is manifest in the great works of art and artifacts that constitute our common cultural traditions, that the cause of architecture be furthered. We must now urgently reconsider the possibility of a radically different ethics as the basis for all human action because of the technological world that we have created. It is a world where we control so much that we can effectively destroy decorous human life through genetic engineering or pollute the universe to death, but individually – both men and women, despite the false political rhetoric to the contrary – we seem to have in fact lost ground with respect to the possibility of making effective choices about our personal existence and destiny. In this context, we simply cannot afford to give up our quest to identify what constitutes a mean-ingful order for human life – the promotion and perpetuation of which has been the inveterate concern of architecture – nor can we simply accept market indicators, personal success, aesthetic fashion, some vague formal mysticism, indices of giddiness and titillation, or mere "difference" as the criteria for an appropriate, purportedly significant, architectural practice in the age of nihilism.

● ▲ ■

The origins of architecture, according to Vitruvius (Cesariano edition, 1521).

Closer to the outset of our architectural tradition, Vitruvius identified the origins of architecture with the origins of language.[1] In a moving passage that re-creates the beginning of humanity, the Roman writer describes how some thickly crowded trees, tossed around by storms and winds, and rubbing their branches against one another, caught fire. Men first ran away like animals, terrified by the fury of the blaze. Eventually they approached the quieter fire and realized that it kept them warm. They subsequently added more wood to the fire and learned to keep it burning. As a result of this social event, they stayed together and uttered their first words, learning to name the reconciliatory act that had kept them alive. With this initial poetic naming came the *poiesis* of architecture, the possibility of making. It should be noted that they did not steal the fire from the gods. This architectural action was an act of affirmation taking place in a space that was, from its inception, social – that is, cultural and linguistic.

Following this realization, Vitruvius also insists that architects *sine litteris* are no good. In the opening passages of Book 1, he establishes that architecture consists of *fabrica et raciocinatione*, terms that have variously been translated as "practice and theory" (Morgan) or "craftsmanship and technology" (Granger). These modern renditions are obviously problematic. Vitruvius is simply alluding to that which is made (from *faber*) and that which names it, which "gives it reason" – its ratio or *logos*. This *ratio* is epitomized by mathematical proportion, the most unambiguous of potential "namings," the clearest sign that architecture embodies *ta mathemata*, the invariable, an order that may enable man to dwell on this earth. For Vitruvius, this is the crucial knowledge that the architect must possess in order to guide his practice. Numerical proportions referred ultimately to the perceived order of the supra-lunar world, an immutable order that functioned as a paradigm for the human orders and that needed to be brought to appearance in the sub-lunar world, ridden by constant unpredictability and change. It is not surprising that the presence of numerical proportions in architecture underlined the tradition of theoretical texts until the late eighteenth century. Vitruvius himself proposed that the discursive order of cosmology was indeed the *significatur* of the constructed work named as *significat*, the architecture that signifies.[2]

That distinction, if taken superficially and without a consideration of the semantic horizon of Vitruvius's own words, seems to condemn the architecture of modernity, particularly after Durand and the French Revolution, to a necessary meaninglessness. As I have elaborated elsewhere concerning the history of architectural theories, one of the major events in the history of epistemology was the disintegration, early in the nineteenth century, of a cosmological picture grounded in divine transcendence.[3] It was not long before Nietzsche could question the age-old distinction between nature and culture. Having lost its cosmological referent, does this mean that a radically secularized architecture either is condemned to become homogenized with technological building or, at best, must pretend to operate legitimately in a space outside language?

Today the *significatur* of architecture can no longer be a discursive *logos*, with its emphasis on clarity and "truth as correspondence"; it cannot be a cosmology, a formal aesthetic, or a functional or technological logic. The signified is a *poetic* discourse, and if we pay close attention to

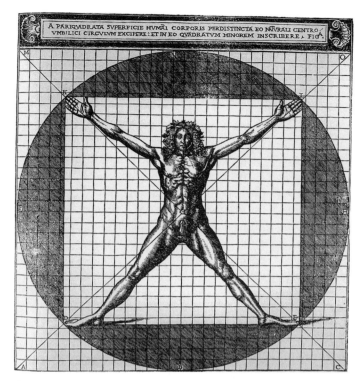

Vitruvius, Man at the centre of cosmic geometry (Cesariano edition, 1521).

the significant work of the last two centuries, we realize that the architect has indeed become a "writer" – implicitly or explicitly, a narrator of events – disclosing "fictional" modes of dwelling by deconstructing and twisting the language of technology, both in his constructions and through his words. This is already a sketchy anticipation of my polemical conclusion, an argument that needs careful elaboration.

Significant, to me, are works in the tradition of Lequeu, Gaudí, Le Corbusier, Hejduk, Lewerentz, and Aalto. This list, no more than an impressionistic sample, is obviously not meant to be exhaustive. My intention, however, is to demonstrate how these works refer to the most authentic tradition of architecture and, at the same time, also respond genuinely to the demands of our own time "at the end of progress" and linear history – a time qualified by Heidegger as too late for the gods and too early for Being, and by some cultural historians as postmodernity. Indeed, as many critics have pointed out, the dilemma ultimately concerns an architecture for a cultural epoch that is defined by a new beginning and yet cannot pretend to overcome modernity and leave behind its fundamental roots in historicity but can only shift and redefine its critical terms, such as the meaning of past and future, reconstituted in a novel shape of time that has been anticipated by artists and writers of the last two centuries.

To shed some light on that dilemma, I will follow the seemingly oblique route of historical interpretation – in fact, our only legitimate means for the articulation of practice. I will discuss the original Greek understanding of the "space" of architecture at the dawn of discursive reason, elaborate on its pre-Socratic connotations, and trace a brief historical sketch of this issue, eventually returning to the first question: How can the architecture of the late twentieth century "represent" and yet aspire to retrieve its status as an architecture of "presence"?

● ▲ ■

For the purposes of this meditation, I will begin with Plato and work backward and forward from his *Timaeus*.[4] Plato, of course, marks the origin of our scientific tradition. We all know of his predilection for ideas over the objects of personal experience that are merely their shadow, and of his low opinion of artists whose work is merely a copy of a copy. Yet Plato's position is infinitely more complex than this. It is true that he championed the cause of "truth as correspondence" – that is, of the presumed identity of truth and Being that marked the two millennia of philosophy and science after him and that led to "enframing" (Heidegger) and perspectival objectification (that is, to the growing concealment of Being until its present occultation). On the other hand, Plato also understood that like the sun itself, absolute truth and goodness – *agathon* – could never be contemplated directly and made objects of pure knowledge, but rather had to be experienced as the "lighting" that makes it possible for the things of our world to be what they are. Any artifact or work of art that allowed such lighting to be experienced was therefore highly appreciated. Both Hans-Georg Gadamer and Eric Voeglin have added much to our understanding of Plato, and I will use their insights in my argument.[5]

Timaeus is the first systematization of the universe, rendered intelligible in a discourse that seems generally autonomous from myth. Plato's formulation of a geometrical universe became the source of inspiration for cosmological pictures in the Western world until Newton, and that universe was thus accepted as the structure of *physis* (nature), the macrocosm that architecture's microcosm was meant to emulate and whose mathematical structure (*ratio*, proportion) was a symbol that assured meaningful work. Being, symbolized by mathematical proportion, was intentionally embodied in man-made artifacts such as machines for war and peace, buildings, gardens, and solar clocks. The aim was to propitiate a virtuous life and ultimately to seduce Fortune (destiny) and frame human institutions (and power!) with *the* true order. Harmoniously taking measure of time and space was the privileged mode of human participation in the order of the real.

Plato's own articulation of reality, however, is not a simple duality of Being and Becoming. As he refines his discourse in *Timaeus*, beginning at section 16, he feels the need to introduce a *third* term to do justice to his experience of human affairs. After identifying this third distinct form, he immediately realizes that this one is "difficult and obscure" to speak about. "In general terms, it is the receptacle and, as it were, the nurse of all becoming and change."[6] Before naming this third term as *chora* (space, place), he endeavours to define it in relation to our common understanding of the world, matter and generation. First, we learn that this term is the "stuff" of the world, that primordial element which constitutes both humans and nature, given that "the names fire, earth, water, air really indicate differences of quality not of substance."[7] As everything in the world is in the process of change and those four most elemental substances are, in the end, never stable, we should speak of them not as "things" but rather as qualities. The receptacle is then compared to a mass of neutral plastic material upon which differing impressions are stamped. This *prima materia* has no definite character of its own, yet it is the ultimate reality of all things.

To explain this, Plato introduces the example of a goldsmith who crafts many different geometrical shapes out of gold, continuously remoulding each shape into another. The most appropriate name for the craftsman's work is "gold" rather than "triangles," "squares," or the like. "The same argument applies to the natural receptacle of all bodies. It can always be called the same because it never alters its characteristics ... We may indeed use the metaphor of birth and compare the receptacle to the mother, the model (Being) to the father, and what they produce between them to their offspring."[8] Following from an ancient misconception of genetics, Plato assumed that the mother was an appropriate metaphor for his neutral receptacle because biological traits were believed to be an exclusive attribute of the male semen. It is also interesting to note that in describing the marrow – the male life-substance and seed, which (he believed) flowed

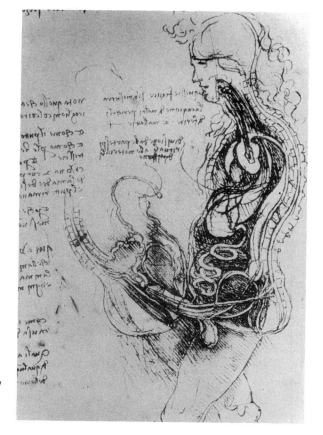

Leonardo da Vinci's image of human
procreation, showing the traditionally
assumed connection between the
brain and the penis (c. 1500).

between the lofty spherical head, seat of ideas, and the penis – he also
describes a substance practically identical to the neutral plastic mass/
receptacle in question, composed of "smooth and unwarped" triangles,
capable of producing "the purest fire, water, air, and earth." Genetic
misconceptions aside, this *prima materia* is androgynous, a receptacle of
all "visible and sensible things" that is itself "invisible and formless, all-
embracing, *possessed in a most puzzling way of intelligibility, yet very
hard to grasp.*"[9]

Thus Plato concludes that there must be three components of reality:
first, "the unchanging form, uncreated and indestructible ... imperceptible
to sight or the other senses, the object of thought" (Being); second, "that
which bears the same name as the form and resembles it, but is sensible,
has come into existence, is in constant motion ... and is apprehended by
opinion with the aid of sensation" (Becoming); and third, *chora*, "which
is eternal and indestructible, which provides a position for everything that
comes to be, and which is apprehended without the senses by a sort of
spurious reasoning and so is hard to believe in – we look at it indeed in
a kind of dream and say that everything that exists must be somewhere
and occupy some space, and that what is nowhere in heaven or earth is

nothing at all."[10] In the following paragraph, Plato identifies this receptacle with the space of chaos, "a kind of shaking implement" that separates the four basic elements out of itself, so to speak, to constitute the world as we know it. Linked etymologically to the Indo-European *chasho*, chaos maintains its connotations as a primordial gap, opening, or abyss, as well as a primordial substance.

What can we make of all this? Plato is describing nothing less than the space of human creation and participation, postulating a coincidence between *topos* (natural place) and *chora*, yet naming the latter as a distinct reality to be apprehended in the crossing, in the *chiasma*, of Being and Becoming. This disclosure is a prerogative of human artifacts, and in the particular context of Plato's tradition it was the province of poetry and art.

Chora is both cosmic place and abstract space, and it is also the substance of the human crafts. In architecture, it would undermine the common distinction – which in fact dates from only the nineteenth century! – between contained space and material container. *Most importantly, it would point to an invisible ground that exists beyond the linguistic identity of Being and Becoming, while also making language and culture possible in the first place.* It is the "region" of that which exists. The problem, as Plato emphasizes, is that its presence and reality can be grasped only with great difficulty – obliquely, so to speak – through a kind of "bastard reasoning."

● ▲ ■

Prior to Plato, there was no name for this third term. Indeed, the absence of this awareness characterizes the world of myth. In the specific context of ancient Greece, we can support this conclusion by observing the pairing of the goddess Hestia and the god Hermes. Jean-Pierre Vernant argues that, among the six major divine couples who appear on the base of the great statue of Zeus at Olympia, only the coupling of Hermes and Hestia cannot be accounted for through genealogy.[11] This pair, in fact, seems to represent a religious articulation of space and movement, of centre and path, of immutability and change. While Hestia refers to domesticity, femininity, the earth, darkness, centrality, and stability – all qualities of interior "space" – Hermes is identified with the masculine values of mobility and threshold, of changing states, openness, and contact with the outside world, the light, and the sky – qualities associated with the external, public spaces of action. What must be emphasized is that the *pair* reveals how space and movement were not detached as independent, abstract concepts in this cultural context. Both were always present, together with other aspects, in the concrete experience of reality as "Thou" rather than as a scientific or philosophical "it."

It is difficult for us to conceive a personified, wilful, and therefore totally unpredictable external reality, identical and continuous with the self, needing constant propitiation through human actions to secure the survival of the world from one instant to the next. Nevertheless, this is precisely the context of ritual. One could indeed argue that external reality – that is, nature – was so thoroughly articulated through myth as a cultural construction that there was a homology between the "mountain" and the "pyramid," between the *tholos* and the cave ... Yet these acts of ritual construction were part of an a priori order, they were affirmations of the "given" – indeed, a gift – through a propitiatory action in the infinite thickness of the present, rather than product-oriented projects. These reflections will be helpful when we return to the problem of the potential meaning of architecture in the context of our technological world – a meaning that perhaps signals, at the end of Western metaphysics, a *ricorso* of history that, while recognizing a distance from the first beginning, seriously acknowledges the collapse of nature into culture as the locus of "political" action.

A well-known ritual in ancient Greece became the historical precedent of Western art and architecture. Aristotle himself gives us a clue when he states that both tragedy and comedy, at first mere improvisation, originated with the leaders of the dithyramb.[12] The dithyramb was originally a spring ritual dedicated to Dionysus. The word itself meant a leaping, an inspired dance, and in its original form was an actual bringing-back of life, a rising-up or calling-up that took the form of *dromena*, actual "things done," such as song and dance.[13] Of course, it is no surprise that the great tragedies of Aeschylus, Sophocles, and Euripides were performed in Athens during early April, at a festival in honour of Dionysus.

The ritual origins of the Western work of art, as manifest in the Greek

Top right: The Minoan ritual dance platform at the Palace in Knossos, Crete (c. 1500 B.C.).

Bottom right: Remains of the Theatre of Dionysus in Athens (fourth century B.C.). Only the foundations of the permanent stage can be seen.

theatre, hold many lessons for architecture. The dramas were most likely played not on the stage but in the *orchestra*, particularly in the early stages of the development of the *dromenon* into drama. The *chorus*, that group of dancing and singing men often in charge of lamenting destiny, was always at the centre of the action. Its actual role is difficult to comprehend and digest for many a modern observer. The focus of the event was the circular dance platform often named after the *choros* itself, a chorus that originally signified a group dance and eventually took its name from *orchesis*, which also means dance.[14] We have evidence from Roman texts of the second century A.D. that such events, combining poetry, music, and dance in their architectural frame, were believed to have a cathartic effect. In fact, both *katharsis* and *mimesis* seem to have been employed quite early in relation to art. *Katharsis* meant a purification or a reconciliation between the darkness of personal destiny and the light of the divine *dike*, as expressed in the tragedy.[15] *Mimesis*, also in relation to the *choreia*, signified not imitation but rather the expression of feelings and the manifestation of experiences through movement, musical harmonies, and the rhythms of speech – an acknowledgement, through the body's presence, of its intermediate location *between* Being and Becoming.

We must now read Vitruvius's description of the theatre in his *Ten Books*, in relation to both the event of the tragedy and the mythical origin of the constructive arts. On the latter question, we must recall some pertinent aspects that appear in the myth of Daedalus, who personified the first Western architect.[16] One of Daedalus's major commissions was the design of a *chora* or dance platform in Knossos. This followed his more famous commission to build the labyrinth; both were unequivocal sites of dance and drama. While the figure of the labyrinth made explicit the mythical co-presence of path (Hermes) and space (Hestia), and became a privileged symbol of cities (and architecture in general) in the Western tradition, the same co-presence remained implicit in the *chora* or dance platform. Although an excursus into the theme of the labyrinth is always tempting, it is only crucial for us to remember that the labyrinth was a condensed symbol of human life (one entry, one centre) and of the presence of order in apparent disorder, and that it originated in the Trojan games as a dance that, according to the *Aeneid*, was performed in Troy on two occasions – to celebrate the founding of the city and to honour the dead.[17] The labyrinth is therefore a frozen choreography that remains present but invisible in the *orchestra* of the Greek theatre.[18]

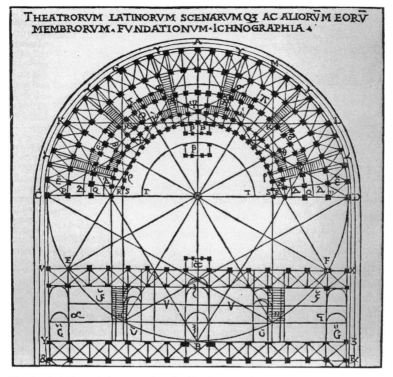

The classical (Roman) theatre as described by Vitruvius (Cesariano edition, 1521).

Whereas ritual enables primitive man to propitiate the external world and dwell in a totality, the Greek theatre frames the transformation of the same task, now in the realm of art. The introduction of the amphitheatre poignantly represents the profound epistemological transformation signalled by the advent of philosophy. This becomes a place for seeing, where a distant contemplation of the epiphany would have the same cathartic effect on the observer as was accomplished previously through active, embodied participation in the ritual. This distance is, of course, akin to the theoretical distance introduced by the philosophers, which enabled a participation in the wholeness of the universe through rational understanding, as a disclosure of discursive *logos*. This, we must remember, is the same distance that created the conditions for the eventual concealment of Being, for the objectification and enframing that resulted in the substitution of the world for its scientific "picture," leading to instrumental rationality and to the crisis of representation that confronts us today.

Emphasizing the importance of a healthy site for the theatre, Vitruvius writes: "When plays are given, the spectators, with their wives and children, sit through them spellbound, and their bodies, motionless from enjoyment, have their pores open, into which blowing winds find their way."[19] The human voice of the actors, being "a flowing breath of air" and moving "in an endless number of circular rounds, like the innumerable increasing circular waves which appear when a stone is thrown into smooth water," demanded that architects perfect the ascending rows of seats in the theatre by means "of the canonical theory of the mathematicians and the musicians."[20] It is in the design of the theatre that the architect must apply his knowledge of harmony, and here Vitruvius introduces musical modes and intervals, followed by tetrachords and a discussion of the sounding bronze vessels to be placed under the seats. The plan of the theatre is then constructed in accordance with the image of the sky, starting from a circle and inscribing four equilateral triangles, "as the astrologers do in a figure of the twelve signs of the zodiac, when they are making computations from the musical harmony of the stars."[21]

Although Vitruvius is describing the Roman (and not the Greek) theatre, his account of its reality as a cosmic place, disclosed through the event of the tragedy, is poignant enough. It is here that architecture "happens," disclosing an order that is both spatial and temporal. Framed by architecture, tragedy inhabits a space of transition, its ultimate theme being the event in-between the Dionysian and the Apollonian. The event takes place in the choir, the space, the *chora*, for an epiphany of the Platonic *metaxy*. If one understands with Eric Voeglin that this Platonic notion defines a human existence that is not a given, static fact but rather "a disturbing moment in the in-between of ignorance and knowledge, of time and timelessness, of imperfection and perfection, of hope and fulfilment and ultimately of life and death,"[22] the issue of meaning for man involves participation in a movement with a direction to be found or missed. Greek tragedy in its gestural frame, the Greek theatre, constitutes the supreme epiphany of belonging and wholeness (meaning) to be attained by individual citizens "at a distance." The well-known effect that Aristotle named catharsis speaks for itself. The re-enactment of the tragedy purified, centred, and appeased the spectators, and in a world where disorders were always understood to be psychosomatic, it is not surprising to find that the tragedy was deemed to have powerful healing effects, as demonstrated by the presence of the great theatre of Epidaurus in the sanctuary of Asclepius the healer.

Drama is experienced as a tight weaving of temporality and spatiality. Its effect must be attributed to the narrative dictated by the poet, as

Remains of the Theatre at the Sanctuary of Asclepius in Epidaurus (fourth century B.C.).

opposed to the plurality and diversity of traditional myths; it is in agreement with the philosophical understanding of the purposefulness of the movements of the cosmos. Catharsis, a recognition of the presence of Being in the events of everyday life, does not rely on ordinary language (prose). The language of drama is a poetic language, the language of metaphor, and it maintains a high-tension gap between the two terms of metaphorical speech, exposing the audience to the nearness of distance. The receptacle, *chora* – dance platform or *orchestra* – takes its shape through *mimesis* from Being and Becoming. We must recall how, in his *Poetics*, Aristotle posits *mimesis* as a function of art: rhyme, rhythm, eurhythmy, and harmony are but attributes of what the spectator recognizes as a universal ground in the possible but improbable plot of the tragedy, always new and striking and yet uncannily familiar.

We are now in a better position to understand the nature of *chora* as paradigmatic architectural work, again recalling its importance in the myth of Daedalus. It is simultaneously the work and the space, its ground or lighting; that which is unveiled, the truth embodied by art, and the space between the word and the experience. It is both a space for contemplation and a space of participation – a space of recognition. It is my contention that in this liminal understanding of architecture as a space for the dance, as a place for the poetic motility that distinguishes human beings from other animals, as a "choreo-graphy" woven by language in a narrative form, we find the ever-present "origin" of the work of architecture, an approximation of its invisible significance.

●　▲　■

During the Renaissance, transformations in theology and architectural theory, and more specifically in their concepts about the theatre, already reflected a different understanding of the Greco-Roman *chora*. Renaissance artists, as is well known, developed an interest in geometrical perspective, or *perspectiva artificialis*.[23] In painting, the visible rendering of reality soon represented geometric space to display the mathematical structure of depth. This event was invariably an ontological disclosure, always given with a "thickness" resistant to monocular vision and homogenization. There is no point at infinity in Renaissance painting. For architects, on the other hand, *scenographia* or *perspectiva artificialis* concerned specifically the design of theatrical space, stages for urban celebrations and the recreated *skene* of theatre buildings. This is demon-

The stage of Palladio's *Teatro Olimpico* in Vicenza (sixteenth century).

"Tableau vivant" from Johannes Bochius, *The Ceremonial Entry of Ernst, Archduke of Austria, into Antwerp* (1594).

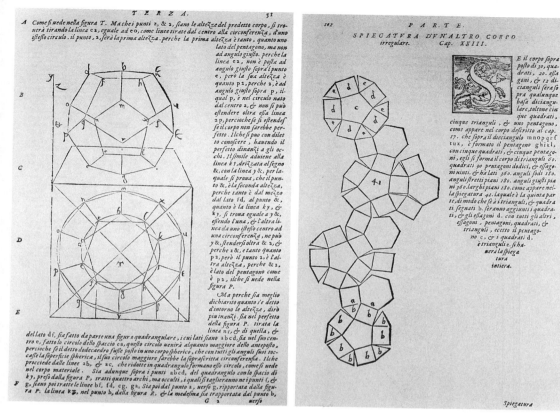

Danielle Barbaro's planimetric studies of solids and their perspective, from *La pratica della Perspettiva* (Venice, 1569).

strated most explicitly in Danielle Barbaro's *La Pratica della Perspettiva* (1569). Barbaro emphasizes that the principal tools of architectural ideation of which Vitruvius spoke did not include *scenographia* (together with plan and elevation); rather, Barbaro says, Vitruvius meant *sciographia*, interpreted by Barbaro as section. Interestingly, though, Barbaro then proceeds to show, like Luca di Pacioli before him, the planimetric development of space-filling bodies that are generated by proportional ratios and that eventually are shown in perspective.

In this regard, we should remember how Pacioli, the brilliant mathematician from Umbria, friend of Alberti and Leonardo, and disciple of Piero della Francesca, recast the Platonic *chora* in his book on the Golden Section (1507). Besides the mystical and Christian properties associated with this unique proportion, Luca emphasizes that the Golden Section is the proportion implicit in the pentagon, which in turn is the basic surface of the dodecahedron, one of the Platonic solids, and the one identified with the "quintessence." We may recall that the four other solids – the tetrahedron, the cube, the octahedron, and the icosahedron – were related

18

Sebastiano Serlio's Tragic Stage, from *Architettura e prospettiva* (1519).

by Plato in his *Timaeus* to the four basic elements: fire, earth, air, and water. The quintessence is the origin of all the other elements (like Plato's *chora*), regulated by a dynamic proportion that can be seen as an empirical regulator of organic growth and as the ultimate symbol of ontological continuity. This dodecahedron, the *prima materia*, is also the receptacle that circumscribes the four other platonic solids in this cosmography. Pacioli believed that knowledge of this secret proportion was crucial for architects, who should employ the regular and space-filling bodies to generate their work. A collection of the latter geometrical volumes appear in his book (probably drawn by Leonardo), invariably represented as solid *and* structure, as bulk and container, recalling the traditional ambiguity of *chora*, while both aspects are depicted in perspective.

Indeed, while Barbaro recognized with Pacioli that for architects the constructive operation was more important than perspective *per se* – that is, the section through the cone of vision – it is clear that he and other Renaissance architects (such as his close friend Palladio and Sebastiano Serlio) believed that the theatre had a particular revelatory power. This is

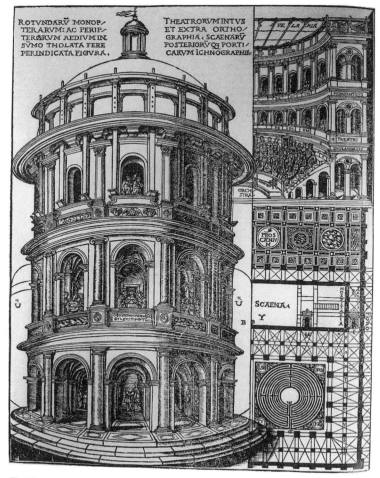

The *Theatrum Mundi* in the Fifth Book of Cesariano's edition of Vitruvius (1521). Notice the labyrinth as a "foundation" of the theatre.

also substantiated by Barbaro's own discussion of the issue in his edition of Vitruvius and by Cesariano's eloquent plate in the 1521 edition of Vitruvius, where the theatre is represented as the cosmic building *par excellence*.

Renaissance architecture therefore never conceives space as a geometric entity. The perceptually exciting depth of the painting or the stage, never subjected to just one viewing point, was incomplete without the *storia*, the eloquent poetic narrative of which Alberti speaks in *Della Pittura*. These narratives were also an integral part of the *tableaux vivants* in urban celebrations, always coherent with the themes and allegories of the events. This fascinating depth is therefore a modification of the original *chora*, still retaining its character as a space of transition. It is indeed akin

A theatrical ephemeral structure constructed in Antwerp for
The Ceremonial Entry of the Archduke Ernst (1594).

to Pacioli's quintessence – simultaneously a substance, a material structure, and its contents.

Giulio Camillo's theatre of memory also bears comment in this regard.
Although a final reconstruction of its physical form is unlikely, this *locus*
of universal knowledge, paradigmatic for Renaissance architecture, posits
a specific relationship between the spectator and the object of contemplation. Whether it was a small amphitheatre into which the operator might
walk or a *machina* in the shape of an ascending spiral, both with compartments alluding to the seven planets and the hierarchically ordered
knowledge of the world, the spectator either occupied the *chora* or
inhabited the ambivalent periphery, like the spectators in Cesariano's
image of the theatre. The search for orientation in the theatre, while it
was a contemplative enterprise (at a distance), also involved an alchemical
process of transmutation of self and world towards the attainment of a
radical orientation, visual and yet participatory.[24]

● ▲ ■

Thus I have argued that until the end of the Renaissance the disclosure of wholeness (the three terms of reality for Plato) had been unquestionably the province of artists and architects, and that this disclosure was always situational. Of particular concern was the ungraspable third term, the very event of ontological continuity, manifested during the Renaissance as a mysterious geometric depth that was disclosed by the work of art but remained concealed and elusive in everyday life. Quotidian experience in the sub-lunar world appeared to be located in *topos*, a natural space. Recall that movement was not a state in Aristotelian physics; objects changed their being when they moved, an ontological difference existed between rest and movement, and *topos* was the locus of Becoming.

Despite his traditional sources and his many contradictions, only Galileo was capable of imagining a truly different physics in which space and bodies could be objectified and in which motion or rest could indeed be only a state incapable of affecting being. Galileo not only brought Platonic space, the original *chora*, down from the supra-lunar heavens to the earth of man; through his scientific cosmology, he also created the conditions for such a space of ontological continuity to be no longer contemplated but instead inhabited or manipulated, concealing the mysterious event itself while allowing for the reduction of Being to the purely ontic – that is, to a re-presented world of objects. Thus Galileo created the conditions for instrumental and technological culture in general.[25]

The differences between Renaissance and Baroque attitudes towards the city, landscape, art, and architecture need not be restated. Baroque architects set out to change the world and accomplished an exciting synthesis of the qualities of natural space and the geometrical reality of *chora*. The potential to transform the totality of the human world into a self-referential cultural entity appeared for the first time, and yet, given the overwhelming presence of a natural ground of meaning, a distinction was established among the points of epiphany, the perspective vanishing points in theatres and churches, and the rest of experience. It was in these theatrical points that the sacred or profane representation attained its supreme coherence and meaning. Much less ambiguously than in the Renaissance, man now contemplated the space of God, re-presented exclusively as a geometric entity. The transformation of the world into a picture took on another dimension. To experience this epiphany, human beings literally had to leave aside their bodies and binocular vision, to assimilate themselves with the geometric vanishing point – now truly a "point at infinity." In Baroque institutions, this epiphany still could be considered part of an embodied ritualized life, both in politics and religion, while the obsession to build human space as infinite or at least indefinite (to observe Descartes's distinction) was undeniable. Despite Descartes's insistence that space and matter are co-substantial and that nature abhors the vacuum, it would be difficult not to notice that in painting it is the presence of geometric space, although still imbued with a mysterious metaphysical light, that becomes the predominant object of representation.

It may be remembered that Descartes himself seemed quite uninterested in the medium of painting. In his *Dioptric* he praises the character of precise copper engravings because they convey the objective form of things. For him, colour is secondary. Only line drawing is capable of

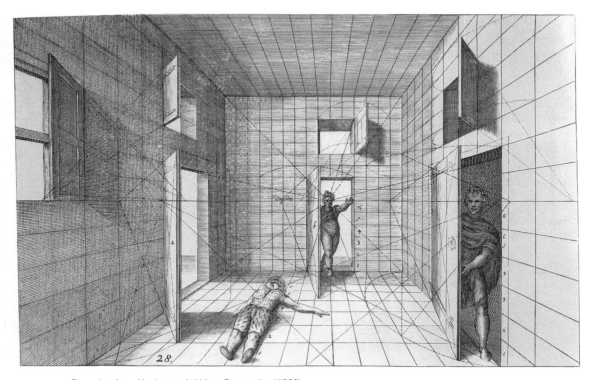

Engraving from Vredeman de Vries, *Perspective* (1600).

disclosing *extension* as the reality of existing things. Obsessed by constructing vision according to epistemic models rather than abiding in perception, Descartes must be held responsible for the thinning and objectification of space, now erected into a positive being, independent of all points of view: *chora* has been objectified, assumed to be transparent to mathematical reason, no longer the in-between Being and Becoming that characterizes embodied existence. As suggested by Merleau-Ponty, this consecration of *perspectiva artificialis* as the prime epistemological model led depth to lose its status as the first dimension, to become merely one of three dimensions, analogous to length and breadth.[26]

In the eighteenth century the whole world was conceived as a stage, and the analogies between architecture and theatre became literal. The proscenium arch separating the stage from the space of real experience seemed to disappear in Bibiena's *Architettura civile*.[27] His *perspectiva per angolo* democratized the theatre; now every individual occupied a place in geometric space, and the space of man became fully a construction. As Richard Sennett has shown, the social conventions for public interaction in the large European cities of the eighteenth century also betrayed the theatricality of everyday life.[28] In the churches, frames of frescoes tended to disintegrate, while Rococo architects collapsed the traditional Renaissance categories of ornament and structure, transforming their work into a subjective formal game that no longer addressed the inveterate quest to erect structures as a frame for rituals that, in turn, demanded appropriate ornamentation. Inhabiting an objectified *chora* and a linear, progressive time, either humanity was on the verge of constructing paradise in a utopic future, now following its old quest for transcendence through technology, or else the vision of paradise in the present here-and-now, represented by traditional artistic endeavours, was possible only as a spectacle through an insurmountable gap, the aesthetic distance of the fine arts, the origin of the well-known paradigm of art for art's sake.

Newton's void was an all-pervasive cosmic space, invisible except for the manifestation of impersonal laws that take place in it. It consecrated the intuitions of Galileo and Descartes, free of the encumbrances of subtle matter (Descartes) or any "necessary" circular motion (Galileo). Human consciousness was expected to become a passive cybernetic receptor in order to do justice to the truths, which for Newton were still transcendental, implicit in the universal law of gravitation taking place in the vacuum. This was the price to pay for intellectual freedom and democ-

Illustration of *perspettiva per angolo*, from F. Galli da Bibiena, *L'Architettura Civile* (1711).

racy: to inhabit an infinitely thin and ungraspable depth – a perspective depth that appears utterly prosaic once it is secularized – as if the truth of the world were indeed conveyed by something akin to documentary photographic images, where lines are believed to meet at infinity as a matter of fact and where tactility is disregarded, where we can be seduced by the promise of cyberspace and cybersex.

● ▲ ■

While all this was taking place, artists and architects became divided about the nature of their work. Some, comfortable with the secularized version of utopia that resulted from science and technology, simply built within this prosaic world and embraced the technological values of efficiency and economy, asserting that meaning was not the concern of the architect, that it would simply follow. Early in the nineteenth century, the École des Beaux-Arts attempted to temper this dangerous proximity to the task of the engineer through a recovery of architectural tradition, but the crucial question of the meaning of art for art's sake was not raised. In this context, architecture could only be the stylistic ornament attached to the shed, at best irrelevant, or even criminal (as Adolf Loos proclaimed)[29], from a social or ethical standpoint. In an attempt to clarify the ultimate status and specificity of architecture as a fine art, it was soon declared, indeed for the first time, that architecture was the art of space; its intentional *raison d'être*, according to Schmarzow, was the artistic manipulation of space.[30] Had we now reached the end of our story, or perhaps a new beginning? Finally, architecture had a proper, "scientific" definition. Its essence had been named. Was this ultimate clarity an utter confusion? This declaration of architecture's spatial essence was soon reduced to aesthetic or formal composition, axes and the *marche à suivre*, design methodologies, typologies and the *mécanisme de la composition*. Its space was indeed the invisible, insidious space of panoptic domination and surveillance.

Other artists and architects, however, adopted a strategy of resistance. Once geometric space had become the locus of social and political life, these architects sought to retrieve the mystery of depth, the transitional event of *chora*, by implementing strategies of destructuration and recollection of embodiment. Piranesi and Ingres were precocious members of this group. Their quest was continued by artistic movements in the twentieth century, intensely informed by Cézanne's obsession with abandoning the external form of objects that preoccupied realism and impressionism in order to retrieve a new depth – a true depth of experience whose paradigm is *erotic* – that traditional illusionism could not convey. The artist's vision is no longer a view of the outside, a mere physical/optical relation with the world. As Merleau-Ponty has pointed out in regard to Cézanne, the world no longer stands before him through perspectival representation; rather, it is the painter (and the observer) to whom the things of the world give birth by means of a concentration of the visible. Ultimately, the painting and, in general, the architectural and artistic work of resistance in the last two hundred years relate to nothing

Etching from the *Carceri* series by G.B. Piranesi (c. 1761).

at all among experienced things unless they are not, first of all, "auto-figurative." They are a spectacle of something only by being a spectacle of nothing. Works by Lequeu and Duchamp, Gris and de Chirico, Giacometti, Le Corbusier, John Hejduk, and Peter Greenaway break the skin of things in order to show "how the things become things, how the world becomes a world."[31]

Given that the paradigm of Renaissance illusionism became problematic once the eighteenth century started to inhabit homogeneous, geometric space, the arts of resistance all became imbued with the traditional concerns of architecture. Once symbolic representation was replaced by

Internal views of Le Corbusier's Dominican seminary of La Tourette in L'Abresle, France (1959).

instrumental representation, the aesthetic distance could only be exacerbated. We need only remember Walter Benjamin's city of voyeurs.[32] The danger for art and architecture is, indeed, irrelevancy through potential closure – the closure to participation that is implicit in instrumental (i.e., aesthetic) representation. But is it possible to contemplate an opening through this paradox that may afford us a new opportunity to understand *chora* as the ground of being, but now in terms of a fully built culture? Are we now in a better position to imagine a *ricorso* of history that starts by acknowledging that culture is our nature, while respecting the irreducible and silent presence of the body as our transhistorical ground?

Hermes Trismegistus stated that art was "an inarticulate cry ... the voice of the light." Rather than a meticulous contextual construction or artifice referring to a world existing outside, art comes to us like Apollinaire's phrases in a poem that seemed not to have been "created," but to have "formed themselves."[33] Art and architecture seem to awaken powers dormant in ordinary perception, demanding a different relationship with things. I believe it is possible to relate the in-between of which I have been speaking to the referent of the work of art in the sense described by Gadamer.[34] He reminds us of the original Greek meaning of symbol as a token of remembrance. The host presented his guest with a piece of an object broken in two, keeping the other piece for himself. If a descendant of the guest should return to the house many years later, the two pieces

Internal views of Le Corbusier's Dominican seminary of La Tourette in L'Abresle, France (1959).

would fit together and the stranger would be recognized. A similar story of breaking into two pieces is told by Plato in the *Symposium*. While all human beings were perfectly spherical wholes at one time, their misbehaviour prompted the gods to cut them in two. Since then, every living being seeks his/her other half, wishing to be made whole again through the experience of love. These stories show how the experience of meaning in art, the experience of the beautiful, is the invocation of a potentially whole (and holy) order of things, wherever it may be found.

Artistic meaning rests upon an intricate interplay of showing and concealing. The work of architecture is no mere bearer of meaning, as if the meaning could be transferred to another bearer. Instead, the meaning of the work lies in the fact that it is there. Above all, Gadamer emphasizes, this creation is not something that we can imagine being made deliberately by someone. It is, first and foremost, of the world, and our experience of it overwhelms us. Rather than simply meaning "something," art and architecture enable meaning to present itself. We recognize the meaning as new and yet we cannot name it; we are invited to silence and yet must proclaim the utterly familiar. Thus art and architecture, as cultural forms of representation, present something that can exist only in specific embodiments. They signify an increase in being, disclosing the lighting that makes the world of things into objects, the event of Becoming-into-Being. This representative power – which is not reducible to replacement, substitution, or copy – distinguishes the work of art and architecture from other technological achievements. Its order, like the Platonic *chora* itself, resists pure conceptualization. It is not linked to an ultimate meaning that could be recuperated intellectually. The work of architecture, properly speaking, preserves its meaning within itself. It is *not* an allegory in the sense that it says one thing and gives us to understand something else. What the work has to say can be found only within itself, grounded in language, and yet beyond it.

● ▲ ■

The work of architecture as *chora* is indeed space-matter, obviously beyond any traditional typology of artistic products that might try to differentiate it from sculpture when constructed, or from painting or even film when issues of depth may involve an exploration of colour or temporality. Philosophers of art have generally avoided speaking about architecture because of the complexities involved by questions of utility and program. Yet it is my contention that architecture must be understood as the paradigmatic cultural product of representation after the demise of Renaissance illusionism. It is the fragmentary artifact *par excellence* that may enable us to identify our opaque nature under the linguistic "house of being," revealing the *horizon* of beings that we recognize (in our wholeness), while we acknowledge that it is never fully present. Here, we may recall our earlier observations about ritual making, perpetuated, for example, in the traditional *opus* of the alchemist. The philosopher's stone, embodiment of wisdom and radical orientation, was never a fixed "product"; it was the process that mattered. This intuition must now be radicalized if we are to transcend the technological enframing.

While marking an intensification of being or embodying truth without objectifying it, architecture is demanding on the spectator or inhabitant. It requires from the architect and the inhabitant a different relationship with external reality. This is what Martin Heidegger has named *Gelassenheit*[35] – an attitude that may stand beyond the dichotomy between ritual participation and intellectual contemplation. Philosophy itself has denounced its traditional claims to an absolute truth in the spirit of a rigorous science. We know from Heidegger's late philosophy that Being is no longer graspable through pure contemplation or pure instrumentality. As an event, Greek tragedy perhaps already held this promise for us, distinct from the scientific implementation of *logos* that resulted

The *chora* or round dance in
"Le Palais Idéal du Facteur Cheval"
in Drôme, France.

from the same cultural origins. While accepting the technological language and body from which it issues, architecture seeks to destructure it; it aims at love and recognition beyond optical seduction, it seeks to demonstrate the mysterious origin of technology and the impossibility of survival in a world of objectified things where personal and collective memory, and future possibilities for a recognizable human life, may finally collapse into pure present (cyberspace), through either a manipulation of external reality or a drugging of human consciousness.

To transcend aestheticism, reductive functionalism, and either conventional or experimental formalism, architecture must consider seriously the potential of narrative as the structure of human life, a poetic vision realized in space-time, in the in-between or *metaxy* implied by *Gelassenheit*. The architect, in a sense, must now also write the script for these dramas. This is, indeed, a crucial part of the architect's design activity, and also the vehicle for an ethical intention to inform the work. Only by accepting this responsibility will it be possible for this work to invite the radicalized individual of the late twentieth century to exercise, with his/her freedom, a reciprocal responsibility to participate in the re-creation of a work of art that is no longer the imitation of a shared, socially validated or transcendental order nor the product of a Romantic imagination attempting a construction *ex nihilo*. Architectural work is therefore articulated as a narrative, metaphoric projection grounded on recollection. On the one hand, the spectator's perception must remain distant – the work, a representation of mysterious depth, the ultimately unnamable presence of the lighting that can be construed as a trace of cultural continuity. On the other hand, the rupture with the cosmological epoch is signalled by the inhabitant's intimate participation in re-creating the work through language, so that it may yield its sense in the high-tension gap inherent in the metaphor. This intensification of Being is what defines the work of art, regardless of its medium and its figurative or non-objective nature. In it, humanity recognizes its purpose.

To repeat: during the past two centuries, all art forms – including literature, music, sculpture, painting, and, more recently, film and other hybrids – seem to be emphatically about space, about *chora*. It is the imagining self (not identical, of course, to the Cartesian *ego cogito*) that, both as creator and as spectator, can inhabit through these works a world already beyond the future-orientation of modernity, where the notion of progress has collapsed and yet the narrative function, with its vectors of recollection and projection, remains the only alternative to articulate ethical action, an appropriate choreography for a postmodern world. *Chora*, an empty gap that is not nothingness, assumed by common sense to be the exclusive space of action, is the meaning of architecture. In works of architecture that transcend the reductions of functional modernism and the pastiches of historicism, however, it is revealed as infinitely dense and impenetrable. *Chora* is the site of darkness, the space of *mimesis* that is our nature and must be preserved for the survival of humanity.

NOTES

1 Marcus V. Pollio Vitruvius, *The Ten Books on Architecture*, tr. M.H. Morgan (New York: Dover 1960), II.i.1. Another translation, published under the work's original Latin title, is also used in this essay: *De Architectura*, tr. F. Granger (Cambridge, Mass.: Harvard University Press 1983).

2 Vitruvius, *De Architectura*, i.i.3.

3 Alberto Pérez-Gómez, *Architecture and the Crisis of Modern Science* (Cambridge, Mass.: MIT Press 1983), ch. 8 and 9.

4 Plato, *Timaeus and Critias*, tr. by H.D.P. Lee (Hardmonsworth, U.K.: Penguin Books 1965).

5 Hans-Georg Gadamer, *The Relevance of the Beautiful*, tr. N. Walter (Cambridge, U.K.: Cambridge University Press 1986); and Eric Voeglin, *Plato and Aristotle* (Baton Rouge, La.: Louisiana State University Press 1957).

6 Plato, *Timaeus*, 66.

7 Ibid., 67. In his late philosophy, Merleau-Ponty refers to this primordial element as the "flesh" of the world. This radical phenomenological understanding of a non-dualistic reality is, in my view, not so distant from Plato's own formulation. See Maurice Merleau-Ponty, *The Visible and the Invisible*, tr. A. Lingis (Evanston, Ill.: Northwestern University Press 1968).

8 Plato, *Timaeus*, 68.

9 Ibid., 69; emphasis mine.

10 Ibid., 70–1.

11 Jean-Pierre Vernant, *Mythe et pensée chez les Grecs* (Paris: Maspero 1965), I, 124.

12 Aristotle, *Poetics*, tr. by S.H. Butcher (New York: Dover 1951), IV, 12.

13 Jane Harrison, *Ancient Art and Ritual* (Bradford-on-Avon, U.K.: Moonraker Press 1978), 40.

14 In modern Greek, Κωρα, often transliterated "hora," is the word for place, used as well as a proper noun to designate the most important city of some islands (there is also a Hora in the Peloponnese, near Pylos). The word for dance, on the other hand, is Κορα, written with omicron (o) rather than omega (ω), and with the accent on the last syllable. In ancient Greek there was most probably a difference in pronunciation that has been lost today.

15 Wladysaw Tatarkiewicz, *History of Aesthetics*, ed. C. Barrett, tr. R.M. Montgomery (Warsaw: Polish Scientific Publishers 1970), I, 16.

16 Alberto Pérez-Gómez, "The Myth of Dedalus," *AA Files* 10 (1985).

17 Hermann Kern, "Image of the World and Sacred Realm," *Daidalos* 3 (1983), 11.

18 It is significant that the foundations of the *tholos* or circular temple in Epidaurus, dedicated to Asclepius, the god of healing, are in fact labyrinthine. The special status that Epidaurus held in Antiquity as a place for healing is well known. The famous theatre in the sanctuary played a most important role in the process of restoring psychosomatic stability to the "patients," who could also undergo a dream cure in the *abaton*. The fact that in the circular temple, of which there were very few examples in ancient Greece, the circular form of the heavens (and the chorus) is physically reconciled with the labyrinth of the underworld (where the three sacred serpents associated with the ritual of Asclepius resided), makes manifest the "function" of architecture as

one of the disciplines that enabled order to appear or, if lacking, to be restored. The theme of the labyrinth as the foundation of architectural order, while seldom realized as literally as at Epidaurus, was a pervasive foundational idea during the Middle Ages and in Renaissance and Baroque architectural treatises. Architecture thus occupies the liminal position *in-between* darkness and light, revealing the true place of human existence.

19 Vitruvius, *Ten Books*, 137.

20 Ibid., 139.

21 Ibid., 140.

22 Eric Voeglin, *The Ecumenic Age* (Baton Rouge, La.: Louisiana State University Press 1974), ch. 3.

23 See Louise Pelletier and Alberto Pérez-Gómez, "Architectural Representation beyond Perspectivism," *Perspecta* 27 (1993).

24 Lina Bolzoni, *Il Teatro della Memoria: Studi su Giulio Camillo* (Padova: Liviana 1984).

25 The most concise discussion of this aspect of the scientific revolution is still Alexandre Koyré, *Metaphysics and Measurement* (London: Chapman & Hall 1968), especially ch. I–IV.

26 Maurice Merleau-Ponty, "Eye and Mind," tr. C. Dallery, *The Primacy of Perception*, ed. J.M. Edie (Evanston, Ill.: Northwestern University Press 1964).

27 Ferdinando Galli da Bibiena, *L'Architettura civile*, intr. D.M. Kelder (New York: Blom 1971).

28 Richard Sennett, *The Fall of Public Man* (Cambridge, U.K.: Cambridge University Press 1977).

29 Adolf Loos, "Ornament and Crime" (1908), in *Sämtliche Schriften* (Vienna: Verlag Herold 1972).

30 August Schmarzow's works on aesthetics date from the late nineteenth and early twentieth centuries. See, in particular, "Raumgestaltung als Wesen der architektonischen Schöpfung," *Zeitschrift für Ästhetik und allgemeine Kunstwissenschaft*, vol. 9 (Stuttgart 1914), 66–95.

31 Merleau-Ponty, "Eye and Mind," 181.

32 See, for example, Benjamin's essay, "Paris, Capital of the Nineteenth Century," in *Reflections*, ed. P. Demetz (New York: Harvest/HBL 1978).

33 Merleau-Ponty, "Eye and Mind," 181ff.

34 Gadamer, *Relevance of the Beautiful*, 31–9.

35 Martin Heidegger, *Discourse on Thinking* (New York: Harper & Row 1966), 55.

The Measure of Expression: Physiognomy and Character in Lequeu's "Nouvelle Méthode"

Jean-François Bédard[1]

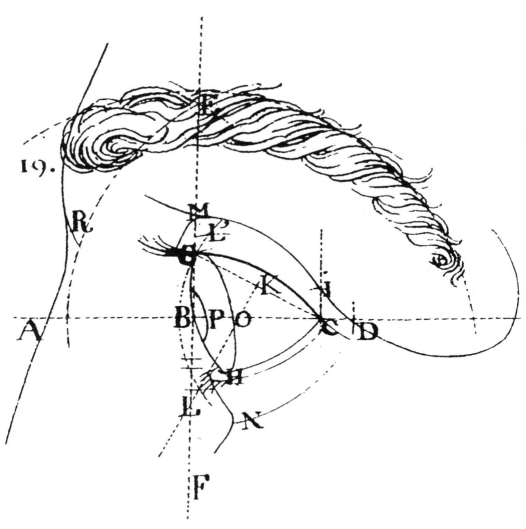

IT WAS NOT UNTIL THE PUBLICATION IN 1933 of Emil Kaufmann's *Von Ledoux bis Le Corbusier* that Jean-Jacques Lequeu was officially ushered into the world of architectural historiography.[2] Both in this book and in a later article,[3] Kaufmann asserted that Lequeu and his colleagues Étienne-Louis Boullée and Claude-Nicolas Ledoux were important forerunners of early twentieth-century modernism. Other historians have analyzed Lequeu's work since then, variously describing him as a romantic, a surrealist, a dadaist, a schizophrenic, and a pornographer; Philippe Duboy even called him the "pataphysical" alter ego of Marcel Duchamp.[4] Beyond these differences of interpretation, all agree that Lequeu's architecture represented the birth of modern architecture at the end of the eighteenth century.[5]

Lequeu, an architectural draughtsman, completed his "Nouvelle Méthode" in 1792, at a time when the convulsions of the French Revolution were reaching unparalleled levels.[6] His treatise on the proportions of the human face was coupled with a drawing method intended to aid draughtsmen in reproducing the harmony of the visage. One year before his death in 1826, he donated the document, along with other manuscripts and drawings – including his spectacular "Architecture Civile" – to the Bibliothèque Royale (now the Bibliothèque Nationale).[7]

Lequeu has often been portrayed as an eccentric who was marginalized by the Old Régime and by the newly founded Republic, an outcast whose mind was constantly vacillating between revenge against the institutions and madness.[8] In this century, modernist, psychoanalytical, or "deconstructivist" students of his architecture have described it as revolutionary and ground-breaking. In this essay, I propose a different interpretation of Lequeu's architectural theory. Contrary to those revisionist speculations, it is my view that his work was firmly rooted in the thought and practices of his time.[9] Through analysis of the "Nouvelle Méthode," I will attempt to show that the emphasis given by Lequeu to the study of proportions and geometry of the human face, to the codification of physiognomy and character, was entirely in keeping with the architectural theory of his era.[10]

Previous critics have assessed the alleged modernity of Lequeu's architecture by comparing it with constructions of a more recent past. But clearly, any appreciation of his work should be based on a close scrutiny of his theoretical discourse, particularly his understanding of geometry and his use of the anthropomorphic metaphor, both of which were cornerstones of architectural theory in the classical age. A careful consideration of the "Nouvelle Méthode" shows that the body studied by Lequeu was not the same as that studied by nineteenth-century medicine and anthropology; Lequeu's architectonic body was still reproduced with the help of the *physionorègle*[11] and the analytical grid of "character." The mimetic architecture generated through this approach was neither modern nor romantic, and it certainly was not surrealist. As Rykwert has observed, the architecture of the classical age was not a "language" of standardized parts that the architect reorganized according to the requirements of a particular commission.[12] As a consequence, the end of "classical" architecture did not, as many have argued, result from the collapse of coherent formal systems. As long as the geometry of the human body remained at the core of a theory of architecture, classical architecture was preserved. But the architecture of the classical age was attacked to its very core when the self-explaining truth of order and its re-enactment in ritual could no longer be sustained, when the representation of truth through character could no longer justify its existence. The arithmetic of proportions and character found in the "Nouvelle Méthode" did not threaten these basic tenets of classical architecture.

THE "NOUVELLE MÉTHODE" AND PETRUS CAMPER'S
DISSERTATION SUR LES VARIÉTÉS NATURELLES

Lequeu begins his "Nouvelle Méthode" by stressing the importance for the arts of the development of a precise method, surpassing those developed by artists of the past, for reproducing the proportions of the human face – a method, he stresses, not only important for the painter but essential to the young architect.[13] After lengthy disquisitions on the ancestry of architecture, its hegemony over the other arts, the dates of the foundation of cities, and the chronology of famous architects, Lequeu exposes the mechanics of his system, beginning with the rudiments of Euclidean geometry.[14] He explains how, by combining simple geometrical figures, one can draw each part of the face to eventually obtain the entire head.[15] Throughout this account, Lequeu notes the anatomical and physiological peculiarities of facial features and comments on the significance of their shapes according to the celebrated theories of the physiognomists.[16] He concludes his dissertation with a brief description of the bones, muscles, and veins in the upper body, and expresses the hope that, if the reader has found this method useful, he will be allowed to adapt it to the other parts of the human body.

Lequeu's treatise bears a number of remarkable similarities with Petrus Camper's *Dissertation sur les variétés naturelles*, a study of the morphology of human and animal species published posthumously in 1791.[17] Like Lequeu, Camper sought to discover rules to help the artist represent the human face harmoniously, and he emphasized the usefulness of these rules for the production of beautiful architecture since, as he stated, beauty in architecture is akin to the well-proportioned body.[18]

To this end, Camper developed the theory of the facial angle. He believed that a careful study of the geometry of the profile – in particular the position of the jaw in relation to the other parts of the head – was fundamental to the correct reproduction of the facial proportions of animals or of men of different ages belonging to different nations.[19] After

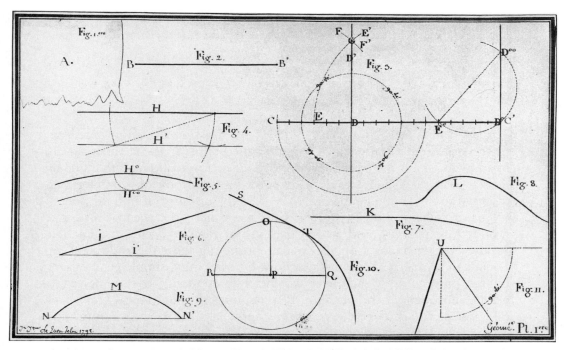

Jean-Jacques Lequeu, geometrical figures, "Nouvelle Méthode" (1792), pl. 1; from Philippe Duboy, *Lequeu: An Architectural Enigma* (Cambridge, Mass.: MIT Press 1987).

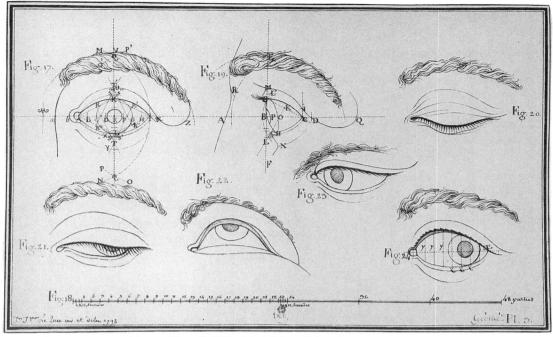

Lequeu, geometry of the eye, "Nouvelle Méthode," pl. 3; from Duboy, *Lequeu*.

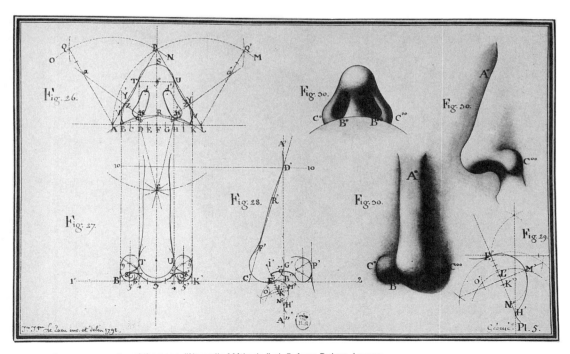

Lequeu, geometry of the nose, "Nouvelle Méthode," pl. 5; from Duboy, *Lequeu*.

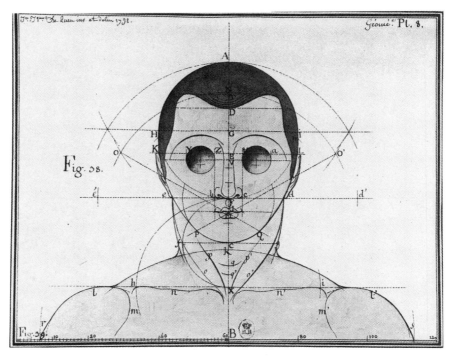

Lequeu, geometry of the face, "Nouvelle Méthode," pl. 8; from Duboy, *Lequeu*.

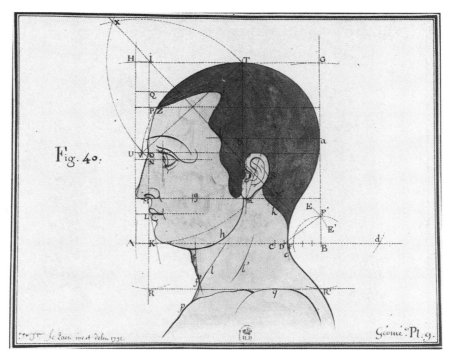

Lequeu, geometry of the profile, "Nouvelle Méthode," pl. 9; from Duboy, *Lequeu*.

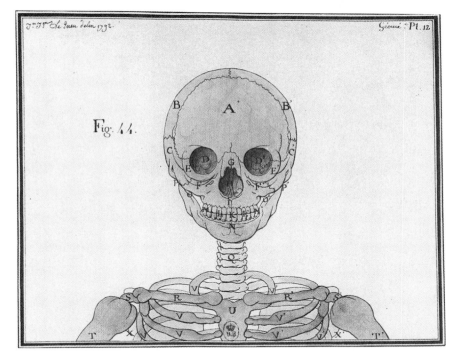

Lequeu, description of the bones of the head, "Nouvelle Méthode," pl. 12; from Duboy, *Lequeu*.

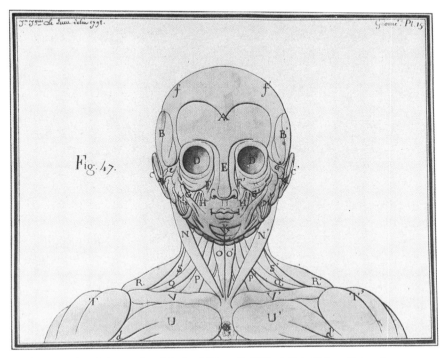

Lequeu, description of the muscles of the head, "Nouvelle Méthode," pl. 13; from Duboy, *Lequeu*.

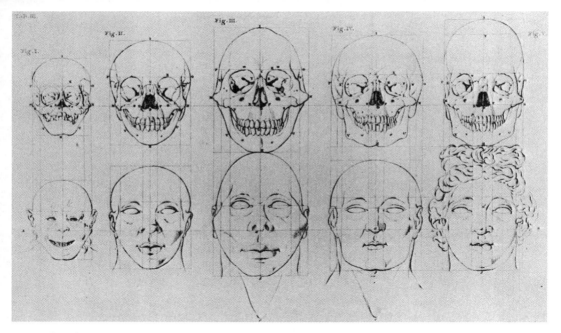

Peter Camper, from ape to Apollo Belvedere, *Dissertation physique* (1791), pl. 3;
from Barbara Maria Stafford, *Body Criticism: Imaging the Unseen in Enlightenment
Art and Medicine* (Cambridge, Mass.: MIT press 1991).

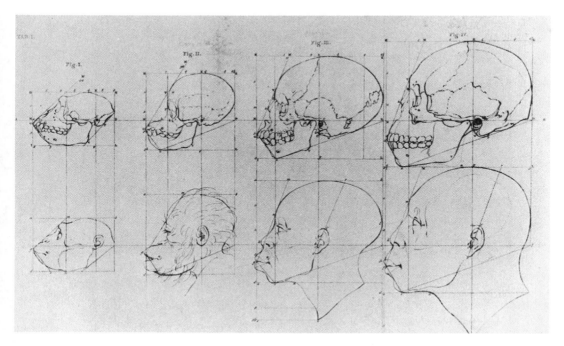

Camper, various measurements of facial angles, *Dissertation physique*, pl. 1; from
Stafford, *Body Criticism.*

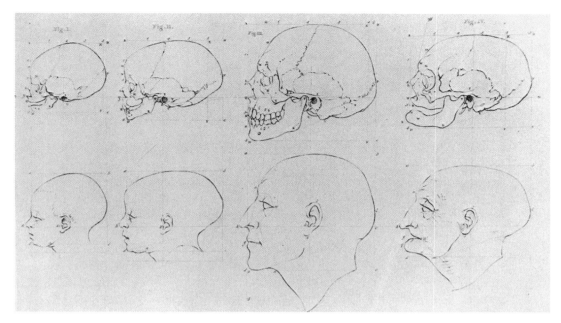

Camper, from youth to old age, *Dissertation physique*, pl. 4; from Stafford, *Body Criticism*.

comparing a vast quantity of skulls cut in cross-section, Camper isolated what he called the "facial line" – an imaginary line stretching from the top of the forehead to the outermost part of the chin. He named the angle between this line and the horizon the "facial angle," which, in his view, determined precisely the character of all animals, humans, and even the gods – from the woodcock to Apollo.[20] When slightly modified, the facial angle, he wrote, could help the artist to convey all emotions.

For most historians of science, Camper's "discovery" of the facial angle signals the beginning of nineteenth-century anthropological and phrenological research.[21] In this view, Camper created modern comparative anatomy, uncovering the geometrical principles on which animal and human morphologies are based and eliminating the arbitrariness present in eighteenth-century studies of anatomy. A few historians have also analyzed Lequeu's interest in the representation of the human figure. By postulating that his work was influenced by renewed interest in physiognomy at the end of the eighteenth century – thanks to the work of the Swiss theologian, Johann Kaspar Lavater (1741–1801) – and by Gaspard Monge's descriptive geometry, commentators have interpreted the "Nouvelle Méthode" as proof of the emergence of "expression" in late eighteenth-century architecture, a theoretical category pushed to an extreme by Lequeu in his architectural designs.[22]

The similarities of form and intent between the "Nouvelle Méthode" and the *Dissertation* contradict this facile dichotomy between Camper, supposedly obsessed by the proto-Darwinian desire to organize nature according to an evolutionary hierarchy, and Lequeu, allegedly overwhelmed by an uncontrollable architectural expressionism. Rather, they demonstrate the unity of interests of the naturalist and the architect in the classical age. The efforts of the two men to establish reliable principles for the representation of beauty – by seeking a mechanism capable of organizing the various characters of animals and humans (Camper) or by focusing instead on the proportions of an "ideal beauty" (Lequeu) – bring together the rigour of ideal proportions and the encyclopedic desire to catalogue the variety of beauties found in nature. Both Lequeu and Camper hoped to organize nature according to the expressive mathematics of character.

PHYSIOGNOMY AND CHARACTER IN THE CLASSICAL AGE

The drawing techniques employed in the "Nouvelle Méthode" and in the *Dissertation* are intimately related to the search for the physiognomic characteristics of individuals. To demonstrate the consistency between expressive and proportional theories at the end of the eighteenth century, one must emphasize the important roles played by representation and order in the structure of knowledge at the time. According to Michel Foucault, who examined this topic at length in *Les mots et les choses*, analogy ruled knowledge during the Renaissance; the marks found by Renaissance scientist on plants, animals, and humans were seen as proofs of the existence of a complex network of affinities linking the most distant star to the humblest terrestrial creature. The classical age began when signs were freed from analogy and were given their own representative nature.[23] This "doubled representation" of the sign, as Foucault called it, placed *order* at the centre of all knowledge in the classical age, when signs were seen as providing a grid through which the secrets of nature could be understood perfectly. This unity of order and knowledge meant that comparative analysis was now the foremost cognitive process; the precise representation of each natural object could thereby be determined and displayed in a taxonomic table according to quantitative or qualitative hierarchies. Knowledge in the classical age was physiognomic; through careful observation and comparative analysis, the natural historian and the artist could determine the character of a specific object and position it correctly in the great table of creation, be it the taxonomic grid of the botanist or the painter's canvas.[24]

The ancient science of physiognomy became an important vehicle in the search for character.[25] In contrast with the physiognomies of antiquity or the Renaissance, which were divinatory sciences founded on cosmo-biological analogies, classical physiognomy attempted to codify, through a comparative analysis of the geometry of the human features, the great diversity of expressions in order to produce a complete alphabet of human "types."[26] The pathognomy of Charles Le Brun (1619–90) is an example of such a physiognomy.[27] In *De l'expression générale et particulière*, Le Brun determined the parameters of the physiognomy of expression that were deemed essential to the practice of historical painting in the seventeenth and eighteenth centuries.[28] The Cartesian theory of the passions was the starting point for Le Brun's physiognomic system. In Descartes's account of the passions, the pineal gland, seat of the soul, with the help of "animal spirits" made the expression of emotions appear at the surface of the human body. This causal relationship between soul and body enabled Le Brun to codify, with the precision of an engineer, the manifestation of each passion on the surface of the "mechanical animal." Le Brun used geometry to establish a precise distinction between the "strong" passions, which mark and sometimes even deface the physical aspect of man, and the "swift" passions, which alter his appearance only temporarily. For the permanent passions, he calculated the measure of the angle between a straight line passing through the long axis of the eyes and a line tangent to the forehead and the nose. For temporary passions, Le Brun calculated the degree of movement of each part of the face, particularly the eyebrows and the mouth, from their still positions.

Le Brun's mapping of the emotions and the temperaments produced a taxonomy of passions wherein the human features were ordered according to the rules of geometry, proportion, and symmetry. Unlike those of his predecessors, his zoomorphic heads do not celebrate the unity of the cosmological and the biological; instead, they show a continuity between the classification methods of natural history and art. The influence of Le Brun's triangulation method on Camper's theory of the facial angle is proof of a continuity in theories about the "geometrization" of character until the beginning of the nineteenth century, and also of the perceived unity, in the artistic theories of this period, of geometry and expression – a unity that is the foundation of Lequeu's "Nouvelle Méthode."

THE THEORY OF CHARACTER IN ARCHITECTURE

During the classical age, character functioned as an index that established the position of each natural object within the hierarchical order of creation. Classical physiognomists used proportion and geometry to codify the human character in order to establish a taxonomy of expressive species. By the act of representation, the architect and the artist contributed to the ordering system of classical knowledge; they represented the appropriate character of their subjects – in one word, they *characterized*. The wide-ranging influence of Le Brun's treatise on the character of passions, coupled with the publication of drawing methods concerned with the geometric principles of beauty and the variety of natural human types, demonstrate the persistence, until the end of the eighteenth century, of the artist's role as the organizer of visible diversity.

Like classical natural history, architectural theory of the classical age was based on representation and order. As the embodiment of mathematical order, architecture organized society with the rigour of the rules of civility it incarnated. Even when new architectural theories appeared in the late eighteenth century, they did not question this link between architectural theory and these principles. For example, while the theory of "natural taste," influenced by English sensualism, emphasized the role of human perception in establishing the truth of architectural rules and denied them a transcendental origin, it did not question the existence of these rules. Far from announcing twentieth-century modernism, the architecture of the late eighteenth century, with its repetitive use of pure solids, demonstrates the enduring symbolic role of geometry in architectural design. Boullée and Ledoux may have transformed or eliminated the orders from their architecture, but they nevertheless preserved the authority of geometry.[29]

What role does the notion of character play in the architectural theory of the classical age? In the "evolutionist" interpretation, architectural theory based on the divine mathematics of neoplatonism was destroyed in the late eighteenth century by the emancipation of the individual.[30] According to this interpretation, character played a crucial role in the transformation of traditional architectural theories, which until then had preserved the meaning of architecture. For evolutionist historians, character was introduced into architectural treatises in two distinct phases. In the first, from 1730 to 1770, character was a mere adjunct to existing architectural notions – in the writings of Germain Boffrand and Jacques-François Blondel, for example. In the second phase, from 1770 to 1800, theoreticians such as Nicolas Le Camus de Mézières, Julien-David Leroy, Jacques-Guillaume Legrand, Antoine-Chrysostome Quatremère de Quincy, Boullée, and Ledoux interpreted character as the very substance of architectural creation, thereby opposing polemically the practice of architecture to that of civil engineering.[31] These developments would have taken place simultaneously with the emancipation of the human subject and the overthrow of all authority, from social rules to Vitruvian principles – an emancipation that reached its apotheosis during the French Revolution.[32] Character, under the influence of the sensualist theories of Archibald Alison, Francis Hutcheson, and David Hume, would not only have destroyed Cartesianism, on which the architectural theory of the classical age was established, but it would have accounted for the "licentious" architecture that crowded gardens from the middle of the century onward. Character's destruction of the authority of proportion therefore opened the way to nineteenth-century eclecticism.[33]

Contrary to this evolutionist position, I believe that character is linked intimately to notions of representation, proportion, and order, as I argued when discussing the *episteme* of the classical age. Character is not a late development of architectural theory, the result of a sudden "psychologization" of the individual; rather, it is at the very origin of architectural theory. From Vitruvius's analogy between the orders and human "types"[34] through the Renaissance interest in the relationship between the cosmological and the biological, character finally became fully anthropomorphic and sexualized in the classical age.[35]

For Blondel (1705–74), character was of primary importance; all segments of architecture were subservient to it, and he encouraged architects to express a building's proper character through the orders and massing.[36] Conscious of a similarity between the classification methods of the natural sciences and those of architecture, Blondel, in his *Cours d'architecture*, inventoried the different architectural characters appropriate to different building types. He summarized his discussion as follows:

This Chapter has been devoted to the Analysis of Art; we have provided new definitions, aimed at giving a precise view of an Architecture possessing a specific style, expression, and character; we have explained what is meant by Architecture that is easy, free, original, beautiful, noble, pyramidal, licentious, cold, sterile, false, arid or poor. These designations should not be confused. The clear distinctions between them guide the conduct of young Artists more than we can imagine and help them to choose the type that fits their many endeavours.[37]

Blondel's ideas concerning the unity of the principles of proportion and disposition under the rule of character were developed by Le Camus de Mézières (1721–92). In *Le Génie de l'architecture*, Le Camus interpreted character as closely related to proportion.[38] He deplored his predecessors' careless study of the effects of the proportions of architecture on people, which, he claimed, had led some architects to use the orders "without taking the opportunity to combine them into a whole with a character all its own, capable of producing certain sensations."[39] For Le Camus, the architect must take his inspiration from the inanimate objects of nature that have the power to influence our emotions. He praised Le Brun for this discovery:

Occupied with such observations since my youth, my zeal has sustained itself by fixing my attention upon the works of nature. The more closely I have looked, the more I have found that every object possesses a character, proper to it alone, and that often a single line, a plain contour will suffice to express it. The faces of the lion, the tiger, and the leopard are composed of lines that make them terrible and strike fear in the boldest hearts. In the face of a cat, we discern the character of treachery; meekness and goodness are written on the features of a lamb; the fox has a mask of cunning and guile: a single feature conveys their character. The celebrated Le Brun, whose talents do honour to his country, has proven the truth of this principle through his characterization of the passions; he has expressed the various affections of the soul, and has rendered joy, sadness, anger, fury, compassion, etc., in a single line.[40]

Convinced that the characters found in nature exert power on the soul, he urged architects to use them in the construction of buildings.[41]

According to Blondel and Le Camus, the architect must exploit the entire range of emotions within the limits established by the rules of *convenance*. Le Camus's reference to Le Brun was evidence that character was not intended to be an incentive for the architect to produce licentious architecture. On the contrary, character was to serve as a framework that determines architectural "species" and systematizes harmony and order. The physiognomic nature of Lequeu's architecture has been well noted.[42]

However, the "Nouvelle Méthode" is not proof of Lequeu's revolutionary modernity. Lequeu's concern with the ancient origins of his art and of drawing, his careful genealogies celebrating the memory of famous artists and builders of antiquity and modern times, his reverence for the theoreticians who had preceded him, his conviction that his work contributed to the "progress" of his art, and his interest in the study of geometry, the human figure, and its character – all were characteristic of contemporary architectural treatises. Nowhere in the "Nouvelle Méthode" did Lequeu corrupt classical architectural theory. On the contrary, his emphasis on the geometry of the harmonious body and the expressive variety of human characters represented a summary of the essential elements of architectural theory in the classical age.

DESCRIBING MODERN MAN

Research on the geometry of the human body and facial expression did not end with the eighteenth century; numerous works that are, at least superficially, similar to the treatises of Lequeu and Camper were published during the nineteenth century. The classical physiognomies of character and expression gave way to other theories in which their authors aimed to discover the truth of "natural" human types. Criminal anthropometry and phrenology, craniometry, and gestural typology all seemed to continue research from the past; in fact, they aspired to obtain the perfect equivalence of man's physiology and psychology.

At the beginning of the nineteenth century, man's new place at the centre of knowledge radically transformed the intention of physiognomic and anthropometric studies. No longer employed in the discovery of order, which had preoccupied thinkers during the classical age, they become an integral part of the new "human sciences." Quételet's anthropometrical treatise, *Anthropométrie ou: mesure des différentes facultés de l'homme*, is a telling example of this transformation.[43]

In his *Anthropométrie*, Quételet studied the harmony of the proportions of the human body. While Lequeu and Camper codified an ideal normative beauty that did not necessarily exist in nature, with their descriptions of the various forms that served the rhetorical interests of representation, Quételet wanted to demonstrate the existence of beauty through statistics. Not content with looking for measurements of beauty only in the literature of the past, he wanted to prove empirically that beauty existed in nature and to validate the proportional systems of past artists by demonstrating that they corresponded to the statistical averages that he had compiled. For Quételet, beauty was not an unattainable ideal; it was a statistical measure that described an entire population. It was the physical appearance of the "average man," the result of statistical research and synthesis arising from Quételet's quest for the physical, moral, and intellectual laws that control the human race. For Quételet, the average man was not an abstraction, a mere statistical mean; he was a type found abundantly in society, characterizing the nation to which he belonged.[44]

Quételet's understanding of character is vastly different from that of Lequeu. By equating beauty to normality, Quételet put an end to classical anthropometry. His proportions were not the embodiment of the beautiful, the evidence of order; they were the sum of arithmetic averages, the result of the kind of quantitative research that was to preoccupy the nineteenth century. Character was no longer understood to be the result of a comparative analysis of appearances, as it had been during the classical age. It was now deduced, according to the laws of biology, from the internal organization of bodies and the ways in which they function. This shift in emphasis from a comparison of external appearances to a study of internal vital processes had been introduced to comparative anatomy by the French scientist Georges Cuvier (1769–1832). For Cuvier, as for Quételet later, the appearance of living organisms was determined by the internal laws that governed them. These laws needed to be understood in order to discover the "types" created by nature itself.[45]

Like Cuvier in the field of natural science, Jean-Louis-Nicolas Durand (1760–1834) initiated a revolution in architecture.[46] Durand rejected architectural theories based on physiognomy and representation, and established the principles of a new architecture using an analysis of the internal organization and function of buildings.[47] Durand developed a *mécanisme de la composition* – a method whereby standardized architectural elements could be used to produce an endless quantity of spatial configurations. With Durand, architectural theory became a method for the efficient production of buildings answering precise functional needs.[48]

It is in man's biological body and in Cuvier's and Durand's functional analyses that modernity is born. Lequeu's delirious encyclopedias are not modern; modernity can be discovered instead on the quiet path of statisticians who understand beauty as the result of statistics and not as the expression of order; of scientists who study digestive systems rather than the proportions of Apollo's profile. Modernity begins when architects no longer see character as the expressive physiognomy of a face or a façade but rather as the functional and economical disposition of building elements.

NOTES

1 This paper was translated and adapted from my master's dissertation (1990) in the History and Theory of Architecture program at McGill University, entitled "La mesure de l'expression: Physiognomonie et caractère dans la *Nouvelle Méthode* de Jean-Jacques Lequeu." I wish to acknowledge the assistance provided by Howard Shubert, Alberto Pérez-Gómez, and Stephen Parcell in the adaptation of my thesis for this essay.

2 Emil Kaufmann, *Von Ledoux bis Le Corbusier: Ursprung und Entwicklung der autonomen Architektur* (Vienna and Leipzig: Rolf Passer 1933). For a list of works on Lequeu before Kaufmann, see Philippe Duboy, *Lequeu, an Architectural Enigma* (Cambridge, Mass.: MIT Press 1987), 66–72.

3 Emil Kaufmann, "Jean-Jacques Lequeu," *The Art Bulletin* 31, no. 1–4 (March-December 1949): 130–5, revised and enlarged in "Three Revolutionary Architects: Boullée, Ledoux and Lequeu," *Transactions of the American Philosophical Society* 42 (October 1952): 538–58.

4 Duboy, *Lequeu*.

5 In addition to the writings of Kaufman and Duboy, the major modern-day analyses of Lequeu's work are, in chronological order: Helen Rosenau, "Architecture and the French Revolution: Jean Jacque [*sic*] Lequeu," *The Architectural Review* 106, no. 632 (August 1949): 115–16; Helen Rosenau, "Postscript on Lequeu," *The Architectural Review* 108 (October 1950): 264–7; Günter Metken, "Jean-Jacques Lequeu ou l'Architecture rêvée," *Gazette des Beaux-Arts* 65, no. 1152–7 (first semester 1965): 213–30; Jacques Guillerme, "Lequeu et l'invention du mauvais goût," *Gazette des Beaux-Arts* 66, no. 1158–9 (second semester 1965): 153–66; Jacques Guillerme, "Lequeu entre l'irrégulier et l'éclectique," *Dix-Huitième Siècle* 6 (1974): 167–80; André Chastel, "The Moralizing Architecture of Jean-Jacques Lequeu," *Art News Annual* 32 (1966): 71–83; Anthony Vidler, *The Writing of the Walls* (Princeton, N.J.: Princeton Architectural Press 1987), 103–23; and Johannes Odenthal, "Lequeu's *Architecture Civile* and the *Kosmos* of Alexander von Humboldt," *Daidalos* 34 (December 1989): 30–41.

6 The full title of the work is "Nouvelle Méthode appliquée aux Principes élémentaires du dessin, tendant à perfectionner graphiquement le tracé de la tête de l'homme au moyen de diverses figures géométriques." Bibliothèque Nationale, Cabinet des Estampes, Kc. 17 in-4°.

7 Son of a cabinet-maker, Lequeu was born on 14 September 1757 in Rouen. After attending the École gratuite de dessin, de peinture et d'architecture, in 1779 he moved to Paris, where he became a member of the Académie d'architecture. While in Paris, he worked on the church of Ste-Geneviève, Parc Monceau, and l'Hôtel de Montholon. He became an associate architect of Rouen's Académie royale des Sciences, des Belles-Lettres et des Arts in 1786. In 1790 and 1791, Lequeu was in charge of the public workshops for the Fête de la Fédération. The following year he began working as a second-class draughtsman at the École Polytechnique, a position he held until 1802. The survey office hired Lequeu as a first-class draughtsman in 1793, and he occupied the same position at the office of public works in 1797. He became first draughtsman-cartographer in the department of cartography of the ministry of the interior in 1802. Lequeu retired from public service in 1815 and died on 28 March 1826, at the age of 69, leaving little but a library well stocked with architectural treatises and works on applied art and science. See Duboy, *Lequeu*, 353–4; and Werner Szambien, "L'inventaire après décès de Jean-Jacques Lequeu," *Revue de l'Art* 90 (1990): 104–5.

In addition to the "Nouvelle Méthode" and "Architecture Civile" manuscripts, the Lequeu archive at the Bibliothèque Nationale includes the following manuscripts: "Mécanique"; "Voyage en Italie"; "Plan et décorations intérieures de l'hôtel de Montholon"; "Coupe et détails de l'église de la Madeleine à Rouen"; "Précis méthodique pour apprendre à graver le lavis à l'eau forte"; "Figures lascives"; "Traité des édifices, meubles, habits, machines, et ustensiles des chinois"; "Architecture de Soufflot"; and personal papers. For inventories of the Lequeu archive since 1825, see Duboy, *Lequeu*, 356–9; Duboy also mentions (p. 360) other works by Lequeu that are kept elsewhere in the library or in other institutions.

8 As suggested in Vidler, *Writing of the Walls*, 103.

9 His work with some of the major institutions of his time – in particular, the Académie d'architecture, the Académie des Sciences, des Belles-Lettres et des Arts of Rouen, the École des Ponts et Chaussées, and the École Polytechnique – and with Jacques-Germain Soufflot clearly suggests that Lequeu was far less of a "revolutionary" and an outcast than is usually believed.

10 The expression "classical age" is used here in the sense defined by Michel

Foucault, principally in *Les mots et les choses: une archéologie des sciences humaines* (Paris: Gallimard 1966; English translation published as *The Order of Things* [New York: Vintage Books 1973]). Foucault defines the essential characteristic of the historical period stretching from the middle of the seventeenth century to the beginning of the nineteenth century as the identification of knowledge with order obtained through the analysis of representation.

11 The *physionorègle* was a grid used by eighteenth-century draughtsmen to situate correctly the different parts of the human face; see Bédard, "Mesure," 20, note 2.

12 "In so far as a tradition in architecture can be called classical, it must rest on two analogies: of the building as a body, and of the origin as a re-enactment of some primitive or – if you would rather – of some archetypal action to which our procedure must refer. From Vitruvius to Boullée, the texts suggest something of the kind, always in different contexts, since such ideas do not contain, or even imply, the repertory of norms and procedures which the constant alteration of circumstances forces you to renew, to rethink and to alter." Joseph Rykwert, "The École des Beaux-Arts and the Classical Tradition," in *The Beaux-Arts and Nineteenth-Century French Architecture*, ed. R. Middleton (Cambridge, Mass.: MIT Press 1982), 17.

13 "Il est bon de rappeler aux amis des arts, que l'art de représenter la stature humaine en général, la connaissance exacte de la géométrie et de la perspective, doivent faire constamment la base des études de ceux qui embrassent l'architecture." Lequeu, "Nouvelle Méthode," 4:1. ("It is appropriate to remind friends of the arts that the art of representing the human figure in general, an accurate knowledge of geometry and perspective, must be the permanent foundation of the studies of those who embrace architecture.")

14 Ibid., 6:5–6:22.

15 Ibid., 31:1.

16 Ibid., 13:1. Lequeu's insistence on enumerating the physiognomic theories relating to the different forms of the face does not prevent him from doubting – as most authors did in the eighteenth century – the usefulness of physiognomy in predicting one's character or destiny. He does, nonetheless, acknowledge that physiognomy plays an important role in the arts. Ibid., 38:4.

17 Petrus Camper, *Dissertation sur les variétés naturelles qui caractérisent la physiognomie des homme des divers climats et des différens âges* (Paris and The Hague 1791). One of the most important anatomists of the eighteenth century, Camper (1722–89) graduated in 1746 from the University of Leyden as doctor of philosophy and medicine. He became professor of anatomy and

surgery at the Athenaeum of Amsterdam in 1755 and held the chair of medicine, anatomy, surgery, and botany at the University of Groningen between 1763 and 1773.

18 Ibid., 79–80.

19 Ibid., 11, 35, 94.

20 Ibid., 37–41.

21 According to Gusdorf, for example, Camper belongs to a "new anthropological age" that began in the second half of the eighteenth century. In the field of the human sciences, this period is characterized, in Gusdorf's view, by the destruction of man's metaphysical status and its transformation into an object that can be scrutinized scientifically. See Georges Gusdorf, *Dieu, la nature et l'homme au siècle des Lumières* (Paris: Payot 1971), 355–90.

22 Jacques Guillerme sees in the "Nouvelle Méthode" not only the influence – rather superficial, in his view – of Gaspard Monge's descriptive geometry as taught at the École Polytechnique when Lequeu was a drawing instructor but also that of the theories of the scientists and engineers whom Lequeu met in the various positions he held. See Guillerme, "Lequeu et l'invention du mauvais goût," 159–60. Duboy interprets the "Nouvelle Méthode" rather conventionally, mentioning the combined influences of Monge's geometry and Lavater's physiognomy. See Duboy, *Lequeu*, 15.

23 Foucault, *Les mots et les choses* (Paris: Gallimard 1989 [1966]), 41.

24 The similarity between the interests of the scientist and the artist, as seen in the works of Lequeu and Camper, was not unusual at this time. Foucault points out that classical linguistics compared the sign to a drawing, an object entirely determined by representation: "Le tableau n'a pour contenu que ce qu'il représente, et pourtant ce contenu n'apparaît que représenté par une représentation." Ibid., 78–9.

25 Physiognomy, from the Greek for "the art of judging someone by his physical appearance," is the science that studies man by analyzing his appearance or behaviour. The physiognomic treatises of antiquity, known in the Middle Ages through their Arabic translations and studied during the Renaissance, placed physiognomy in the lineage of the astrological and the divinatory sciences. *De Humana Physiognomonia*, by Giambattista della Porta (1535–1615), first published in Naples in 1586 and often reprinted during the seventeenth and eighteenth centuries, systematized medieval and Renaissance physiognomies but also announced their decline. As the inspiration for all physiognomies of the classical age – of which the most important French examples are the

Caractère des passions (1642) and *L'Art de connoistre les hommes* (1659) by Marin Cureau de La Chambre and *De l'expression générale et particulière* (1698) by Charles Le Brun – *De Humana Physiognomonia* shifted the discourse of physiognomy from divinatory uses to the study of passions and expressions. See Jurgis Baltrušaitis, "La physiognomonie animale," *Aberrations: quatre essais sur la légende des formes* (Paris: Olivier Perrin 1957); Jean-Jacques Courtine, *Histoire du visage: exprimer et faire taire ses émotions, XVIe–début XIXe siècle* (Paris: Rivages 1988); P. Dandrey, "La physiognomonie comparée à l'âge classique," *Revue de synthèse* 104, no. 104 (January–March 1983); Patricia Magli, "The Face and the Soul," *Zone* 4 (1989): 87–127.

26 Courtine, *Histoire du visage*, 43.

27 Le Brun's *Conférence sur l'expression* was given at the Académie de Peinture in 1678 and published in 1698 under the title *De l'expression générale et particulière*. While it is the principal source of his physiognomic thinking, Le Brun also published a *Conférence sur la physionomie comparée des hommes et des animaux* and a *Conférence sur la physionomie*, both given in 1671. See Dandrey, "Physiognomonie comparée"; and Jennifer Montagu, "Charles Le Brun's *Conférence sur l'expression générale et particulière*," unpublished thesis, University of London (1959), 52.

28 Ibid., 73–4.

29 Alberto Pérez-Gómez, *Architecture and the Crisis of Modern Science* (Cambridge, Mass.: MIT Press 1983), 159–60.

30 Werner Szambien, *Symétrie, goût, caractère* (Paris: Picard 1985), 20; Baldine Saint-Girons, *Esthétique au XVIIIe siècle: le modèle français* (Paris: Philippe Sers 1990), 516.

31 Werner Szambien, "Bienséance, convenance et caractère," *Cahiers de la recherche architecturale* 18 (1985): 41.

32 Ibid., 40–1; Szambien, *Symétrie*, 165.

33 Louis Hautecœur, *Histoire de l'architecture classique en France* (Paris: Picard 1953) V, 91.

34 See Werner Oechslin, "Émouvoir: Boullée et Le Corbusier," *Daidalos* 30 (December 1988): 42; and Ignasi de Solà-Morales, "The Origin of Modern Eclecticism: The Theory of Architecture in Early Nineteenth Century France," *Perspecta* 23 (1987): 125.

35 See George L. Hersey, "Associationism and Sensibility in Eighteenth-Century Architecture," *Eighteenth-Century Studies* 4 (Fall 1970): 71.

36 Oeschlin, "Émouvoir," 42; Szambien, *Symétrie*, 179; Anthony Vidler, "The Idea of Type: The Transformation of the Academic Ideal, 1750–1830," *Oppositions* 8 (1977): 100.

37 Jacques-François Blondel, *Cours d'architecture ou traité de la décoration, distribution & construction des bâtiments* (Paris 1771–7) II, xii; tr. by J.-F. B.

38 Nicolas Le Camus de Mézières, *Le Génie de l'architecture, ou l'analogie de cet art avec nos sensations* (Paris 1780); translated into English as *The Genius of Architecture, or the Analogy of that Art with our Sensations*, tr. D. Britt (Santa Monica, Cal.: Getty Center for the History of Art and the Humanities 1992). See, also, Szambien, *Symétrie*, 181–2.

39 Le Camus, *Genius of Architecture*, 69.

40 Ibid., 70.

41 Ibid., 41–2.

42 "Lequeu was extremely preoccupied with physiognomy; attentive to the possibilities of the expressive structure of facial characteristics, he tries to find complementary and opposite types. What we think of as eclecticism in his inspiration as an architect derives from the same principle. It is a question of producing models that develop, to their highest degree of effectiveness, the various 'expressive' properties of architecture." Chastel, "Moralizing Architecture," 72.

43 Lambert-Adolphe-Jacques Quételet, *Anthropométrie ou: mesure des différentes facultés de l'homme* (Brussels 1871). Quételet (1796–1874), an important nineteenth-century social statistician, was the founder of the Observatory of Brussels and the secretary of Belgium's Académie Royale. He published numerous works on geometry, physics, astronomy, and meteorology but is best remembered for his researches on human statistics. The novelty of Quételet's study of human proportions is emphasized in Paul Rabinow, *French Modern: Norms and Forms of the Social Environment* (Cambridge, Mass.: MIT Press 1989).

44 Quételet, *Anthropométrie*, 64.

45 Rabinow, *French Modern*, 24.

46 For Rykwert, Durand was the only true "revolutionary" architect, in contrast with his colleagues Boullée, Ledoux, and Lequeu. See Joseph Rykwert, "In the Nature of Materials: A Rational Theory of Architecture," *Solitary Travellers* (New York: Cooper Union 1980), 99.

47 Pérez-Gómez, *Architecture*, 299–300; Rykwert, "In the Nature of Materials," 109.

48 Pérez-Gómez, *Architecture*, 302; Solà-Morales, "Modern Eclecticism", 126.

Michelangelo: The Image of the Human

Body, Artifice, and Architecture

Helmut Klassen

Chora

The holy books are open wide
The doctors are working day and night
But they'll never find that cure for love

Leonard Cohen
"Ain't No Cure for Love"[1]

PREFACE

When the image of the human body first appeared in Greek art, it was as an anthropomorphic projection by which unknown and ambiguous powers in the world were identified and could be recognized. Form and gestures, joined with a name, delineated a physiognomy that made apparent a characteristic mode of action and behaviour in the world.[2] More than a representation or picture of man, the image of the body was thus a mask or figure with which something invisible and ultimately unknown was grasped and made familiar. It was a construction that represented the achievement of a certain understanding of reality rather than a fundamental presupposition of it. The emergence of the human form as a stable construction followed a long period characterized by the projection of animal forms and attributes, or theriomorphy, with intermediate stages of mixed or monstrous forms.[3] The achievement of a pure anthropomorphism in Greek art meant not so much that the image of man conquered and erased earlier forms of projection as that man first discovered his unique image, not with a self-directed gaze but as reflected in the mirror that was the world.[4] An objective description of man could be conceived only when the achievement of anthropomorphic projection lost the trace of its own coming-forth, its self-disclosure, and was taken for granted as a stable, pre-existing reality. Then the focus of attention for the construction of the image of man shifted away from the mirror of the world to the direct examination of man himself. Anatomy – the structure and relation of the parts of the body to the whole that are revealed by systematic dissection – was a product of this new philosophical strategy.[5] However, a completely self-consistent physical description of the body remained an elusive end, first conceived only during the Renaissance and achieved with Vesalius's *De humanis corporis fabrica* (1543), almost two millennia after the first dissections were carried out. The development by the artists of the Renaissance of the means of representation with which

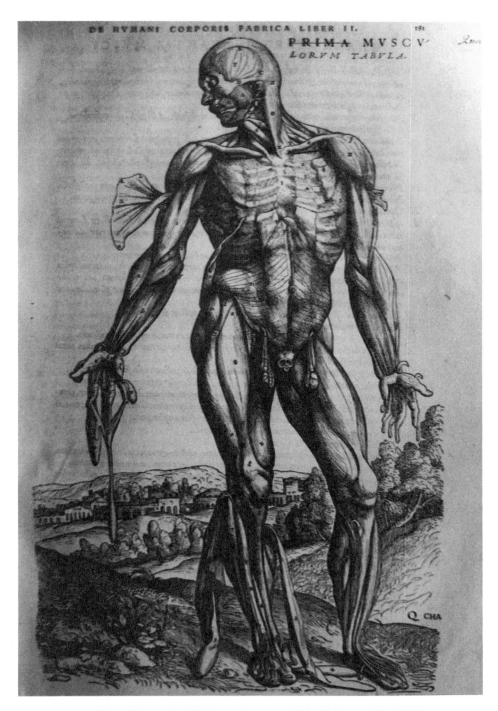

Andreas Vesalius, "Plate of the muscles," *De humanis corporus fabrica libri septum* (Basel 1543). Courtesy Osler Library of the History of Medicine, McGill University.

to coordinate and fix the results of research in an intelligible picture – a fixed frame of reference against which to measure, judge, and ultimately manipulate experience – was decisive for the new image of man. With this framework was created an image that could be improved, transformed, made ever more consistent and precise – but not contradicted or forgotten.[6]

ONE

Traditionally, figuration in architecture was explained as a proportional relationship with the human body. As the source of the measure of architecture, of geometry and proportion, the body during the Renaissance was believed to display the inherent order of the classical tradition.[7] With this perceived authority, it became the object (artifact) of an active re-search into the nature of architectural reality.[8] While the human body was almost universal in Renaissance elaborations of the theory of art and architecture, it would be impossible to construct from this work an objective image of the body, complete and unambiguous, that could form a fixed plan for the elaboration of architectural practice. Though the production of such a representation formed the implicit program for anatomical research initiated by the artists, there existed simultaneously the understanding that an exact reproduction – the conformity of a copy with a model – was an intention that contradicted nature. Every human being who has ever lived is different from every other in some respect. Since God created man in his own image, this differentiation is not an accident of matter to be overcome but a subtle intention that is also observed in the works of man. Filarete suggested that this obvious, yet hardly noticed, first principle of similitude existed for "greater beauty."[9] Thus among the works of each artist, the image of the human body was defined by differentiation. Moreover, a particular interpretation in a work had precedence over a universal image as the site where the diversity of beauty became apparent.

The distortion from the universal standard of the human body to the multiplicity that characterized its particular incarnations was recognized in Renaissance art as the trace of a particular quality of judgment and a complementary manner of working – a trace of artifice.[10] Given this emphasis on the open possibility of differentiation, figuration in architecture did not conform primarily to a fixed image of the human body but was produced within a reciprocal and dynamic relation of interpretation and making – architecture interpreted through the form of the human body related to architecture as a construct framed by man.

In Michelangelo's *œuvre*, we are confronted to the point of enigma with the human body as a universal theme that is, however, revealed polymorphically within a multiplicity of works. Moreover, the works themselves appear to be without a complementary theoretical articulation of their intentions and do not reflect a direct attention to the predominant theoretical concerns of numerical proportion, geometry, and perspective. Obscure to the new theory, the architectural artifice of Michelangelo is revealed through the shadows of the distortion that inherently characterizes all the works of man. In his work, there is an endless display of the human body in movement – figures in which extreme physical movement is joined to the movement of the passions in the form of gestures. Because they are fundamentally singular, gestures evade the grasp of an objective representation of the body. The image of the body is, rather, a possibility through the specificity of all bodies – demanding, for its construction, not so much a set of ideas as an efficacious process of artifice. In Michelangelo's *œuvre*, the phenomenon of figural distortion, characterized by excess, achieves the status of the spurious principle of an unparalleled conception of artifice.

TWO

Form is the fundamental defining character, or nature, of a thing.[11] In the evolution of the concept of anatomy in relation to art theory, form is increasingly interpreted as a physical description of the reality of the body. This inclination is the assumption of the method of dissection and the basis upon which the modern physiological image of man is constructed. Before the achievement of Vesalius, however, it is not accurate to speak of the body as an autonomous reality defined by physical form. Rather, man, and all worldly phenomena, were perceived to be a joining of visible and invisible dimensions. Thus "body" was the corporeal complement of an animating soul – a force beyond all physical explanation that accounted for life and movement. Form was thus a vital force.

In the medicine of Marsilio Ficino, effective artifice was the action of adjusting (or distorting) the course of our lives to correspond, fit, or agree with the vital forces of the world.[12] In this view, fit and agreement are neither a linear conformity nor a one-directional prescription between the world and our bodies but a joining through which body and world complete each other.[13] Ficino defines joining dynamically as an appropriate being-moved and a responsive movement[14] – at first, a passion rather than an activity. This notion is further supported by the complementary characterization of fit or agreement as the influx of a vital heat.[15] Movement (*tempo*) and passion (*temper*) are the vital signs of the body's nature or character defined as a temperament – an aggregate of qualities joined fatefully to a particular individual. Rather than a stable composition, temperament as form is a creative force that is actualized at birth as the plan directing growth, corruption, and death. Not a pre-existent principle, it is the quality of character that exists in, and persists through, the metamorphoses of life, as the force of a seed is revealed in a plant. Physical description grasps only a momentary state of reality and is thus inherently blind to the force of life. Thus medical thought and action are a figuring of the vital powers in the world, based upon a careful measure of the signs and symptoms that reveal formative character. Understood in terms of passion, measure in medicine is defined as pathognomy – (e-)motions that indicate temperament or nature. In nature, because of its corporeal weight, the potential of temperament tends towards a sickness of the passions, or pathology, and exists in an imperfect state, scattered and incomplete.[16] The work of medical artifice is to gather together the incomplete and scattered natures of things, crafting a multi-natured temperament. This is an action of perfecting the natural temperament, suggesting a positive meaning of health for which there exists no equivalent in modern thought – the perfected passion.[17] What is important for effectiveness, more than the specific powers within things, is an action of artifice that imitates invisible nature, or character. That is, artifice that conforms to an inchoate creative force.[18] Thus care and attention to the procedures or motions of artifice, to joining and connecting, have precedence over a method leading to a fixed end or result. Defined from beginnings rather than ends, the measure of form eludes the grasp of human reason, yet is accessible to the imagination. In its earliest form, medicine was an art of divination in the diagnosis of a state of things, and an art of prophesy, or foresight, in the practice of healing.[19]

THREE

For Ficino, the fabric of medical thought was consistent with the intelligibility of astrology, the measure of things from beginnings, and magic. He affirms this fundamental presupposition with the assertion that the sciences of astrology and magic describe what may readily be seen as natural forces of attraction between every thing in the world: "Nature ... is everywhere a magician."[20] He remains ambiguous, however, about the implication that astrology and magic might refer to the world as a fixed order that may be transformed and manipulated – that is, that they are primitive forms of technology.

This ambiguity undergoes a distortion in the medical practice of Paracelsus. He affirms a form of naturalism that rejects astrology and magic as deterministic and, moreover, almost all tradition as delusory preconception. However, the naturalism of Paracelsus does not reject certain forms of knowledge about the world in favour of others; rather, it rejects the idea of knowledge as intelligibility. Astrology and magic are thus rejected to the extent that they are products of human speculation or reason – fragments of man's own mind rather than an understanding of the world.[21] In short, he rejects the traditional supremacy of contemplative theory for an effective understanding of reality. With the supremacy of theory, an order of nature defined by intelligibility inevitably becomes the standard for measuring the reality of the world. Understanding, on the other hand, refers to the world as its standard – a self-forming reality that continually exceeds any speculation about it. Thus understanding reality takes precedence over a knowledge of its intelligibility. Reality exists in the world, and it is directly from the world itself that effective understanding may be learned. The world is an irreducible whole in which each element, including man himself, is defined within its entanglement with everything else. Each element of the world is not an independent object, a physical body, but the focus of a labyrinthine web in which every other phenomenon is mirrored.[22] From the presumption of this complex web, an elementary representation is precluded. Instead, understanding phenomena demands imaginative insight or recognition to figure their reality.[23] Theory means a representation that is a picturing of reality – a frame constructed to procure and challenge from things their conformity to an order of intelligibility, only a fragment of their life in the world.[24] To posit the supremacy of theory is a delusion of the human mind with the gravest consequences for life, the fundamental measure of things. Vesalius's *Fabrica* may be called such a construction – one that to Paracelsus would appear arbitrary and thus would contribute nothing to medical understanding.[25]

FOUR

For an understanding of things, Paracelsus lays emphasis upon observation, or travelling with open eyes. Observation is not simply perception, which is prone to deception, but it is also an understanding of the significance of perceived things, or experience.[26] Unlike modern empiricism, which filters what is seen through a fixed representational frame, observation is not an active objectification of reality but a passion by which reality is perceived. Yet a process of separation, differentiation, and discernment exists between perception and experience that defines observation as a perfective passion. Thus observation is a heuristic process that perceives and with this activity is productive; it figures within the physical world the appearance of the invisible force of character, or virtue. This force is equivalent to each thing's name, a quality that defines each thing as a specific species or kind. It is the knowledge with which "a pear tree grows pears and not apples."[27] This understanding is of a potential reality that is not real, autonomous from its actualization in the world. Thus complementary to the divination of the name is the need for a careful cultivation of the symptoms of character within matter – an understanding of what makes each individual of a kind specific and particular. Within the complex of the world, the understanding of creative force in its joining with matter is, for Paracelsus, the "anatomy of life."[28] In contrast to reason, the heuristic power of observation is associated with the imagination: fantasy is speculation.[29] As something imagined, or a phantasm, the anatomy of life is figured in a manner homologous with its action, as it becomes effective, in the world. Thus imagination is a form of speculation that presumes the opacity of the lived world. Emphasizing the world as a whole before any of its contents, imagination excludes neither reason nor astrology and magic. Rather the potential sovereignty of each is distorted. All belong to the world, and speculation that conforms with the world discovers the appropriate time and place of their exercise, or praxis. Thus Paracelsus's naturalism is an inclusive and synthetic speculation that encompasses all as it appears in the world.

FIVE

> Painting ... demands fantasy and skill of hand,
> to find [trovar] things not seen, seeking them
> beneath the shadows of the natural, and fixing
> them with the hand, showing that which is not,
> to be [quello che non e sia].

> Cennino Cennini
> *Il Libro dell'Arte*[30]

Michelangelo's profound sense of artifice may be found in the understanding of painting extended to mean universal painting, or the fundamental power of the production of images. This specific sense of *disegno* developed by Michelangelo concurs with the heuristic power of observation in Paracelsus. Closely tied to the imagination, "it is superior to sense in that, with no external stimulus, it yet produces images, not only present, but also past and future, and such as cannot be brought to light by nature."[31] Furthermore, "it can form, and reform, combine together and separate; it can blend together the most distant objects or keep apart the most intimately connected objects."[32] *Disegno* is thus inventive, transforming rather than imitating visible nature. Rather than a relation of visible appearances, the analogy between *disegno* and nature is one of creative processes, *disegno* being a force of artifice proportionate to the formative powers of nature.[33] Thus *disegno* is a power parallel, rather than antithetical, to nature: man's painting mirrors God's "painting." As such, *disegno* has access to all things both seen and unseen. In this formulation, nature and *disegno* supplant the traditional norms of theory and practice in the arts. If nature is everywhere proportionate, then it is necessary simply to practice *disegno* in order to reveal proportionality in the world. Thus the appearance of nature supplants an intelligible order of nature as the standard. This is the foundation of naturalism in the arts – a process that paradoxically meant a transmutation – an augmentation (or distortion) of appearances through personal craft or vision, precisely in order to conform to nature. That Michelangelo was never directly concerned with an autonomous articulation of theory is thus consistent with naturalism.

Not merely physical drawing, *disegno* named both the inner power of fantasy and its joining to matter by the work of the hand in the "arts of design" – painting, sculpture, and architecture. *Disegno* was the guiding force of speculation that, with Michelangelo, came to transcend the media that defined the specificity of the arts. Yet if *disegno* was defined by fantasy, it remained implicitly a potential reality until it surfaced into experience – the unseen made "as if" it were real. Thus complementary to imaginative speculation was embodiment, demanding a process of concretely visible work.[34] Theoretical principles that were elaborated autonomously from their material embodiment formed an arbitrary speculative construction that ultimately did not bear fruit.

While *disegno* is critical of theory, it is simultaneously critical of practice understood as skill of craft, or technique. The productions of craft arise from repetitive action, or habit – methods that produce foreseen results. *Disegno*, however, is a force defined by invention – a disruption of existing processes that precedes the action of craft as its plan. Sparked by desire, we are led to imagine beautiful things that motivate us and draw us forward, to make the visions of our imagination real. *Disegno* is the imagining power that guides the action of craft – not the prescription of technique towards end results but the initiating movement as the beginning, or intention. Thus *disegno* is a power beyond the expertness of craft: if the artist's "*fantasia* should be able to imagine beautiful or masterly (things), his hand could not be so inexpert as not to reveal some trace of his beautiful desire (*desejo*)."[35] Thus someone who possessed *disegno* knew more about an art than someone who was expert at craft. This explains how a painter or sculptor could practice architecture with a success exceeding that produced by skill alone. Linking thought and material experience, *disegno* defined by imagination was a distinct faculty in-between traditional theory, or contemplation, and action.

SIX

For Michelangelo, the power of *disegno* was elaborated through a drawing of the human body. Though he is reputed to have laboured patiently over the study of anatomy for twelve years,[36] there does not exist an independent articulation of his research. This is in contrast to Leonardo's anatomical studies, which constituted a body of research even though they were never given systematic form. Rather, Michelangelo's understanding of the body and the nature of his research are framed by the circumstances of the work – that is, as the body appeared in painting, sculpture, and architecture.[37] In these works, there exists no evidence of a knowledge of dissection – of the inner structure of the body as revealed by cutting. Moreover, there is no direct indication of a knowledge of the body and of its structure, and of gestures derived from historical works such as antique sculpture. Instead, the figures conform primarily to what is visible – the imagined reality of the work created by *disegno* that is complementary to the reality of the observed world. *Disegno*, as a form of speculation that mirrors the action of the world, is superior to specific or specialized speculation – not only to mathematics and geometry but also to history and science. Thus *disegno* is not tied to an order of analysis but to a synthetic dimensionality defined by observation. Michelangelo's figures are not drawings from life but are defined as constructions of diverse parts and members derived from various sources – life, dissection, and historical works. Yet primary to the work's identity is the integration of the parts into, and their inseparability from, an observed whole. Consistent with observation as a perfective passion, his figures are thus images of a perfected or healed human frame. Observation is an attention to things, a care of the flesh.

The image of the human body has been revealed in Michelangelo's work as a recurring set of gestures (approximately 2,000) that encompasses the significance of human movement as a fabric, or theatre, of man's passions. This theatre is a complete image, yet is not defined by a systematic intentionality such as seen in Vesalius. It is a laborious construct that exists polymorphically within the multiplicity of specific works. Thus gestures exist within a finite whole, yet are never fixed or even consistent. Not formed with reference to a pre-existing model, in Michelangelo's anatomy the human body is continually remade or interpreted – an open project through which the nature of human experience is explored and ever newly revealed.

SEVEN

The live body is mobile from "beginning to end"[38] – defined by continual physical movement but more fundamentally by metamorphosis from birth to death. Thus it continually exceeds or surpasses attempts at precise and fixed measurement. It is significant that the mathematical and proportional description of the human body during the Renaissance was elaborated in association with the practice of anatomy, in which the presupposition of order is the physical structure of the body deserted by life. Stiffness and immobility is exactly Michelangelo's criticism of Albrecht Dürer's *Four Books on Human Proportions* (1528),[39] in which a complete mathematical and geometrical description of the body is elaborated first in terms of plan, section, and elevation. However, such theoretical work had a limited use in the practical task of art. The incomparability of the self-exceeding reality of the body and consistency of numerical measure was traditionally resolved with individual judgment in practice.[40] With Michelangelo, this is the site where a different principle of measure is elaborated.

The problem of bodily measure leads Vincenzo Danti to concede that the human body has no fixed proportions.[41] Danti emphasizes a distinction between quantitative and qualitative measure, and defines the latter as that which conforms to life. Quality is understood as a force rather than a physical attribute of the body – as an intentional reason that accounts for the growth and movement of things to their fulfilment as specific individuals. Qualitative proportion is the understanding of order as a creative force of animation, the cause by which things actively take shape, understood as a relation of form to purpose. With this understanding of forming power, the parts of the body could be constructed with the same reasons as nature rather than from life or from memory. Moreover, understanding of qualitative proportion enables the construction of things not as they are seen but to their intended fulfilment – perfection as a healing of things in the world. Qualitative proportion describes a coming-to-be of things – their image as an active appearing. Thus resemblance is defined as the presence of life rather than as a representation, a copy of a somatic reality. However, the emphasis upon qualitative proportion does not preclude quantitative or numerical proportion.[42] Rather, proportion is revealed as something produced, the result of the force of quality. This is exactly what has been forgotten since the beginning of the theoretical tradition in architecture, in which quantitative relations predominate in the definition of order.[43]

The relation of intentional form to purpose was not a formula to be optimized but was understood as a relation revealed in the fabric of the human body. Consistent with the definition of its nature as a temperament, the body is a complex *compositum* of intentional forms and functions that is not subject to a single system of proportion. The order of the body, rather than a composition, may be described as a mode or disposition that presents a quality of movement as the sign of life. Yet the representation of life and movement paradoxically is produced from a discordant relation of the parts to the whole – a *compositum* of parts and members existing at different tempos. A single system or tempo paralyses movement. Thus Michelangelo rarely draws whole figures but constructs the body from dynamically articulated parts – volatile elements open to joining and connection. The image of life and movement is thus paradoxically the result of an artificial construction, the inverse of the representation of natural movement.

EIGHT

Though artifice was defined by invention, Michelangelo's fidelity to the classical tradition of architecture was as great as his fidelity to the physical fabric of the human body. He did not invent the ornaments of architecture[44] but transformed their being into volatile elements, as he had done with the parts and members of the body. They too were capable of being "formed and reformed, combined and separated" as his desire moved his imagination. Invention thus presumed an existing situation or background as the circumstance or occasion for the beginning. Upon this situation, observation imagines something new and desires to make it as a completion of what was already existing. Thus invention is a creative process of imagining things "not seen" as a critical superimposition of two distinct realities. Leonardo's entreaty to find new things in spots on walls or in cloud formations is an expression of this process.[45] Invention defines a new reality that is a projection that separates, or is born, from the background of another – an appearance as emergence or relief. This dynamic sense of invention is maintained only when both elements inexplicably act together, each revealing the trace of the other, like the body and the soul. This is demonstrated in Michelangelo's *Slaves*, where stone and figure intertwine, and in his architectural drawings, where the superimposition of elements reveals a potential new construction. Most importantly, the metaphorical reciprocity of the human body and architecture delineates a reality that brings together distinct entities into an imaginative

Above left: Michelangelo, architectural study for the Porta Pia and Figure; inv. no. 106A recto, Casa Buonarroti, Florence.

Above right: Michelangelo, elevation and plan studies for the papal tomb at S.Lorenzo; inv. no. 128A, Casa Buonarroti, Florence.

Opposite: Michelangelo, "Awakening slave"; Galeria dell' Academia, Florence; from *The Complete Work of Michelangelo*, ed. Mario Salmi (New York: Reynal & Co. 1967).

relation.[46] This relation is not defined by equivalence, the basis of a humanization of architecture with its substitution by the body. Rather, it is defined dynamically by tension or discordance – a relation of "is like" or "as if" in which the body and architecture pass dynamically in and out of identification with each other. More than the direct meaning of any one thing, or the combination or composition of things, invention is the discovery of something new as an imagined reality. Defined by excess or superimposition, by appearance rather than physical depth, figuration is a completion by means of a transformative act of imaginative seeing.

NINE

Disegno was understood to be not only a physical drawing but also an internal drawing by the power of fantasy – the imaging of a possible world that the external *disegno* actualized, made as if real. Because of the contact with matter, the first externalization of the image (idea) is inherently imprecise and distorted. The task of *disegno* is to cultivate a completed appearance from a confused, imprecise image. This process of generation is not a linear method determined from the beginning by the idea, but a process of transmutation in which the work is clarified paradoxically by becoming further distorted.[47] The powers of the world "are not immediate, like the rays of a lantern, but like ... sensual things they shine through the eyes of living bodies."[48] That is, physical incarnation is not materialization in conformity with an idea but a process of work in contact with matter. The idea fulfils itself as a living entity, its self-actualization defining its perfection. It is a process in which something contradictory to itself, new and unforeseen, may be produced. *Disegno* fundamentally described the process with which appearances were determined. Thus *disegno* was not fixed to any medium or determined by any method but was defined by the problem of embodiment, itself open to invention. In the architecture of Michelangelo, as with the body that was described by the visible surface, clarification by *disegno* was to adorn – a process of ornamentation as architectural ideation. Michelangelo's architectural drawings are predominantly elevation details and profiles in plan and elevation, reflecting the concern for the appearance of the surface relief of the work. Geometry and number, craft and the techniques of construction do not constitute fundamental aspects of drawing. Rather, drawing corresponds to the construction of the idea, an image formed by fantasy, while all problems of construction, both theoretical and practical, are resolved within the craft of building.[49]

TEN

> All the reasons – of geometry, or arithmetic, or proofs of perspective – were [of] no use to men without the training of the eye ... this whole art ... and its whole end is to know to draw all that is seen with the same reasons that one sees.
>
> Lomazzo[50]

The introduction of the method of section in anatomical representation may be seen clearly in the work of Leonardo da Vinci. This is revealed

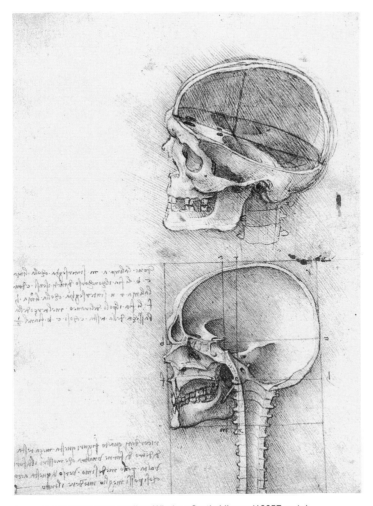

Leonardo da Vinci, skull studies; Windsor Castle Library (19057 recto).

most notably in a series of studies in which the structure of the human skull is drawn in sectional perspective. These, in turn, have been related to his architectural studies for ideal churches.[51] The evolution of section in anatomy, and in relation to perspective, involves the construction of a plane of reference, or norm, against which the inter-relationships of the parts of the body, or between things in space, may be measured consistently. This method for measuring and constructing a conformity between the parts and the whole may be extended further to create a conformity between a model and a reproduction. Leonardo's work is the inspiration for Dürer's three-dimensional description of the body as a systematic,

Leonardo da Vinci, studies for *tempietti*, with sectional perspective drawing of church in upper left corner; Codex Atlanticus, folio 205v, Biblioteca Ambrosiana, Milan.

measurable relationship between plan, section, and elevation.[52] In this manner, the mathematical and proportional description of the body founded a new potential for architectural representation. With this potential followed an inherent tendency towards reductionism – an overcoming of the subtle differentiation that Filarete defined as the first principle of similitude by the precise control of the physical description of things, and their appearance, within a visual or a mental construct.

Michelangelo, however, forgoes this means of geometric or visual construction in favour of a drawing characterized by foreshortening – a drawing of height, breadth, and depth that significantly does not determine interrelationships among things.[53] Foreshortening has been described as drawing where proportions do not correspond or agree with each other, and also as drawing "made to seem monstrous," or distorted.[54] However, distortion may be defined as such only against a measurable norm. In Michelangelo's work the intermediary measuring construct is intentionally absent. Instead, foreshortening measures things with the judgment of the moving eye – a tracing of things within the dynamic connection of seer to seen. Distortion defines the indefinite point of view of someone engaged with the world, not from a static or abstract point of view, but within a dynamic entanglement.

Foreshortening is a vision of things circumscribed by an angle of vision in which the interrelation among things is delineated by the profile separating one thing from another, rather than by three-dimensional depth measured against the cut of a section. Thus things are known by their

Above left: Albrecht Dürer, from *Vier Bücher von menschlischen Proportion*. Courtesy Osler Library of the History of Medicine, McGill University.

Above right: Michelangelo, studies from the Crucifixion of Haman; black chalk and red chalk, 252 x 205 mm., inv. no. A16 recto, Teylers Museum, Haarlem, The Netherlands.

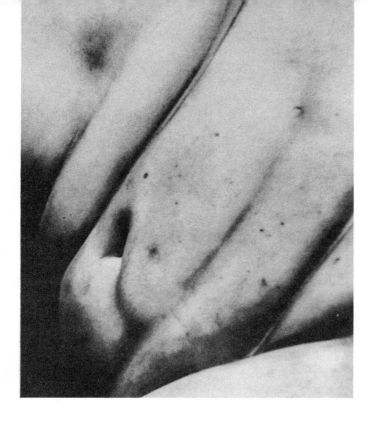

Michelangelo, Abdoman of Night; new sacristy of San Lorenzo, Florence; from *The Complete Work of Michelangelo*.

Opposite: Michelangelo, ten profiles of cornices; black chalk and red chalk, 331 x 229 mm; inv. no. A34 verso, Teylers Museum, Haarlem, The Netherlands.

outside,[55] their appearance, rather than through a depth achieved by a violation of their life. With the measure of profile, focused upon the twisted and distorted figures traced with foreshortening rather than figures flattened to conform to perspective, Michelangelo transcribed the dynamism of human existence into the work of architecture.

ELEVEN

In architectural theories since Vitruvius, "optical corrections" made explicit the inevitable transmutation of ideas through the processes of artifice. Optical corrections focused upon the difference between a building's theoretically generated proportions and the inescapable deformation of their ideality in the appearance of the work. Though proportions could be quantitatively correct, the ideality of proportion and measure was necessarily distorted from particular points of view. The meaning of a pathology inherent in human perception is apparent in Vitruvius's characterization of this phenomena as optical "deception."[56] The cure for this "disease" was not the correction of the perceived distortion by a rational demonstration of ideality to the mind but a perfection of the proportions

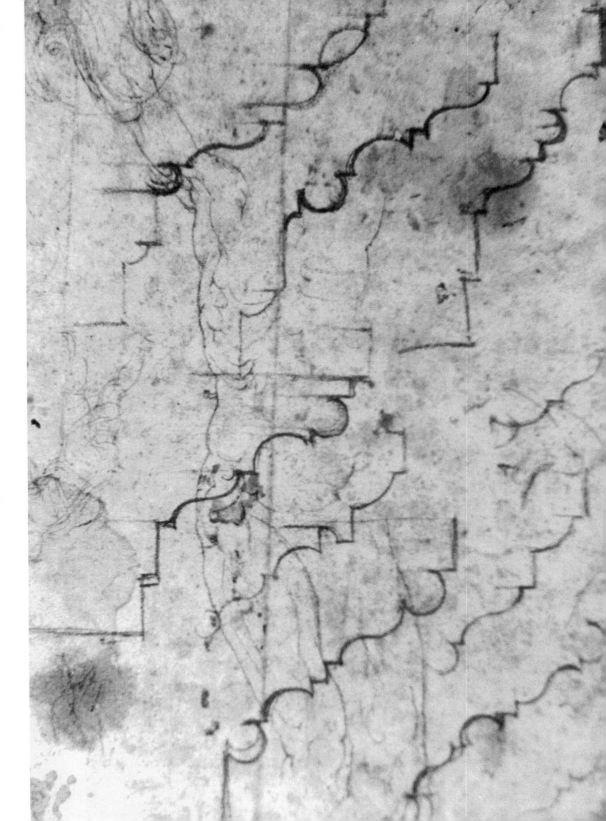

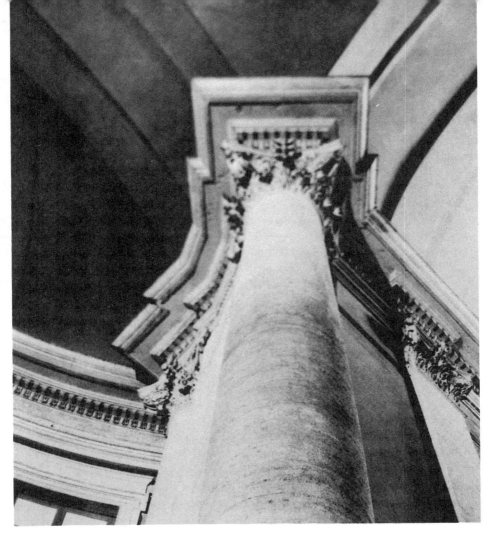

Top left: Michelangelo, upper apse of Sforza Chapel in Santa Maria Maggiore, Rome; from Paolo Portogesi, *Michelangelo Architetto* (Torino: Einandi 1964).

Bottom left and above: Michelangelo, details of columns, Sforza Chapel in Santa Maria Maggiore, Rome; from Portogesi, *Architetto*.

such that they appeared correct, by an adjustment or actual distortion of the measured proportions. That is, the cure was not an elimination but a further exaggeration of the disease – a surplus, an excess.

The ability to perfect the work determined the proper *métier* of the traditional architect: it was not enough to know and apply theoretical principles. Perfection was not a transcendence of experienced reality but suggested a sense of ideality achieved in, and founded upon, appearances.

Bound up with perception, always particular to someone, the achievement of perfection was thus linked to the unique capabilities of the architect to separate and discriminate differences – that is, to make "judgments of sense" particular to every situation. It is this adherence to appearances that bears the traces of artifice that characterize the site of figuration in the work of architecture. Thus buildings were adjusted, or distorted, to acknowledge the presence of the human body and reciprocally became phantoms constructed in relation to the image of man. One of the defining symptoms of modern thought arises when the illusion of perceptual perfection is no longer taken seriously in architecture, when distortion becomes a pathology that must be eliminated. Perfection then ceases to be an immanent healing of the flesh and is transformed into a transcendent prescription – a remedy, or drug, as a "cure" for our delusions. Characterized by a radical excess, the artifice of Michelangelo itself distorts the problem of optical deception and its corresponding correction. Deception defined from the point of view of theoretical correctness otherwise describes the human condition within a ceaseless entanglement with the world. In this situation, the distinction between pathology and perfection cannot be fixed, both being symptoms of the same ambiguous and ambivalent reality. It is to this slippery experience of reality that the dual meaning of artifice corresponds, suggesting both skill and ingenuity but, today, predominantly, cunning, trickery, and shiftiness of character. "There ain't no cure ..."

NOTES

1 Published by Stranger, Music Inc. (BMI), 1986, 1987.
2 For physiognomic projection, see Hans Blumenberg, *Work on Myth*, tr. R.M. Wallace (Cambridge, Mass.: MIT Press 1985), part 1, ch. 2 and 4.
3 Ibid., 117.
4 Ibid., 117.
5 The connection between the evolution of anatomy and philosophy is discussed in Ludwig Edelstein, *Ancient Medicine: Selected Papers*, ed. and tr. O. and C.L. Temkin (Baltimore: Johns Hopkins University Press 1967).
6 See Georges Gusdorf, *Les origines des sciences humaines*, vol. 2 (Paris: Payot 1967).
7 See Vitruvius, *Ten Books on Architecture*, tr. M.H. Morgan (New York: Dover 1960), III.i.1–5.

8 I refer specifically to the relationship between anatomical research and artistic and architectural practice during the Renaissance. See Bernard Shultz, *Art and Anatomy in Renaissance Italy* (Ann Arbor, Mich.: UMI Research Press 1985).

9 Filarete, *Treatise on Architecture*, tr. J.R. Spensor (New Haven: Yale University Press 1965), 11–12.

10 During the Renaissance, every work was recognized as having a *maniera*, or character, that reflected the judgment and hand of the artist. See, for example, ibid., 12.

11 See "form," *Compact Oxford English Dictionary*.

12 See Marsilio Ficino, *The Book of Life*, tr. C. Boer (Dallas: Spring Publications 1980), 83. In this section, I refer to both implicit and explicit expressions that reveal the fabric of the live world, primarily in Book 3, "On Making Your Life Agree with the Heavens."

13 Ibid., 140.

14 Ibid., 125.

15 Ibid., 12.

16 Ibid., 128.

17 Perfection is based upon the measure of time and place. Ibid., 125.

18 Ibid., 140.

19 Ibid., 160.

20 Ibid., 179.

21 See Walter Pagel, *Paracelsus: An Introduction to Philosophical Medicine in the Era of the Renaissance* (Basel and New York: Karger 1982), 57.

22 Ibid., 67.

23 Ibid., 60–7, 120–4.

24 On representation as a picturing of reality, see Martin Heidegger, "The Age of the World Picture," *The Question Concerning Technology and Other Essays*, tr. W. Lovitt (New York: Harper & Row 1977).

25 On Paracelsus's rejection of anatomy, see Pagel, *Paracelsus*, 108.

26 Experience refers to the German *Erfahrung*. See ibid., 60–7.

27 Ibid., 60–7.

28 Ibid., 108.

29 Ibid., 120–4.

30 Quoted in David Summers, *Michelangelo and the Language of Art* (Princeton, N.J.: Princeton University Press 1981), 133.

31 G. Pico della Mirandola, *On the Imagination*, quoted in ibid., 113.

32 C. G. Norena, *Juan Luis Vives*, quoted in ibid., 113.

33 On the relationship between nature and *disegno*, see David Summers, *The Judgment of Sense* (Cambridge, U.K.: Cambridge University Press 1987), 283–310, particularly 306.

34 Ibid., 300.

35 Michelangelo, quoted in Summers, *Michelangelo*, 104.

36 See ibid., 12.

37 On the character of Michelangelo's understanding of the body discussed here, see James Elkins, "Michelangelo and the Human Form: Knowledge and Use of Anatomy," *Art History* 7, no. 2 (June 1984): 175–87.

38 Vincenzo Danti, *Treatise on Perfect Proportions* (1567); quoted in Summers, *Michelangelo*, 292.

39 A. Condivi, quoted in ibid., 380 and 406.

40 Ibid., 72.

41 For further views on "quality," see the discussion of Danti's *Treatise* in ibid., part 2, ch. 5.

42 Ibid., part 2, ch. 11 and 12.

43 See Vitruvius, *Ten Books*, I.ii.1–2. Order, given as the first principle of architecture, is subsequently defined in terms of quantity and modularity.

44 See Summers, *Michelangelo*, 161–2.

45 See H.W. Janson, "The Image Formed by Chance in Renaissance Thought," in *Essays in Honor of Erwin Panofsky*, ed. M. Meiss (New York: New York University Press 1961).

46 See Paul Ricœur, *Interpretation Theory: Discourse and the Surplus of Meaning* (Fort Worth: Texas Christian University Press 1976), part 3.

47 See Summers, *Judgment of Sense*, 300.

48 Ficino, *Book of Life*, 138.

49 See the discussion of Michelangelo's architectural evolution in Summers, *Michelangelo*, 360 and also 161.

50 Quoted in ibid., 372.

51 See Shultz, *Art and Anatomy*, 75.

52 See Walter Straus, *The Human Figure by Albrecht Dürer: The Complete Dresden Sketchbook* (New York: Dover 1972), 32.

53 Summers, *Michelangelo*, 254.

54 Francesco de Hollanda, quoted in ibid., 479.

55 See Maurice Merleau-Ponty, "Eye and Mind," tr. C. Dallery, *The Primacy of Perception*, ed. J.M. Edie (Evanston, Ill.: Northwestern University Press 1964), 180.

56 Vitruvius, *Ten Books*, III.v.11.

Architecture as a Site of Reception

Part I: Cuisine, Frontality, and the Infra-Thin[1]

Donald Kunze

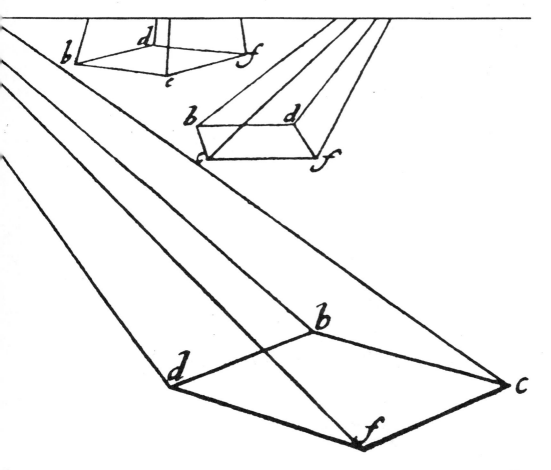

The second level of the theatre shall have its doors painted with one image, and this will be a banquet. Homer has Oceanus give a banquet for all the gods, nor was it without the greatest mystery that this loftiest of poets invented such a fiction, concerning which, with the grace of God, we shall say something.

Giulio Camillo
L'Idea del theatro (1550)[2]

ONE

In *The Gastronomical Me*, M.F.K. Fisher noted that our three basic needs for food, security, and love are so intermingled that we cannot think of one without encompassing the others.[3] There are two important truths here. The first is that the human mind works so much through a logic of displacement, whereby concerns of one kind are written in the language of another, that in fact mind itself might be regarded as nothing more than the process of displacement.[4] The second truth is that hunger, its object (food), and its functions (ingestion and digestion) figure prominently in that process.

Displacement occurs in ways that suggest it to be a universal, integrative phenomenon. Play displaces aggression and emotion onto a bounded field restrained by rules where reality, by being attenuated, may be even more real. Social groups that act as microcosms displace ambiguous desires and fears into the immediacy of face-to-face transactions. But, for us, the most important category of displacement is art, which offers the greatest range of action within the realm of the totally artificial. In art, in architecture as art, we have the topical freedom of being able to speak of one thing through another – in fact, to speak of everything, even through the trivial and abject details of anything that happens to be at hand.

TWO

In general, the task of thinking through the problems posed by the phenomena of architecture is formidable. Architecture is mute, even when its stones narrate the lives of the saints, as in Victor Hugo's famous example. Architecture's principal property is its *emptiness* and its evasion of categorical definition. Like human language in relation to speech, it enables formations to take place intelligibly, but it is never wholly identifiable with any one of those formations. We can point only to buildings, not to the architecture that makes the buildings memorable, meaningful, or awe-full. Our Cartesian intellectual inheritance imposes an ultimately paradoxical division between mind and body, observer and observed, sign and referent. This puts architecture at a distinct disadvantage. Its practical objects will forever remain alien to our theoretical thoughts. Criticism is forced to treat the residuals of the rationalist process of dichotomous division, to provide commentary and captions. Under such conditions, architecture as inquiry is impossible.

Alternatives to the caption-and-commentary process may be found by excavating around, or between, the buried blocks of the current tradition. The situation is much as it was in the sixteenth and seventeenth centuries, when a syncretic intellectual tradition was developing in the wake of Aristotelian scolasticism and in the midst of the Inquisition. The texts of those days were mannerist in their use of irony not so much out of a taste for obscurity as out of a need to survive.[5] It was the duty of the reader to read *actively*, to conspire with the author to realize the unsayable. Conclusions could not be given; they had to be carried into, and reformed within, the secret interior of reflection. Something like this situation exists today, not because of a tyranny exercised from without but because of the internalized self-vigilance imposed by our collectively felt anxieties. No police are needed. Like the sluggish inhabitants of Piranesi's *Carceri*, we sense the futility of ever reaching the exit of our windowless prison of concern. Our subjection is mental, topical. Trapped by the categories of concern, we fail to reach the condition that Umberto Eco called "unlimited semiosis" – the ability to jump with the legs of metaphor from one point of our imaginative universe to any other, however distant.[6]

Like our sixteenth- and seventeenth-century confrères, we must resort to approaches that give necessary arguments an opportunity to be made collaboratively. To use writing as an example, the author must depend on the reader to finish the work, and must above all be able to lead the reader through territory where things are not all that they seem. Though this act of transferring discourse from its literal context to an unfamiliar and unexpected one may be forced by some impossibility of current thinking, it is not at all unfortunate. We are in the homeland of thought, the place of displacement, the site of what Duchamp was to identify precisely as "delay." Although displacement is a response to crisis, its strategies of analogy and circumlocution are the same as those which enabled mythic thought to develop secular forms. In a sense, displacement gives us access to the inner logic of the historical process by which an age or culture succeeds another. While we cannot recover the essence of architectural origins simply by wishing ourselves into a mythic frame of mind, we can step a second time into that river which concealed the secrets of our origins. The same river? Heraclitus might ask. Well, yes and no.

Modern displacement occurs in a condition of abjection, where something cannot be said. Historical displacement recasts the unsayable (e.g., myth) into forms where it maintains its negative though effective presence (monster, denial, *aporia*). By definition, the unsayable cannot be communicated, but it can be comprehended. Displacement thus depends not on a theory of communication or interpretation but on a theory of reception – a theory about how meaning occurs at the "site" of the reader, the audience, or the thinker rather than being fully formed in the workshop of the artist. The idea of reception contradicts and confounds models based on communication because reception violates the spatio-temporal conditions by which communication portrays meaning as projected via a medium. Projection for architecture has a specific sense of graphic geometries that ground acts of representation. But like other projects of the technological consciousness, projection also stands for the instrumentalization of the process of architectural invention, accomplishment, and consumption. Any theory about the reception of architecture and its "sites" is also a critique of projective and instrumental modes of architectural production. It is not about hermeneutic interpretation or response-oriented methods that isolate the subject and object in a Cartesian, information-theory manner.

THREE

Art, essentially, is delay and displacement; and delay and displacement are the basis for art's claim to be a means of thought. But how might we regard this as a justification for examining architecture in terms of the seemingly remote concerns of cuisine? Marco Frascari suggested some ten years ago that "architecture and gastronomy employ similar procedures of production ... The process by which a hut built to house a holy image is refined into a temple, or a covered market transformed into a basilica, is the same as that by which a boiled neck of mutton is refined into *cotelettes à la Marengo*. In both disciplines taste, an interpretive procedure, is at the base of sign production ... Taste is thus a reasoning which suggests what something may be; it is a knowledge which does not know as opposed to a knowledge which knows."[7]

Frascari's interest in cuisine as a phenomenon parallel to our architectural imagination is based on his use of an analogical method of study – a knowledge that does not know as opposed to a knowledge that knows. Analogies as such are not new in architecture (architecture as language, function, narrative, topology, etc.), but they have typically bred reductionism, not the topical freedom of unlimited semiosis. Frascari's analogical realms, such as monsters and medicine, surprise at first but then reveal ancient bonds with architecture, just as George S. Hersey's *The Lost Meaning of Classical Architecture* shocked geometricizing classicists with the bloody allegorical truths of the first temples. Displacement occurs *de facto* as we are led into unfamiliar alliances, but then displacement itself reveals the rules of metaphor that guide architecture and its doubles *de jure*. A displacement of topics reveals their reality – that they are made to be displaced, and only through displacement can we learn their inner logic. And because displacement is about reception rather than interpretation, the terms by which architecture produces meaning are direct, new, and polymorphous. Architecture is no longer the Ruskinian residual of the practical building but, quite simply, the "site of reception."

Frascari's choice of cuisine as a subject for analogical thinking is both serendipitous and serious. The point is that cuisine itself works through an analogical method, and analogy is, principally, a means of tasting to find out what is "there," to make "there" real. Cuisine would be significant to architecture if only for the reason that the language of taste and cooking, ingestion and digestion gives clearer guides to the understanding of reception. But cuisine goes further than other topics might in forcing us to revise our ideas about space and time. Reception in general violates the rules of projective communication. Where is the reader reading a book? Where is the audience of a play? What is the form of time that belongs to a poem? Perhaps our only real resources for answering these questions are works of art that address questions of spatiality and temporality in a surprisingly direct way – Proust's *Remembrance of Things*

Past; the last section of Nabokov's *Ada*; the use of anthology, episode, and dream in Cervantes's *Don Quixote*. But there is a consistent pattern.

Works that address the spatiality and temporality of their own reception inevitably address the role of the body. The body, in short, is about the audience's body as the site of reception for the work, but it is also the material existence of the work as an artifact – not, one should note, just the literal stones, canvases, and pages of the physical entities of art but the transactions that occur in the process of reception – transactions that work within their own specialized spatio-temporal conditions. "Body," here, does not mean the Renaissance use of idealized body geometries but rather the relationship of art to reception, and of reception to the analogous domain of cuisine – hunger, eating, ingesting. This is not the abstracted body but the body displaced, the body realized through displacement. To talk about the reception of the work of art, we must talk about art as if we were eating it.

Another possibility is to study architecture's resources for displacement through the language of *eros*. Pérez-Gómez has portrayed reception in terms of the quest, an architectural version of the amorous Poliphilo in Colonna's *Hypnerotomachia Poliphili*.[8] In the spirit of this ambitious, speculative, and open-ended work, the idea of "presencing" evokes architecture's essential temporality, and Pérez-Gómez has relied on venatic time, Polyphilo's "hunt" for Polia, to shape his quest for the revitalized feminine city. Hunger and its related subjects are companions to this study of architecture as *eros*, if only for the reason that festivals (and antifestivals such as periods of fasting or mourning) themselves constitute a form of time that has influenced architecture as much as the hunt. A fully analogical study of architecture as a site of reception has to do with two complementary studies, one of erotics, the other of cuisine. I would summarize both in terms of a revised dimensionality of art. That this dimensionality is based on the body and not on the abstractions of projective geometry has to do with its temporality, and this temporality, in turn, is based on the more fundamental algorithms of the hunt, the festival and the anti-festival, each with its own unique, space-building form of time.

Furthermore, perhaps the study of one is the study of the others. In his short story, "Under the Jaguar Sun," Italo Calvino tells the following tale.[9] In a little room leading to the bar of a hotel that has been converted from a convent, a painting and inscription communicate the story of a young abbess and the convent's chaplain who loved one another without carnal contact for thirty years. When the priest died, the abbess, twenty years younger, died within a day. The narrator and his wife speculate about how love had found a different medium from the usual one. They ask their Mexican companion about conditions in the abbey:

"*Tenían sus criadas*," Salustiano answered. ("They had their servants.") And he explained to us that when the daughters of noble families entered the convent, they brought their maids with them; thus, to satisfy the venial whims of gluttony, the only cravings allowed them, the nuns could rely on a swarm of eager, tireless helpers. And as far as they themselves were concerned, they had only to conceive and compare and correct the recipes that expressed their fantasies confined within those walls – the fantasies, after all, of sophisticated women, bright and introverted and complex women who needed absolutes, whose reading told of ecstasies and transfigurations, martyrs and tortures, women with conflicting calls in their blood, genealogies in which the descendants of the conquistadores mingled with those of Indian princesses or slaves, women with childhood recollections of the fruits and fragrances of a succulent vegetation, thick with ferments, though growing from those sun-baked plateaus.

Nor should sacred architecture be overlooked, the background to the lives of those religious; it, too, was impelled by the same drive towards the extreme that led to the exacerbation of flavors amplified by the blaze of the most spicy *chiles*. Just as colonial baroque set no limits on the profusion of ornament and display, in which God's presence was identified in a closely calculated delirium of brimming, excessive sensations, so the curing of the hundred or more native variety of hot peppers carefully selected for each dish opened vistas of a flaming ecstasy.

The idea of a carnal love adequately communicated by displacing itself into the sensual agency of spicy food or architectural ornament is an answer to the Cartesian mind/body problem; perhaps it is – for reasons that lack of space prevents me from enumerating here – *the* answer. In the process of desire and ingestion, the body and mind merge in their interests. Hunger and sex may be thought, reductionistically, to exist initially as "drives," in the same way that psychoanalysis would have us interpret all mental activity as psycho-chemical states. However, hunger and sex are quickly converted into specific desires for the certain forms of nourishment that will satisfy them. The needs of the body are conflated with those of the mind or soul. We do not experience a distinction between mind and body, thought and place. We experience, rather, a discontinuity, a small space of time and moment of space that Duchamp was to name, aptly, the "infra-thin."[10] This amounts to an "open set" or empty category that different cultures fill in different ways. Even after being so filled by custom, there is a little something still left over, something empty, that makes this gap an important site of art.

FOUR

Julia Kristeva relates a story about a psycho-culinary geometry in the phobia of a young girl discussed by Anna Freud.[11] After the girl was separated from her mother, she feared that she would be eaten by a dog. At the same time, she became prodigiously garrulous, enthusiastically incorporating into her conversation strange and difficult words. A series of displacements formed a tight web: the hungry girl generated the hungry dog lying in wait. The missing mother was the food missing from the mouth that took up "eating language." Time was divided into a "now" filled with language and a future menaced by the hungry dog. The subject, the young girl, was divided by the phobia into a dog-girl whose mother's absence accelerated her towards a future catastrophe, where a dog's meal symbolized not so much death as the collapse of her temporarily divided personality.

The girl's formula for hunger mirrors in negative a claim once made by Salvador Dalí (cited by Frascari) that "the tactile dimension of taste expresses a desire to learn through cannibalism; that is, to incorporate the outside world into oneself."[12] In art, the internal hunger of the senses is relocated to a point antipodal to the self, both spatially and ontologically, a hunger turned around and aimed at us, awaiting us at a future rendezvous, towards which we accelerate according to the clockwork mechanism of the work of art. Strangely, this "logic of doubles" is to be found within the practice of cannibalism itself. Montaigne's essay, "Of Cannibals," offers this anecdote:

I have a song composed by a prisoner which contains this challenge, that they should all come boldly and gather to dine off him, for they will be eating at the same time their own fathers and grandfathers, who have served to feed and nourish his body. "These muscles," he says, "this flesh and these veins are your own, poor fools that you are. You do not recognize that the substance of your ancestors' limbs is still contained in them. Savor them well; you will find in them the taste of your own flesh."[13]

The architecture of this displacement and return is about thresholds that are made to be violated. Fear or hunger, generalized and all-penetrating, like the "evil eye," has one antidote – discontinuity (*apotrope*). Only through the device of a threshold separating the subject from threat can the subsequently divided world be articulated, civilized, inhabited. Thresholds as such are the basic stuff of architecture, but their complexity can too easily evade the eye. Following Frascari's reminder that taste is a matter of touch – and remembering the more ancient example of the Cretan labyrinth (a building that is literally "all threshold"), where a thread rather than a plan did the trick – we must see the threshold in terms of the double structure of displacement, the antipodal division, where the closest and most feared becomes the most remote, *plus* the palpable return, where the protected centre and the feared periphery meet. The wall, the gate, the threshold are thus about both a division of space and a re-incorporation of space that necessitates the ingestion of the body within the wall.

This is the compact logic of Maya Lin's Vietnam Veterans' Memorial, where the body of the visitor is taken up into the wall in a venatic and forensic movement – the visitor hunts for names; the wall hunts for the visitor – towards a dark centre. The visitor "gets cooked" by ending up further inside the wall than anticipated. The reflections, eventually encompassing the visual field of the site, overwhelm. The space on the virtual "other side" behind the names becomes more substantial than its "real" twin.

The wall may be the ultimate signifying condition of architecture, but the opening in the wall, however formally posed, is about the condition of our entry into the literal work of architecture as such. The threshold is the piece of building that is correlative to the act of displacement, the moment at which the formal distinctions between the self and the world are momentarily effaced. The building eats us, diagrammatically, but in the act of comprehending its architecture, we eat it. The important features of entry have to do with the way that the "frame" of the act of entry takes on a simultaneously neutral and gnostic value. It is supposed to disappear from view. But in reality, it conditions the nature of this initiatory act. The frame imposes a frontality that initiates a process of eating, and being eaten by, the building. To understand it further, we must examine in some detail the way in which frontality structures (or un-structures) space and time.

FIVE

Mikel Dufrenne, writing about the relation of works of art to their witnesses:

The witness, without leaving his post in physical space, penetrates into the world of the work. Because he allows himself to be won over and inhabited by the sensuous, he thereby penetrates into the work's signification – we may say that the meaning penetrates him, so close is the reciprocity of the subject and object. In front of a figurative painting ... no lighting is impossible, because the lighting belongs to the painting ... This does not mean that the painting partakes of the unreal. It means that I have derealized myself in order to proclaim the painting's reality and that I have gained a foothold in the new world which it opens to me, a new man myself.[14]

Frontality, as its etymology suggests, is the face-to-face. In human relations, the face-to-face can take an erotic course or engage a potentially violent rivalry. In art, frontality is essentially the imaginative displacement of the subject into the illusory world of the painting, play, or book into which one must figuratively travel. The work's surface, whether literal or not, becomes the face for the spectator by standing in *for* the face of the spectator, whose eyes are now the transparency of illusion, whose feet are now the rhythms of the work's narrative flow, whose hands are now the tactile and palpable substances of the work. Entrance into the world of the work of art is initiated by this frontality, which digests and reconfigures the subject as a zombie in the service of a poem-god.

Frontality might be taken up from two points of view, in terms of its spatio-temporal dimensionality or of its relationship to cuisine. Either way, we must first discuss how it is that we "know without knowledge," in Frascari's terms. This I would translate as the need for a kind of logic that might be dubbed "proofs of the body." The work of art, to be received, does not demand our philosophical agreement; it demands our *participation in its realization*. This participation has its own form of validity, comparable to philosophical agreement. It is a validity felt rather than thought, but felt in such a way that the proof of the body over-whelms any purely intellectual viewpoint. But even in the dry cabinet of philosophy, the idea of a proof of the body has been put forward as the strongest – perhaps the only – means of securing truth.

There are four philosophical sources useful for discussing proofs of the body. The first comprises rhetorical/theatrical ploys, ordinarily considered to be fallacies, that nonetheless are useful. The *argumentum ad personem*, the argument that ridicules the person, and the *argumentum ad boculium*, the argument "with a club," are the best known. Rabelais provides good examples of both. In the section of *Gargantua and Pantagruel* entitled "Why Monks Love to Be in Kitchens," Antigonous, the king of Mace-donia, finds his official camp poet Antagoras in the mess, standing over a pan of fried conger-eels. Wishing to insult the poet, he speculates aloud whether Agamemnon's poet, Homer, was frying conger-eels when he described Agamemnon's great deeds. Responding, Antigonous speculates whether Agamemnon, when he was performing his great deeds, ever bothered to find out if anyone in his camp was frying conger-eels. In this *argumentum ad personem*, the physical presence of Antigonous is proof of the poet's point – that they both know who Agamemnon was and that Antigonous is "no Agamemnon." The effectiveness of the *argumentum ad boculium* is demonstrated in the story of the mock wedding set up by the Lord of Basché to outwit the bum-bailiffs assigned to serve him with a warrant. I will let readers find this delightful tale on their own.

The three remaining sources of arguments of the body are more "offi-cial." The first is from Diogenes, the cynic, or "dog philosopher." The second is the sixteenth-century skeptic Francisco Sánchez, who wrote in his most famous work, *Quod Nihil Scitur* (That Nothing Is Known), that all proofs are necessarily internal. The third source is Giambattista Vico, who put forward the radically postmodern idea that to understand his text, *The New Science*, the reader had to narrate it to himself. The relation between those three philosophical proponents of the resurrected poetic body is striking. I can review these seminal sources only in the briefest terms and entirely from the point of view of the idea of a proof of the body. I will take the liberty of creating a philosophical monster by amal-gamating these three very distinctive personalities into a composite being. Following Diogenes, this "school" takes philosophy to the level of the body. Contradiction, *aporia*, and other forms of mental abjection are written in the scars of the scourged body: one lives in a tub, begs for food, wears rough clothing, simplifies, mortifies. The tub itself is mortified. Although he has been exempted from the draft, presumably on account of his "insanity," Diogenes patriotically prepares for the siege of Corinth by encyclopedically scourging his tub.[15] The motion is from *nomos*, custom, to *physis*, nature, in the sense of the perennially true. Diogenes is not adopting abjection on behalf of an abstract idea, he is using gesture and pain to get beyond the categories of social custom. He demonstrates that the body is the only site for the reception of the true – *physis* as opposed to *nomos*.

Sánchez puts this in terms of three objects of cognition: first, the object of which we see only an image, an aspect – the object of the external world; second, the object of purely internal sensation, such as anger, anguish, pleasure; third, the object that is a composite of the external and the internal, an observable phenomenon complemented by what the mind "imagines is taking place, as when we form an image explaining the effect of a magnet on a piece of iron."[16] For Sánchez, the only knowledge is that which is able, paradoxically, to blend the solidity of the external world with the certainty of the internal, impossible in logic but not beyond cuisine.

Vico's contribution is a theory of reading that is also a theory of thinking. To understand his *New Science*, Vico argues, one must meditate it on the inside, as the second of Sánchez's objects.[17] In this infra-thin environment of ingestion/digestion, a sympathy is discovered between who eats and what was eaten – the same sympathy, one thinks, as that suggested by the victim of sacrifice and subsequent cannibalism who warns his future diners that they will be eating "their kin." In this third world of Sánchez's, in this three-dimensional reality, categorical oppositions collapse. *Physis* is discovered.

SIX

The proof of the body in architecture takes place within a space and time generated by the essential frontality of architecture as a site of reception. To understand this space and time, we have to revise our notions of dimensionality. The Euclidean progression of dimensionalities (point, line, plane, solid) bites so deeply into architectural critical and technical practice that their truth seems self-evident. The difficulty of this system is its well-documented lack of correspondence to sensual experience. Our three-dimensional body rarely experiences three dimensions or three-dimensional objects as such. Its limitation to the ground plane is escaped only by flying or dreams of flight. Our skin does not recognize three-dimensional patterns of sensations accurately. Our eyes have to be taught culturally to recognize the third dimension in nature, and such learning makes one blind to often quite distinct ways of seeing and portraying space found in other cultures. Points and lines are abstract, not perceivable in nature's patches and horizons. While the Euclidean system is useful, predominantly for manipulating space as well as the people and objects in it, its building-block approach to spatiality is nonetheless inadequate to our quotidian experience.

Real primacy belongs to the surface, which in the body is the medium of the senses that have the tightest grasp of spatial reality (the skin or the retina). The surface, like the skin, is capable of dividing regions, such as inside and outside, self and world. Because of its service as a boundary, the skin is both a medium of signs (tattoos, scars, writing) as well as vulnerable to violation. The dimension perpendicular to the skin is, appropriately, named the "sagittal," the arrow-like. An act of penetration is either erotic or deathly; the ambiguity of the sagittal with respect to the body is revealed in full in Bernini's statue of St Theresa, where destruction and ecstasy are simultaneous. Skin and the image on the retina are frontal in the sense that they initiate an actual or imagined motion in the sagittal direction, into the depths of the image or illusion. This is the dramatic aspect of all art – its movement beyond a threshold imagined as screen, curtain, or façade. We face what faces us, our senses are met fully by the images and sensations before us. We are in a position to receive them, and they us.

Frontality is also art's culinary aspect because, beyond the moment of frontal encounter with art, subsequent relations are in terms of one thing containing another. The point of the sagittal dimension becomes the mouth that inverts the geometry of the hunt's penetrating arrow or spear. The table or plate presents food as display – as presentation. Its arrangements form a chiaroscuro of flesh through which we eat until we reach the bones. When a Roman burned his dead father, notes Onians quoting Varro, "as soon as he came upon a bone, he said that he [the dead] had become a god."[18]

We cannot simply add up the two-dimensionalized experiences of the body (of the flesh) to create an experience of a three-dimensional world.[19]

The two slightly different images of the retinas are not combined or unified to produce the sensation of depth. The whole somehow "resides in" our two-dimensionalized experience, but it does not determine it. Studies of depth perception in non-Western cultures reveal our knowledge of the third dimension to be the product of cultural learning and personal experience. This has to do not only with understanding graphic cues of depth, such as perspective, overlap, or size diminution, but with the immediate perception of space. Peoples accustomed to forest environments are reportedly terrorized by open spaces. Women's perception of depth differs from men's. Children's idea of the third dimension develops in paradigmatic fashion, not continuously. Studies of fictional narrative space reveal what is even more evident in painting and cinema – that depth is a dependent variable rather than a fixed constant; and that it is influenced by a broad spectrum of experiences, including fear, desire, and time.

Depth, the flesh of the world, is less a Cartesian matter of quantitative extension and more an atmosphere or temperament that affects small objects and local events even more intensely than large landscapes. Its discontinuities (horizons, shadows, *terrae incognitae*) infect our locale to the extent that we prefer objects that conceal their contents (books, boxes, drawers, cabinets) as more adequate representatives of global order. They, like the world, postpone our inspection by elaborate folds, closures, and compartments. "Solid" seems to be a synonym for "real" in terms of pure extension, but objects – whose solidity is a means of concealment, whose faces hide some interior mystery – are the chief suspects in the "crime" of signification.

Depth, the flesh of the world, does not seem to be so thick, but the transition between appearance and reality, surface and interior, image and world is conceptually almost impassable. The image of the labyrinth summarizes the many metaphors of reality as "near, but very far away" by compressing a long meander within a tight space. Duchamp's term, *infra-mince*, or "infra-thin," borrowed from Jouffret's discussions of the "sections" between continuums of different dimensions, is apt.[20] Duchamp linked *infra-mince* to chance, discovery, and possibility – traditional components of this idea under its previous flags. The infra-thin is simultaneously very thick and very thin. Its thinness is due to fact that the actual difference between the spaces it connects is negligible, even in some sense non-existent; it is thick because getting across it is no simple matter.

Duchamp, and others of his generation interested in the role of the fourth dimension in art, based their ideas on analogies constructed by extending Euclidean geometry one step further, from the three-dimensional world to a four-dimensional hyper-reality. By this analogy, one can see the relationship between ordinary and hyper-real space in terms of the relationship between the closed, curved surface of the earth and three-dimensional Cartesian space. Just as our life on the surface is finite yet unbounded, so is three-dimensional space finite and unbounded. We cannot perceive it as such because our senses are conditioned by the use of one dimension as a projective line (the sagittal), and this line must be included in four-dimensional space.

I would alter this analogy by using a different comparison. If we allow the solid (three- dimensional) world to stand for the congruence between appearances and reality that is realized in acts of perception as concrete understanding – and if we allow that this sort of three-dimensionality is not projectable – then it is possible to talk about the relation between our sensations/perceptions and our knowledge in terms of a fictional space separating two-dimensionality from three-dimensionality – a space between planes and solids, in Euclid's terms. This fictional space is infra-thin and still very thick. The infra-thin is a fourth dimension in that the lore that accrued to this term in the early 1900s is applicable – its relation to the discovery of the real, to processes of initiation and revolution, to chance, to poetry, and to art. This fourth dimension is a metaphor of the difference between the worlds of the senses and the world as enduring. It is actually less of a space and more the idea of a mode of time that anticipates, in one way or another, an act of passage.

My revised fourth dimension, my infra-thin, is thus something lying between two-dimensionality and three-dimensionality. It is not the exclusive property of non-Euclidean geometries or avant-garde art but of cultures, in the selective building-up of perceptually shared worlds; of the imagination, in its elaboration of virtual worlds; and of the quotidian experience of chance, delirium, necessity, and fate.

The surfaces of architecture and art – now defined in terms of frontality, incorporation of the body, and passage – reveal directly the nature of the infra-thin. In fact, the artistic frontal surface is perhaps the best definition of the infra-thin. But how is frontality interpreted as dimensionality? Is frontality not essentially the orientation of the artistic work to its audience?

1 The audience, inherently, has a collective quality, but the sensual experience of the work is directed to the individual as if he or she were the sole recipient. This is clearly seen in theatrical performances, where the viewer maintains a dual status as a member of the audience and as a single person. In the case of the painting, the shape of the canvas privileges the space directly in front, but the two-dimensionality of the canvas allows this front to be experienced broadly, even at acute angles. The famous effect by which the eyes of portraits "follow" the viewer in motion shows how frontality is effectively present even when its literal condition is absent. The collective is therefore implicitly present in the public nature of the work and sometimes literally, in the presentation to an audience. But the relation of the work to the individual, specifically to the body of the individual, is an element maintained by the work's frontality, an element whose literal features are geometric, architectural, and technical, and whose aesthetic features are related to the work as *something to be received* – the time and the figurative space of reception.

2 The recipient's status is sublimated – raised to a level of maximum ambiguity. It is too easy to say that the work paralyses the viewer in such a way that the metaphors of sleep or death can be applied. Rather, the work makes the question of the viewer's death or life as indeterminable as possible. The corresponding reference in popular culture would be the zombie, except that zombies, to act like zombies, have to play more at being dead than alive. True ambiguity, in this case, requires being lively when one should, technically, be dead. One must look as if one had just returned from the Seychelles. When Macrobius retells Cicero's story of Scipio's dream encounter with his dead uncle, he underlines the extreme good health of the inhabitants of this farthest region of Elysium.[21] In contrast to our all-too-frequent experience of noticing the unpleasant wrinkles, sags, and fatty mortal burdens on living friends, Scipio sees what happens to the soul after undergoing the ultimate weight-loss program.

SEVEN

A brief illustration may serve to tie up the relationships among the revised dimensionality of reception, frontality, and *infra-mince*. I hope it will also secure, within this web, a place for cuisine.

The exhibition *Picasso & Things* was cooperatively organized by the Cleveland Museum of Art, the Philadelphia Museum of Art, and the Galeries Nationales du Grand Palais in Paris. In this collection of still-lifes (*natures mortes*), one could discover a series of topics and techniques that Picasso used to give neutral objects a chance to speak of art as a whole and of painting in particular. One of the recurrent themes of Picasso's still-lifes is food, so much so that Marie-Laure Bernadac's essay on this subject was included in the catalogue.[22] Food – usually just fruit and vegetables, but sometimes bottles of wine, fish and other meats, and the accompaniments and furnishings of a good meal – are traditional subjects for painting. The student chooses to paint such subjects, first because they cost less than live models, but also because their shapes, textures, and colours challenge the beginner's skill in depicting form, shade and shadow, colour, and spatial arrangement.

Part of Picasso's intention in adopting this mode of painting is parody, for instead of developing the realistic appearance of such arrangements, he transformed his still-lifes into hieroglyphic emblems, cubist monograms, and *memento mori*. Given that still-lifes constitute the most traditional and mundane province of art, Picasso saw to it that his own creations were revolutionary lessons in the dimensional and symbolic capacity of the canvas. These lessons went over much the same material that cubism had laid out for the twentieth century – the temporalization of the space of painting, the revision of seventeenth-century perspectival realism, and the active use of anamorphosis. But it seems that the theme of food enabled Picasso to strengthen the cubist themes through an even broader range of possibilities.

A *nature morte* ("dead nature") is pregnant with suggestions of what happens to the eye that is displaced into the realm of the work of art. From Macrobius to Calvino, poets and philosophers have compared this experience with that of death, or the dream of death. Picasso's still-lifes abound in skull imagery, and skulls are sometimes the literal subject matter of paintings or studies. As preliminary studies for *Les Demoiselles d'Avignon* show, Picasso regarded this traditional *memento mori* as the appropriate accompaniment to any passage into the space of painting. The predecessor of the masked figure of the final version was a medical student, skull in hand, holding back the curtain to reveal the interior of a room in a brothel. The skull opened on to the space of art because, like the traditional *memento mori*, the viewer was to encounter a self-image from a timeless perspective, death and life combined. Other skulls appear anamorphically within a puzzle of shapes and shadows. Once one discovers a face or skull in one of the still-lifes, it is hard not to see it. But, as the catalogue attests, art historians have great difficulty in seeing beyond the literally present image. Even the famous face of the *Mandolin and Guitar*, painted sometime after 1927, goes unmentioned. More adventurous anamorphic skulls lie exactly on the edge of what can be claimed or disclaimed. This, of course, is the point of anamorphosis.

The neutral quality – the sheer meaninglessness – of the fruits, vegetables, and other items in Picasso's still-lifes provided the freedom to displace topics of dimensionality, mortality, eroticism, and temporality into objects that had absolutely nothing to say on the matter. Only the skull spoke directly, and Picasso chose most often to conceal it anamorphically. What is offered to the viewer is a completely gratuitous venture. The scenes are trivial in the extreme. Their painterly mannerism, which the late twentieth-century eye now finds entertaining, was first intended to be (and was) daunting. After being put off by the subject and the manner of painting, the viewer did well to ask, Why bother? This is the perfect moment for frontal engagement with the work of art, for it disconnects all claims on the interests of its future recipient. Picasso's neutral still-lifes are therefore very much akin in tone to architecture's engagement of the site of reception.

What does painting talk about when its subject matter has no relevance whatsoever? It talks about itself. Here, a dimensional issue comes up. The phrase "looking at looking," used by artists to discuss the self-reflective matter of how looking works, has a problematic geometric aspect. The classic illustration associated with Desargues's perspective is that of a gentleman gazing at a geometric object, at the angles of which strings have been tied. At the other end, all the strings are gathered together by the gentleman, who pinches them taut just in front of his eye to demonstrate the action of the "rays" of vision as they converge on the eye.

We see all this from the side; we see the sagittal dimension in its full length, from subject to object, viewer to viewed. The cubist opinion on the matter was that this view was impossible. The sagittal was the principle of projection and was not in itself projectable. The sagittal was –

From Abraham Bosse, *Manière Universelle de Mr Desargues pour Pratiquer la Perspective par Petit-Pied comme le Géométral* (Paris 1647).

and can only be – an invisible point, portably carried about by every eye, present in the act of looking as transparency and transfer: the agent of visual displacement. Just as we can see someone seeing something but still have no idea exactly what he or she really sees, there is an epistemological chasm between looking at things and looking at looking. Looking can be portrayed, however fictionally, by the projective logic of perspective. Although we know that this way of looking is culture-specific, its claim to be a natural way of representing is usually accepted without question. But looking at looking itself pushes perspectivism to collapse. This self-reflective act requires some version of Duchamp's idea of the infra-thin – space in terms of skins and violations of those skins; a sagittal dimension that never appears but is the condition of appearing.

We can see Picasso put this case in his own terms. Although other paintings, such as *Les Demoiselles d'Avignon* (1907) and *The Dryad* (1908), had explored this issue in terms of erotic images, the still-lifes provide even better evidence that Picasso, too, was considering the reception of painting in terms of non-Euclidean dimensionality, displacement, frontality, and the metaphor of death. It is really not so far from these still-lifes to Duchamp's concise *The Bride Stripped Bare by Her Bachelors, Even*. First, regard the issue of frontality, which in Duchamp's case is deconstructed by re-presenting the horizon, the boundary between the visible and invisible, as a bi-folded plane, Bride on top. Picasso's small gouache, *Table before an Open Window (Nature morte sur une table devant une fenêtre ouverte)* shows a table with guitar, palette, and tobacco humidor in front of an open window whose curtain and doors are open to reveal a balcony railing and sky beyond. The frontality of the painting is a natural quality of the canvas, of flat presentations. One is "in front of" the picture even if standing at an odd angle, since the perspective and other depth cues remain in constant ratio, no matter how oblique the view.

An earlier painting (1916?) of a fireplace in Picasso's apartment showed two anamorphic transpositions of the idea of frontality – a fireplace whose beveled surfaces mimicked the receding lines of a one-point perspective, and a mirror above. Other sketches of the same scene show that Picasso thought of the fireplace and mirror as being in counterpoint: one was a perspective in perspective, the other a representation within a representation. The status of the image in the mirror or the fireplace is equal to looking at looking – an act trumped by itself, a double ingestion. Frontality was something that Picasso did not take for granted.

In small cardboard maquettes prepared for *Table before an Open Window*, frontality is developed in terms of making the view into a stage set. To perfect the illusion, the logical locations of the various planes within the painting are manipulated. The sky stands in front of, not behind, the window. The guitar is shown as a void cut through the sky, not as an object silhouetted before it. But the most important clue that frontality is being actively manipulated is the reversal of the angle of the sides of the table, which in usual perspective would be shown as vanishing to a point on the horizon lying between the upper third and lower two-thirds of the painting. The edges form a top-heavy rhombus and converge on a point near the bottom edge of the painting. This edge does not belong to the scene, for it is divided into two shades. Although the author of the catalogue finds this "quite illogical," it is clear from the way this surface is not attached to the window or its dressings that it is not the wall but,

Pablo Picasso, *Table Before an Open Window*, gouache on paper (26 October 1919); Paris, Musée Picasso.

instead, the field of vision, coded to indicate the binocularity of the viewer. I say "clear," but the point of such encoding is not clarity but a maximum ambiguity. The bicolour patch works well enough for a wall, without which the window and table combination would float uncomfortably in the void, but not so well – there is no line where it meets the floor, for example – that doubts are not entertained.

Frontality is dealt a few more rough shakes that compound the violence of the reversed vanishing point. Two elements work together to establish the anamorphic quality that represents all paintings as anamorphs. The French doors open at an angle. This could be a happenstance of the scene as Picasso found it, but it is too close to the analogy of the picture plane as a window not to think about the way in which this frontal stage set opens up to let us inside its space. The doors do not symbolize this: they actually facilitate it by forming the edge of the painting's subtle anamorphic image of the skull, whose eyes are painstakingly arranged by placing the thumb-hole of the palette and the sound-hole of the guitar just the

right distance apart. The second-most evident clue is the grillwork forming the toothy upper mandible and the chalky, blue-white sky that doubles
as bone. We are "inside" the thin space of painting at this point, looking
at our own self-image. We have been caught *flagrante delicto* at our own
looking-act. The vanishing point where we stand is where the painting
ends. Semiosis is open because the difference between us – the new us,
that is – and the painting is insignificant.

EIGHT

The interrogation of a painting such as Picasso's *Table before an Open
Window* adopts a forensic strategy. Clues are sought to find a truth
concealed in the past, in the remote moment of painting. But for us
actually to receive the painting as such, the painting itself must operate
in a venatic mode. We attempt to prosecute its significations at the same
time as it seeks to destroy us – the us, at least, that is exterior, alien, and
abject within the painting's phenomenal world order. The painting and
the prosecution's case arrive at the same point at the same time –
Golgotha, the "place of the skull."[23] The site of reception of art involves
an architecture of the infra-thin that defines a site in terms of a place that
is, doubly ingested, a "place of places," where the hungry young girl and
the girl-dog meet.

The image here is of a point of convergence and of two converging
processes that are at first unknowingly synchronized. The initial event of
one process seems to trigger an event in a remote antipodal corner – an
event that can be ignored because of the great distance and irrelevance
involved. But as the implications build that these processes are linked (the
process of art and the process of pursuing art), serendipity turns into
fatalism. The work that we contained within our view now contains us
within its view. We look at it. In return, it looks at us – in Picasso's case,
with the eyes of a skull.

NINE

The conditions of frontality – the singling out of an individual witness;
and the maximization of the ambiguous status of the witness (dead or
alive? god or prisoner? hunter or hunted?) – seem appropriate for the fine
arts, but what of architecture? Frontality, as it turns out, is what distin-

guishes architecture as such from the normative building. Take the case of the art work's engagement of the individual as body. In building *per se*, without architecture, the body is accommodated by suiting its mechanical, biological, psychological, and symbolic needs. For the building to be present as architecture, the body must assume a different relationship to the building. Instead of being the building's client, the body identifies with the formation of the building as a work of art. The body becomes the personal recipient of architecture, and the imagination establishes the site of reception. This is not a matter of identifying mentally with the architect and his/her intentions, but of thinking one's way into the often inaccessible parts of the building; of envisioning the building as an analogue not just of *a* body but of the receiver's particular body. The *poché* of the building and other shadowed parts must be inhabited – nourished – imaginatively. Often the architect provides a means of anticipating this impossible task, as in Soane's creation of a mercurial reticule of thin spaces through the use of mirrors, narrow hallways, and spaces-within-spaces.[24]

The second condition – the maximization of the ambiguous status of the receiver – is achieved in architecture quite easily because of the likelihood that a building's normative use is the only symbolizable content. A door denotes entry, and its decorousness symbolizes the kind of patron and activity for which it is intended. Other elements relate to the normative uses of the building as well, a speech turned in two directions at once – in one direction towards utility (as in the case of the door, "going in and going out"), and in another direction towards the necessary material conditions of that utility (structural support, resistance to weathering, attention to related functions such as security, and to related symbolic content, such as decorum). The receiver of architecture must first be a "client" of normal usage. Anything other than normal usage is assigned a zero degree of meaning, which is to say that it is written in the language of negation. The maximally ambiguous recipient of the art of architecture is, metaphorically, dead; able to inhabit the *poché* of the building much like the traditional foundation sacrificial victim, the recipient receives the building by identifying with it bodily: as it incorporates him or her, he or she incorporates it. The act of comprehension is an eating of the building, and the building's eating of the recipient.

The ambiguous state of the recipient provides the conditions for the unlimited topical meaning of the building to unfold, for once the hold of the prior hierarchies of categorical spaces and functions is broken and the infra-thin space of architecture is entered, the dichotomous oppositions such as solid/void, interior/exterior, and motion/*stasis* become fluid. Any value may be exchanged for its opposite.

The condition for moving from the perception of the building in normative terms and a process of receiving architecture at the site of building depends on re-defining that site in terms of frontality. This requires a shift from the Euclidean geometry of the normative building to the infra-thin geometry of skins and the sagittal dimension temporalized as the event of reception. Frontality in architecture thus designates a moment in the encounter with a building where an act of fascination takes place. Fascination enables the client's interest to be displaced into the imaginative anticipation of the future recipient of the architectural idea, within a site that must be constituted during the act of reception. In this constitution, the identities of the architect and the recipient merge – or rather, it would be more accurate to say that the single identity of architect/recipient is born for the first time, out of its prior constituent parts.

NOTES

1 This is the first part of a two-part article. Part II, in the form of a cook book, is entitled "Sea-Food and Vampires," and will appear in the next volume of this collection.

2 From Lu Beery Wenneker, "An Examination of *L'Idea del Theatro* of Giulio Camillo," Ph.D. dissertation, University of Pittsburgh (1970), p. 217.

3 M.F.K. Fisher, *The Gastronomical Me* (San Francisco: North Point Press 1989), ix.

4 This claim is not as astounding as it may seem if one recognizes the wide use of displacement, in one form or another, in the spectrum ranging from Freud's *The Interpretation of Dreams* to Derrida's *Of Grammatology*. See *Displacement: Derrida and After*, ed. M. Krupnick (Bloomington, Ind.: Indiana University Press 1983). I would propose a different, but not wholly unsympathetic, spectrum of my own, ranging from Diogenes ("anti-building") to architecture.

5 See Ernst R. Curtius, *European Literature and the Latin Middle Ages*, tr. W.R. Trask (Princeton, N.J.: Princeton University Press 1953), 273–301. A more personal view may be found in Vico's *Autobiography*, tr. M.H. Fisch and T.G. Bergin (Ithaca, N.Y.: Cornell University Press 1944), 20–60.

6 The best example one might find of "unlimited semiosis" has been identified in Calvino's piquant essay on "Lightness," which narrates Cyrano de Bergerac's invention of a ruse to delay the suitors by falling before them "from the moon" and giving an account of how one might, if one wished, reach the moon. Literature is in essence such a delay. Italo Calvino, *Six Memos for the Next Millennium*, tr. P. Creagh (Cambridge, Mass.: Harvard University Press 1988), 22.

7 Marco Frascari, "*Semiotica ab Edendo*: Taste in Architecture," *Journal of Architectural Education* 40, no. 1 (Fall 1986): 2–7. As in all things, I am indebted to Professor Frascari for opening up the "cuisine connection," which the trends of subsequent years have served to strengthen. I would advocate a return to that original and stimulating work, which lays the groundwork for any further development.

8 Alberto Pérez-Gómez, *Polyphilo, or The Dark Forest Revisited: An Erotic Epiphany of Architecture* (Cambridge, Mass.: MIT Press 1992).

9 Italo Calvino, *Under the Jaguar Sun*, tr. W. Weaver (New York: Harcourt Brace Jovanovich 1986), 3–29.

10 Marcel Duchamp, *Notes and Projects for the Large Glass*, ed. A. Schwarz (New York: Abrams, 1969), nos. 1 and 26.

11 Julia Kristeva, *The Powers of Horror: An Essay on Abjection*, tr. L.S. Roudiez (New York: Columbia University Press 1982), 38–9.

12 Salvador Dalí, "De la Beauté terrifiante et comestible de l'architecture modern style," *Minotaure* (December 1933); English translation as "Art Nouveau Architecture's Terrifying and Edible Beauty," in *Architectural Design* 2/3 (1978): 139–40.

13 Michel de Montaigne, *The Complete Essays*, tr. D.M. Frame (Stanford, Calif.: Stanford University Press 1965), 158.

14 Mikel Dufrenne, *The Phenomenology of Aesthetic Experience*, tr. E.S. Casey et al. (Evanston, Ill.: Northwestern University Press 1973), 57–8.

15 "He twirled it, whirled it, scrambled it, bungled it, frisked it, jumbled it, tumbled it, wheedled it, scratched it, stroked it, churned it, beat it, bumped it, banged it, battered it, up-ended it, tempered it, tapped it, stamped it, stopped it, unstopped it, shifted it, shook it, thumped it, pummelled it, waggled it, hurled it, teased it, staggered it, tottered it, raised it, rinsed it, nailed it, tethered it, veered it, steered it, stuffed it, bustled it, lifted it, soiled it, tackled it, shackled it, mocked it, spiked it, patted it, plaited it, fondled it, armed it, speared it, harnessed it, penoned it, caparisoned it, rolled it from top to bottom of the hill, and precipitated it from the Cranium." François

Rabelais, *The Histories of Gargantua and Pantagruel*, tr. J.M. Cohen (New York: Viking Penguin 1955), 283.

16 José Faur, "Francisco Sanchez's Theory of Cognition and Vico's *verum/factum*," *New Vico Studies* 5 (1987): 136.

17 Giambattista Vico, *The New Science*, tr. T.G. Bergin and M.H. Fisch (Ithaca, N.Y.: Cornell University Press 1968), §345.

18 William B. Onians, *The Origins of European Thought* (Cambridge, U.K.: Cambridge University Press 1951), 267. The citation is from Varro's *Fragments*.

19 I cannot cite here the representative range of writings that have a bearing on this subject. My primary source is Maurice Merleau-Ponty, *The Phenomenology of Perception*, tr. C. Smith (London: Routledge & Kegan Paul, 1962).

20 Craig E. Adcock has much of interest to say about this and related subjects in *Marcel Duchamp's Notes from The Large Glass: An N-Dimensional Analysis* (Ann Arbor, Mich.: UMI Research Press 1983). My initial inspiration on this subject, however, came from Octavio Paz, *Marcel Duchamp, Appearance Stripped Bare*, tr. R. Phillips and D. Gardner (New York: Seaver Books 1973).

21 Macrobius Ambrosius Theodosius, *Commentary on the Dream of Scipio*, tr. W.H. Stahl (New York: Columbia University Press 1952).

22 Marie-Laure Bernadac, "Painting from the Guts: Food in Picasso's Writings," in *Picasso & Things*, ed. J. S. Bodds (Cleveland, Ohio: Cleveland Museum of Art 1992), 22–9.

23 Hegel wrote extensively and seriously about Golgotha as the nexus of philosophical reflection. Verene notes: "Calvary or Golgotha is literally the place of the skull. This literal meaning is preserved in the German word *Schädelstätte* (*Schädel*, skull; *Stätte*, place) as it is not in English, although *calvaria* is the Latin root of Calvary and Golgotha reflects the original Aramaic *gulgultha*, of which the Latin *calvaria* is the translation. Calvary is the proper name of the Mount on which the Christ was crucified. Figuratively it is an experience of intense mental suffering. Hegel uses the term to describe the process of the *Phenomenology*." See Donald P. Verene, *Hegel's Recollection: A Study of Images in the Phenomenology of Spirit* (Albany, N.Y.: State University of New York Press 1985), 89. See also Alasdair MacIntyre, "Hegel on Faces and Skulls," in *Hegel: A Collection of Critical Essays*, ed. A. MacIntyre (South Bend, Ind.: University of Notre Dame Press 1976), 225.

24 For an overview of the work of Sir John Soane (1753–1837), see Susan F. Millenson, *Sir John Soane's Museum* (Ann Arbor, Mich.: UMI Research Press 1987).

Fictional Cities

Graham Livesey

Chora

THE PRACTICE OF ARCHITECTURE in the postindustrial city is both a difficult and an essential task, given the conversion of the public realm into an alien and endless world of ambient images.[1] Through a brief examination of literary works by Bruno Schulz and André Breton, and the architecture of Aldo Rossi, this essay discusses the role that fiction and, hence, narrative can play in the redefinition of the contemporary city. To frame this inquiry, I will propose that there exists a hidden fictional and dialectical counterpart to the real city. This suggests the often overlooked role that narrative plays in the order of the city and the integral relationship between architecture and story-making. To address these ideas, I will concentrate on two principal components of both fiction and the city – narrative and background. In this case, background can be considered as the material aspect of a city, the setting for narrative action. Inevitably, these two components are united by the people who inhabit fictions, architecture, and cities.

A narrative may be an account, a history, tale, or story – a structured collection of events. An event, as the fundamental component of a narrative, may be defined as a happening or occurrence, however banal or monumental, an intersection of trajectories in real or fictional space. Therefore, the city may be understood as a collection of stories that have been recorded and continue to be written over time. The city becomes analogous to a book, a repository into which events are written. Architecture is vital to the recording and writing of the narratives of the city. Nevertheless, it is the individual and collective stories that provide the enduring legacy, for buildings come and go.

The recognition that our lives are immersed in narrative and that our understanding of the world is given greater coherence by narrative order, is one way of beginning to address the deficiencies of the modern city.[2] Our lives as a continuous sequence of more or less memorable events take on the qualities of a story; and the writing of our life stories has, in the past, often coincided with the larger and essential stories of the collective through participation in public events. It is important to stress the fundamental distinction made by Paul Ricœur between historical and fictional narratives. History records events that have actually happened, whereas fiction, while drawing from the material world, describes what might happen. Our understanding of how narrative underlies actions in the everyday world, of the making of histories, can be learned from the worlds of fiction and fiction-writing: works of fiction can lead us to "what is essential in reality."[3] It is the role of a literary work of fiction to explore events that parallel those of the everyday world. Michel Butor calls the novel the "phenomenological realm *par excellence*" and the "laboratory of narrative."[4] Fiction writers endeavour to reveal new aspects of existence often overlooked by other fields of inquiry (science, philosophy, etc.), and as such, literature has often provided an important voice in the modern world.

The relationship between real and fictional worlds is investigated in *The Street of Crocodiles* by the Polish writer Bruno Schulz, who effectively combines both autobiography and dreams. Schulz writes stories drawn from his early childhood, based on actual events but overlaid and transformed by his fantasies and fears – stories that attempt to reveal the primordial narratives that underlie everyday actions common to us all. This quest is suggested in an essay in which Schulz discusses the work of Thomas Mann: "Mann shows that beneath all human events, when the chaff of time and individual variation is blown away, certain primeval patterns, 'stories', are found, by which these events form and re-form in great repeating pulses."[5] This search for primeval stories is an effort to uncover a mythical basis for existence, a parallel and hidden order, an attempt to reconcile everyday reality with mythology through a poetic regeneration of language.

In a series of interrelated vignettes, Schulz portrays his family and the small provincial Polish town where they lived. It is a town in which there persists a mysterious, dream-like quality: the squares are empty, victim to the fitful winds that often bring in strange and exotic qualities. It is a town of dreams under a large and shifting sky that reflects the great and magical order of the heavens. Seeking to reveal a mythical or "parallel" reality,[6] Schulz celebrated the poetic and elusive nature of the world: "It is exceedingly thoughtless to send a young boy out on an urgent and important errand into a night like that, because in its semi-obscurity the streets multiply, becoming confused and interchanged. There open up, deep inside a city, reflected streets, streets which are doubles, make-believe streets. One's imagination, bewitched and misled, creates illusory maps of the apparently familiar districts."[7]

What is particularly striking in the stories, apart from the sumptuous and sensual poetry of the writing, is the way in which the city and the family house are portrayed as fully alive, responsive to the imaginations of the characters. Trivial and ordinary occurrences often take on a mon-

Bruno Schulz, drawing; from *The Fictions of Bruno Schulz* (London: Pan Books 1988).

umental or magical dimension: a stamp album can become a passkey to all the nations of the world; openings into other worlds suddenly appear. Characters and places are transformed by mysterious forces; what is seemingly ordinary and material can display wondrous tendencies: "Matter has been given infinite fertility, inexhaustible vitality, and, at the same time, a seductive power of temptation which invites us to create as well. In the depth of matter, indistinct smiles are shaped, tensions build up, attempts at form appear. The whole of matter pulsates with infinite possibilities that sends shivers through it."[8]

As in the stories that Schulz recounts, the city plays a central role in the surrealist writings of André Breton. The surrealists advocated the necessary reconciliation of dream and reality, relying heavily on psychic automatism, a method of auto-analysis influenced by Freud's psychoanalytical work. Automatism enabled the artist to tap into the world of dreams, and possibly into a greater subliminal collective order. Other methods developed by the surrealists to liberate the imagination from the strictures of logical thinking and to explore the realm of desires included: hypnosis, recital of dreams, investigations into the methods of esoteric and magical arts, the recording of chance encounters, the staging of unusual events, and the collecting of found objects. Surrealism positioned itself in reaction to the positivistic outlook of the modern era – to what Breton called the "reign of logic." It strove to provide a glimpse of the hidden order that surrounds us, recognizing the inherent ambiguity and mystery of the world.

Breton and other members of the surrealist group sought "surreal" encounters in the streets of Paris. They affirmed these moments of chance, coincidence, and premonition "as the only true reality, as expressive of both the randomness and the hidden order that surrounds us,"[9] demonstrating the existence of a great dream order to the city. Surreal qualities were often discovered in the banal, in trivial and ephemeral things such as billboards and shop signs, and in more enduring objects such as statues and public places. The surrealists' search thus established a fictional map of the city.

Breton's "novel," *Nadja* (1928), vividly suggests this hidden topography beneath the city of appearances. Paris is portrayed as truly engaged in a surrealist manner, with certain places and events experienced by Breton forming a loose and mysterious story. One of his accidental encounters, in this wandering narrative, is with the statue of Étienne Dolet on its plinth in the Place Maubert, a monument that had always fascinated him and that inevitably "induced unbearable discomfort."[10] The most important chance occurrence in the story, however, takes place when Breton encounters the strange and tempting woman whose name provides the title for the book. The first meeting initiates a series of unusual rendezvous that leaves Breton both enchanted and disturbed. Nadja displays a surreal ability for predicting events that are about to occur and is particularly resonant with certain places and people. Gradually, her behaviour becomes more erratic and she is committed to an asylum, leaving Breton to muse over their few meetings.

In a number of works, Breton uses Paris both as a backdrop and as an active participant in the narrative. The city is a great playground where unusual intersections of people, objects, and places become the basis for a narrative structure that reveals an otherwise invisible dimension to the city – an intermingling of individual and collective narratives. The city of dreams is a fictional city that sustains and is sustained by the verifiable city of appearances: "Fever-cities traversed in every direction by women alone, abandoned cities, cities of genius too, whose buildings had animated statues on top, whose freight elevators were built to resemble human beings, cities of sorry storms, this one more beautiful and more fleeting than the others, all whose palaces and factories were in the form of flowers: a violet was a mooring for boats."[11]

Statue of Étienne Dolet, Place
Maubert, Paris; from A. Breton,
Nadja (Paris: Gallimard 1964).

The theories and methods of surrealism suggest that a work of architecture in the city can both enhance the stories of the city and act as a
doorway to the world of dreams. The works of both Schulz and Breton
describe a shift into another reality – one that emerges from the everyday
life of the city either by chance or by searching carefully for the entry
points. This realm is an underworld, an encounter with the self, the city
of dreams – a necessary and hidden other.

●　▲　■

The relationship between architecture and fiction has preoccupied a
number of contemporary architects, including Peter Eisenman, Bernard

Tschumi, and Nigel Coates.[12] This relationship can be manifested in a number of ways: an architect may incorporate narratives and narrative structures into his work; a work of architecture in the city may be a backdrop that allows for the unfolding or modification of narrative action; or architecture, through memory and association, may physically embody stories.

An example of the exploration of the fictional qualities of the contemporary North American city may be found in a number of projects executed during the 1970s for the city of New York by the Office for Metropolitan Architecture (OMA). The history of New York explored by Rem Koolhaas in *Delirious New York* is an investigation of the "culture of congestion" and a retroactive manifesto for a city that lacks definition.[13] After examining a number of seminal New York institutions (Coney Island, the skyscraper, Radio City Music Hall, and so on), the book ends with an appendix entitled "A Fictional Conclusion," in which Koolhaas proposes a number of projects for the city.

The conceptual and metaphorical project entitled "The City of the Captive Globe" (1972) by OMA is a series of discrete skyscraper blocks ordered on a grid. Each "in the absence of real history develops its own instantaneous" folklore "through the double disconnection of *lobotomy* and *schism*."[14] An intuitive depiction of New York, this theoretical project is a surreal tribute to the sciences, arts, and manias of the city, using explicit references to the European avant-garde seduced by the skyscraper city – Le Corbusier, Dalí, constructivism, Mies van der Rohe, Dr Caligari, and so on. Together, these projects provide an "enormous incubator" for the story of the Captive Globe lying at the centre of the city: "The City of the Captive Globe is devoted to the artificial conception and accelerated birth of theories, interpretations, mental constructions, proposals and their infliction on the World. It is the capital of the Ego, where science, art, poetry and forms of madness compete under ideal conditions to invent, destroy and restore the world of phenomenal Reality."[15]

Projects such as the City of the Captive Globe provide an example of how the narrative order of a city can be changed by the addition of an architect's story, developed from a reading of the city. This approach is very different from that found in the work of the contemporary Italian architect Aldo Rossi. Rossi's career offers a profound examination of the European city, in terms of both narrative and form making. In the opening pages of *A Scientific Autobiography*, Rossi notes the double meaning of

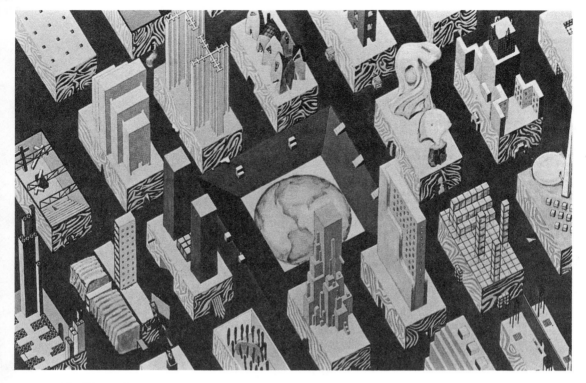

The Office for Metropolitan Architecture, "The City of the Captive Globe" (1972); from
R. Koolhaas, *Delirious New York* (New York: Oxford University Press 1978).

the Italian word *tempo* – which refers to both atmosphere and chronology – which suggests to him the fundamental confrontation in architecture between enduring forms and chance encounters with unforeseen events.[16] Throughout his career, Rossi has tried, through his ongoing examination of a limited number of typological forms, to realize forms that are enduring and essential for the everyday drama of human lives. Architecture is a vehicle for the unfolding of events; it represents a society's efforts to make new stories and embody history. Rossi describes Filarete's column in Venice, a fragment from a never-completed palace, as a "symbol of architecture consumed by the life which surrounds it."[17] He strives for an architecture alive with memories that will help to understand human actions and the making of fictions, history, and architecture.

Although Rossi has long been associated with the promotion of a rationalist and scientific examination of cities, a strong surrealist undercurrent is evident in his architectural explorations. His work (in particular, his drawings) has often been compared to the "metaphysical" paintings of Giorgio de Chirico. Rossi's projects share with de Chirico's work qualities of enigma and suspense, the making of stark places waiting for dramatic and unexpected events to unfold – what Daniel Libeskind has called the "constructivism of emptiness."[18]

Rossi tries to "stop the event just before it occurs," to understand intimately the action that may unfold, to explore the potential for architecture to be inhabited and engaged. Although inspired by a number of writers, Rossi invokes theatre as his primary means for understanding the role of the event in thinking about architecture: "Without an event there is no theatre and no architecture."[19] He has used theatre projects – in particular the "Little Scientific Theatre," inspired by Raymond Roussel – as laboratories for understanding the connections between architecture, event, and memory. The Little Scientific Theatre was devised as an experiment to explore these relationships. Rossi describes the project as follows:

The invention of the Little Scientific Theatre, like any theatrical project, is imitative; and like all good projects, its sole reason is to be a tool, an instrument, a useful space where definitive action can occur. The theatre, then, is inseparable from its sets, its models, the experience of their combinations; and the stage can thus be seen as reduced to an equivalent of an artisan's or scientist's worktable. It is experimental like science, but it casts its peculiar spell on each experiment. Inside it, nothing can be accidental, yet nothing can be permanently resolved either.[20]

Although not as temporary as a stage set, Rossi's architecture of the city is theatrical and stage-like. He thinks carefully about the public spaces of the city and the possibility for event-making – and, therefore, for narrative. Rossi's most famous theatre project, the "*Teatro del Mondo*" (1980), commissioned for the Venice Biennale, addressed the difficult problem of making an architecture of the city. As a piece of urban architecture for staging events and as a typological character acting against the backdrop of Venice, the theatre was an ephemeral *machina*, overtly reminiscent of the fantastic constructions made for Renaissance and Baroque festivals and processions. Through its very temporality and its wealth of references to the city's festive tradition, this floating theatre demonstrated Rossi's concern for event, architecture, and the city. As in all of Rossi's important projects, once the work is set free it gathers the numerous and constantly shifting events that it encounters. As an urban project, the *Teatro del*

Aldo Rossi, "Little Scientific Theatre" (1978); from *Aldo Rossi: Buildings and Projects*, ed. P. Arnell and T. Bickford (New York: Rizzoli 1985).

Mondo functions in a manner similar to Breton's description of certain Parisian monuments: it engages the city of Venice in a great play, giving new impetus to the architecture of the city.

Exploring how historical memories of the collective overlap with his own personal memories, Rossi devises the "analogous city" as a metaphorical method for understanding and designing the city. The analogous city confronts reality, memory, and the imagination – a collage of the real and the ideal, the historical and the fictional. Rossi uses a painting by Canaletto to describe his method. The painting depicts an imaginary view of Venice that incorporates three works by Palladio – the Rialto bridge project and two buildings in Vicenza. This analogous Venice is a city that we recognize even though it does not exist in reality. A drawing by Rossi

Aldo Rossi, "Composition" (1981); from *Aldo Rossi: Architetture,
1959–87*, ed. A. Ferlenga (Milan: Electa 1987)

replicates Canaletto's *Capricci* by depicting several of his projects contemporary with the *Teatro del Mondo*, including a temporary entrance portal erected for the 1980 Biennale and an unrealized project for Cannaregio West. The juxtaposition of these projects forms an analogous and imaginary city. In this way, paintings and drawings enable Rossi to explore the boundaries between the real and the imaginary, the permanent and the ephemeral, and to generate authentic, unforeseen, and original meanings: "The analogous city meant a system of relating the city to established elements from which other artifacts could be derived. At the same time, the suppression of precise boundaries in time and space allowed the design the same kind of tension that we find in memory."[21]

Rossi's works – the Gallaratese housing project (1969–73), the Modena cemetery (1971–84), and the *Teatro del Mondo* – have the potential to act as doorways to the invisible city of the imagination, the fictional city. Rossi is not interested in writing stories to be added to the city. Instead, through its ability to make significant events, his work engages in the narrative order of the city. Through its very emptiness, his work achieves duration in memory and imagination.

In many older cities, a dialectical relationship has been maintained between the real city and its imaginary or fictional counterpart. This is evident in the literature written about such cities as Paris, London, and Rome – and in their dense histories. There has been an ongoing embellishment of the narratives of these cities, a continuous re-examination and modification of individual and collective stories. The contemporary postindustrial condition that threatens all cities has led to the erosion of the public realm, and the traditional importance of urban architecture is being undermined by the tendency of modern technology to reduce everything to surface. The postindustrial city is no longer able to maintain a balance between the material and the imaginary. Cities are becoming entirely fictional, mere representations of some other place or time. The simulated postindustrial city is nowhere more evident than in the ubiquitous sprawl of Los Angeles, an automobile city truly defined in the flatness of ever-changing images. The home of Hollywood and Disneyland, Los Angeles is a collapsed reality, a city of fiction where history and architecture do not matter:

It is not the least of America's charms that even outside the movie theatres the whole country is cinematic. The desert you pass through is like the set of a Western, the city a screen of signs and formulas ... The American city seems to have stepped right out of the movies. To grasp its secret, you should not, then, begin with the city and move inwards to the screen; you should begin with the screen and move outwards to the city.[22]

In the works mentioned above, there is evidence, I think, of a keen sensitivity to the city and its fictions, an understanding of how the real and the imaginary support one another, and of how the material can be magical. Although a work of fiction operates in the space of the imagination – and therefore cannot be but can only describe the real world – there is much that fiction can indicate about, or modify in, the everyday world. Conversely, there is much about the material city that resembles the world of a book. Butor defines the city as a "sum of trajectories"[23] – as the sum of narratives that it embodies, as its collective history. The city inevitably becomes a palimpsest on which a complex record of events is inscribed over time.

The contemporary condition requires architectural projects of substantial depth that, much like a surgical operation, can carve through the seamless web of images generated by modern communications technology. Architecture gathers, modifies, and distorts the narratives of our lives in the city, and it is the architect who engages in a careful exploration of the urban realm to discover glimpses of the invisible. To this end, the work of fiction acts as a metaphorical guidebook. Analogously, the work of architecture provides openings and the architect establishes passages between the material world and fiction: "Then, without feeling reluctant any longer, I set about discovering the face of the infinite beneath the concrete forms which are escorting me, walking the length of earth's avenues."[24]

NOTES

1 For a detailed examination of this problem since the eighteenth century, see Richard Sennett, *The Fall of Public Man* (London: Faber 1986).

2 See David Carr, *Time, Narrative, and History* (Bloomington, Ind.: Indiana University Press 1986).

3 Paul Ricœur, "The Narrative Function," *Hermeneutics and the Human Sciences*, tr. J.B. Thompson (Cambridge, U.K.: Cambridge University Press 1981), 296. Ricœur's essay contains a discussion of the relationship between history and fiction.

4 Michel Butor, *Inventory*, ed. R. Howard (New York: Simon & Schuster 1968), 27.

5 *Letters and Drawings of Bruno Schulz*, ed. J. Ficowski (New York: Fromm 1990), 114.

6 Ibid., 88. Schulz found the notion of a "parallel" reality in the work of Franz Kafka.

7 Bruno Schulz, *The Fictions of Bruno Schulz*, tr. C. Wieniewska (London: Pan Books 1988), 61.

8 Ibid., 39. From a story entitled "Treatise on Tailors' Dummies, or the Second Book of Genesis."

9 R. Shattuck, "Love and Laughter: Surrealism Reappraised," in Maurice

Nadeau, *The History of Surrealism*, tr. R. Howard (New York: MacMillan 1968), 21.

10 André Breton, *Nadja*, tr. R. Howard (New York: Grove Press 1960), 24.

11 André Breton, "Soluble Fish," *Manifestoes of Surrealism*, tr. R. Seaver and H.R. Lane (Ann Arbor, Mich.: University of Michigan Press 1972), 81. "Soluble Fish" is an early automatic text by Breton.

12 Studio explorations carried out by Tschumi and Coates at the Architectural Association during the 1970s are examples of this.

13 Rem Koolhaas, *Delirious New York* (New York: Oxford University Press 1978).

14 Ibid., 244.

15 Ibid., 243.

16 Aldo Rossi, *A Scientific Autobiography*, tr. L. Venuti (Cambridge, Mass.: MIT Press 1980), 1.

17 Ibid., 6.

18 Daniel Libeskind, "*Deus ex Machina/Machina ex Deo*: Aldo Rossi's Theatre of the World," *Oppositions* 21 (1980): 18.

19 Rossi, *Autobiography*, 48.

20 Quoted in *Aldo Rossi: Buildings and Projects*, ed. P. Arnell and T. Bickford (New York: Rizzoli 1985), 185.

21 Aldo Rossi, *The Architecture of the City*, tr. D. Ghirardo and J. Oakman (Cambridge, Mass.: MIT Press 1984), 176.

22 Jean Baudrillard, *America*, tr. C. Turner (London: Verso 1988), 56.

23 Butor, *Inventory*, 36.

24 Louis Aragon, *Paris Peasant*, tr. S.W. Taylor (London: Pan Books 1987), 130.

Instrumentality and the Organic Assistance of Looms

Indra Kagis McEwen

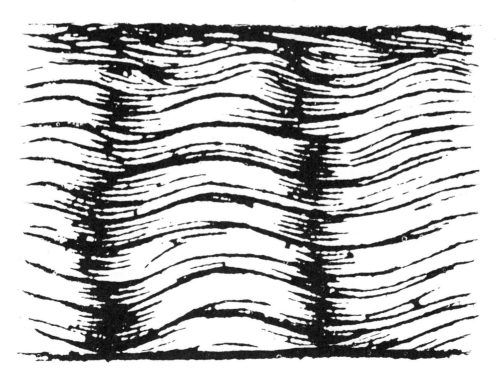

Chora

> Let us then consider what was first discovered
> from necessity: clothing, for example, where, by
> the organic assistance of looms, the warp is
> bound to the weft, not only so that the body
> might be covered in order to protect it, but also
> so that ornament might enhance its honour.
>
> Vitruvius
> *De Architectura*[1]

THE CRITIQUE OF MODERNISM that so preoccupies contemporary architectural discourse has entailed a fundamental re-interpretation of the history of Western architecture. The critique and the re-interpretation together have led to the discovery that architecture, initially and throughout most of its history, was understood as anything but a functional or formalist undertaking. It was found that until very recently, *all* architecture – not only (albeit especially) that of church or temple buildings – was essentially religious, inasmuch as it confounded the immanent and the transcendent in built, corporeal reality. Architecture was like the human body itself, which – as Vitruvius demonstrated with all the rigour and certainty of geometrical proof – was bounded by both the chthonic, terrestrial mystery of the circle and the celestial, ouranian rationality of the square.[2]

The discovery, or rather the *re*-discovery, that such a fusion was the essential dimension of architecture until the eighteenth century, has been accompanied by the bitter realization that, in a world where the evocation of transcendence plays virtually no legitimate role in discourse, the fusion of the immanent and the transcendent in architecture appear to have become impossible.[3] The square and the circle – and indeed all that made architecture the paradigm of meaningful human undertakings throughout Western history – have, it is claimed, been instrumentalized to the point where the possibility of meaning in architecture has been all but eliminated. The search goes on for some aspect of the architectural tradition that may have escaped instrumentalization and that might yet save architecture from the threat of complete non-sense.

I do not propose to participate in that particular search. Rather, what I propose to do is to examine the notion of instrumentality itself in order to see if, within an expanded understanding of the instrument or tool –

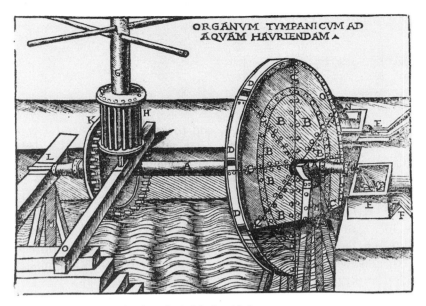

Vitruvius, water-lifting device; from *De Architectura Libri Decem* (Cesariano edition, 1521), Book x, fol. CLXIXr.

within the notion of what the Greeks, and Vitruvius who followed them, called *organon* – there may be found possibilities other than those which seem to lie at the root of all manipulative or instrumental thinking.

Book x of Vitruvius's *De Architectura* – which, as he says, "constitutes the final division of the *corpus*" that is his work – deals with "what the principles of machinery (*principia machinarum*) are and the methodical arrangement of their rules."[4] He begins his discussion by distinguishing between "mechanical" and "organic" machines: "Of these [machines] there are some which are *mechanos* and some which are *organicos*. This seems to be the difference between *machinae* and *organa*, that *machinae* are operated by many workmen since their effect has greater power; for example ballistae and wine presses. *Organa*, on the other hand, operate by the skilful touch of a single workman; for example the turning of scorpions and screws."[5]

On first reading, the distinction that Vitruvius makes in this passage seems to imply that *organa* are more efficient than *machinae*: many workmen are needed to operate machines, whereas tools or implements need only the *prudens* (skilled, knowing, far-seeing, or experienced) touch of a single person. The notion of efficiency is most certainly inseparable from the instrumental view of architecture implicit in all contemporary architectural practice, where the speedy production of flawless drawings by a single, skilled CAD (computer-assisted design) operator has become the *sine qua non* of a "successful" office. Moreover, whatever the postmodernists may claim, the marketplace, and the architects who dwell in it, continue to demand, as the ultimate criterion of architectural worth, not only that CAD drawings, in turn, be efficient in bringing about the production of efficient buildings but also that buildings be efficient in the production of revenue – i.e., that the skilled or knowing investor obtain a return (monetary or other, but preferably monetary) on his investment. Indeed, the incorporeal currency of modern finance makes investment itself (small input, large output) the very model of an ideal, disembodied efficiency. All this would appear to be latent in Vitruvius's seemingly ingenuous definition of *organon*.

Vitruvius uses the Greek word *organa* to speak of what seem to be tools or instruments because there was no Latin equivalent. Cicero, who prided himself on his knowledge of Greek and who first interpreted Greek thought for the Romans, supplied Latin equivalents for many Greek words[6] – but not, it would appear, for this one. Therefore, since there was no Latin way of saying what he wanted to say, one must assume that when Vitruvius spoke of *organa*, the implicit evocation was of the Greek, not Roman, meaning.

Now, the notion of efficiency was not an endemic feature of Greek thought. In fact, although cultivated Romans admired Greek culture, Romans tended, in general, to find the Greeks lazy, verbose, and inept – to consider them rather *in*efficient as a race.[7] The implication, in the context of this argument, is that the *organon*, as the Greeks understood it, must have had little to do with efficiency. But since none of Vitruvius's Greek sources have survived, it is impossible to refer to the *organa* of early Greek architectural treatises in search of corroboration. However, Vitruvius uses the noun *organon* and the adjective *organicos* more than once in Book x, and there is ample lexical information on Greek usages as well – other than the missing architectural ones, that is. And as we shall see, just as instrumentality is not the exclusive dimension of instruments, neither is efficient production (whose inexorable product is more efficient production) the exclusive dimension of *organa*.

POLEMIKA ORGANA

When Vitruvius distinguishes between *machinae* and *organa* in the passage cited earlier, he mentions ballistae as examples of the former and scorpions as examples of the latter. Machinery includes the machinery of

Vitruvius, engines of war; from *De Architectura*, fol. CLXXXr.

war, some of which is "mechanical" and some of which, "organic." Vitruvius himself was a military architect, and the last six chapters of Book X are devoted to such machinery. When Vitruvius opens his discussion, however, there is no mention of war: "Now indeed I will set forth the things that are invented for protection against danger and in the interest of safety, which is to say the proportions of scorpions and ballistae, by which their symmetries may be constructed."[8] Ballistae and scorpions – what the Greeks called *polemika hopla kai organa*,[9] the equipment and tools of war – have, for Vitruvius, to do not with aggression but with safety and protection. Rome's declared mission was *pax romana* (Roman peace), not *bellum romanum* (Roman war).

Vitruvius and the poet Virgil were contemporaries and shared the same patron in the person of Augustus Caesar, author of the Augustan peace that followed a long period of bloody civil war. Like Virgil, Vitruvius sustained the Roman faith summed up in the solemn hexameters that Anchises utters from the underworld near the end of Book VI of the *Aeneid*:

tu regere imperio populos, Romane, memento
(hae tibi erunt artes), pacisque imponere morem
parcere subiectis et debellare superbos.[10]

Engines of war, like all architectural artifacts, must, Vitruvius says, be constructed according to certain "symmetries," according to fixed proportions. He describes these proportions with great care and in considerable detail. In fact, his solicitude here is in no way less than when he set out the proportions for the orders in the earlier books of the treatise. Oddly enough, the one thing he does not stress is that, if the proportions in question are not followed, the catapult or ballista will not work. One must, of course, assume that these engines were intended to be operational, but this would appear to be a secondary consideration.

Proportio (proportion) is the Latin equivalent that Cicero supplied, when translating Plato's *Timaeus*, for the Greek word *analogia*. According to Plato, *analogia* is what binds the universe, the *kosmos*, together and enables the corporeal world of appearance to appear.[11] That architecture, as the very art of proportion, is the analogue for this, is the overriding theme of Vitruvius's *De Architectura*.

Roman legions kept the Augustan peace. Through ordering of the Roman world, they, with their *polemika organa*, allowed that world to appear corporeally, as a unified body with Rome as its *caput*, its head and capital directing things from the top. Thus, of all the parts of architecture, the quintessential analogue for the binding action of *analogia* in Plato's cosmos lies in the proportions of those machines that, in the last six chapters of Book x, constitute the final part of the "final division of the *corpus*" of Vitruvius's treatise. Vitruvius did not conclude his treatise with the chapters on *polemika organa* because he considered these the least important part of architecture. Vitruvius was not only a Roman who shared the faith underwritten by the Virgilian prophecy just cited, he was also, as already mentioned, a military architect. And if Book I, with its outline of general principles, constitutes the head of *De Architectura*, these last chapters are the feet on which it stands.

TA PERI TAS AISTHESEIS ORGANA[12] AND OTHER ORGANS

The point here is that although *polemika organa* had an undeniable aggressive dimension, that dimension was, in the ancient world, mitigated by the understanding that the engines of war enabled the world to appear as a coherent body, as corporeal appearance. This would account for the Greeks' being able to use the same word, *organa*, both for weapons and for the organs of sense perception. *Organa* as weapons guaranteed the continued appearance of the body of the world to the political collectivity – and conversely, enabled the political collectivity itself to appear as a coherent body. Similarly, eyes, ears, nose, tongue, and skin together guaranteed (as they continue to guarantee) the coherent appearance of the world to the individual person, and vice versa. It is important to recognize that these organs did not *make* the world appear but *allowed* it to appear. They are, together, at once receptive and transitive. A single organ, alone, was not:

Wherefore, dealing first with the vessel of the head, they [the gods] set the face in the front thereof and bound within it organs [*organa*] for all the forethought of the soul [*psychēs pronoia*]; and they ordained this, which is the natural front, should be the leading part. And of the organs [*organa*] they constructed first light-bearing eyes ... For they caused the pure fire within us, which is akin to that of day, to flow through the eyes in a smooth and dense stream.[13]

Sight, for Plato and for those who followed him, was the source of knowledge and by far the dominant sense. It is here described in terms of male generation. Only the father, according to ancient belief, was the parent of a child: the mother merely nursed the seed deposited within her.[14] Thus for Plato the visible world is, like the human child, brought into appearance by the effluence, in a "smooth dense stream," of what sounds very much like seminal fluid. This fluid, moreover (as the ancients believed), originated in the head and was concentrated around the eyes.[15]

The author of sight is the sun.[16] Sight – like the sun, the generator of the visible world – occurs when the fire within seeks the fire without, when like is attracted by like. Not surprisingly, for Plato as for many of the ancients, women were a necessary evil, and the best form of love was that between seeing (intelligent) males. The ancients could not quite prove that women, whose heads (necessarily, since they were female heads) contained no semen, were utterly stupid and blind. However, every effort was made to prove that they did not see clearly – that their intelligence was at best inferior.

The action of the eyes, like the action of the organ for which they

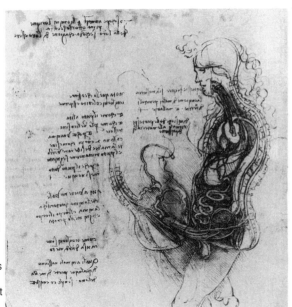

Leonardo da Vinci, coition of hemisected man and woman (c. 1488); anatomical drawing from the Royal Collection, RL19097V. The drawing clearly illustrates the belief that semen originated in the head. It might be noted, furthermore, that the woman is headless.

appear to be an analogue, was understood as essentially male and productive. The other senses, being receptive, were seen as female. Sight can be controlled. To make the visible world disappear, one has only to close one's eyes or, more drastically, to tear them out, as Oedipus did. The receptive senses are more difficult to do away with. To plug one's ears or to tear them off does not obliterate sound, nor does holding one's nose entirely obliterate smell. And it is difficult to imagine how one might even attempt to obviate the other two senses of taste and touch without attempting complete self-annihilation.

In his act of self-inflicted blinding, Oedipus expiated the blind aggression of his parricide by effectively removing himself from the visible world of which his father's act of generation had made him part.[17] Seen in the light of the classical Greek understanding that sight, like ejaculation, engenders, this same self-blinding also becomes an act of symbolic self-castration – expiation for the crime of his incestuous marriage with his own mother. Indeed, as Anthony Vidler has pointed out, Freud interpreted the fear of losing sight as representing the dread of castration, citing "the substitutive relation between the eye and the male organ, which is seen to exist in dreams and myths and fantasies."[18]

This substitutive relation appears to have been reciprocal, at least in fifth-century B.C. Greece. Not only was the eye understood as phallic; the phallus itself was understood as ocular, judging by the evidence of many erotic Greek vase paintings of the period that represent the erect member as seeing, its head equipped with an eye.[19] Like the wide-eyed owl, emblem of classical Athens and mascot of Athena, goddess of wisdom, an aroused phallus could, presumably, see in dark places.

ORGANA CHRONOU

Sight is the source of knowledge and the chief of the senses because, according to Plato, it enables people to see the sky and observe the heavenly bodies through which are revealed the notions of time and number.[20] God brought the sun, the moon, and "the five other stars" (the known planets) into existence so that time "might be born."[21]

Thus the stars, into which human souls are sown or to which they are attached as chariots, are referred to in the *Timaeus* as *organa chronou*,[22] the organs of time. In narrating the myth of Er, at the end of the *Republic*, Socrates tells Glaucon (whose name, incidentally, means bright, or seeing, one) that human souls, having chosen their fates and drunk of the River of Forgetfulness, are then discharged upwards to their birth "like shooting stars."[23] The description of the generation of human souls, like the description of sight, is decidedly male in its imagery.

The attachment of human souls to stars that, as the "organs of time,"

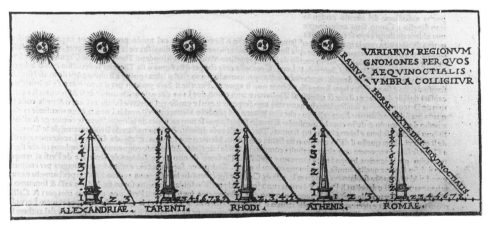

"The different places where the equinoctial shadows of gnomons are reckoned." Vitruvius, *De Architectura*, fol. CLVIIr.

let time appear, would seem to imply a partnership between people and stars in the revelation of time. Because of their attachment to the heavenly bodies, humans too are "organs of time." But as Merleau-Ponty has insisted in our own century, the human person does not create or produce time, any more than, for Plato, the sun, the moon, and the planets created or produced it. Time appears *through* the person or the stars:

It is indeed clear that I am not the creator of time any more than of my heart beats. I am not the initiator of the process of temporalization ... Time flows through me, whatever I do. Nevertheless, this ceaseless welling up of time is not a simple fact to which I am passively subjected, for I can find a remedy against it ... We are not in some incomprehensible way an activity joined to a passivity, an automatism surmounted by a judgement, but wholly active and wholly passive because we are the upsurge of time.[24]

MUSICAL INSTRUMENTS

There are three classes of machines, says Vitruvius – those which are *acrobaticon*, those which are *pneumaticon*, and those which are *baru ison*.[25] "In the pneumatic class are those musical instruments (*organicos*) which, by the influx and expression of air, imitate instruments that are struck (*plagae*) and even human voices (*voces*)."[26] The reference is, of course, to pipe organs. These and other musical instruments would seem to be purely instrumental, pure means to an end; for what *is* a musical instrument except an instrument for producing music? But the musical instrument too is an "organ of time," for music is surely the most temporal of the arts. Like the organs of time (people or stars) that do not, in fact, produce time, musical instruments do not so much produce music as let it appear.

The whole of chapter v, Book v of *De Architectura* is devoted to bronze sounding vessels (*vasa aerea*), which are also musical instruments of a kind. These are placed between the seats of a theatre, where, if properly made, "the voice, spreading from the stage as from the centre and striking by its contact the hollows of the several vases, will arouse an increased clearness of sound, and, by the concord, a consonance harmonising with itself."[27] The action of these vessels, which were Greek rather than Roman, was the musical enhancement of the civic harmony for which the theatre itself was an analogue.

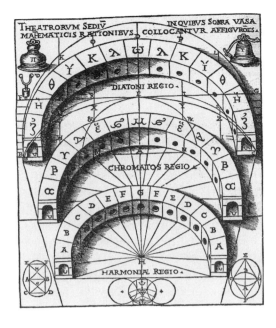

The placement of bronze sounding vessels in theatres, from Vitruvius, *De Architectura*, fol. LXXXV.

Bronze vessels reappear in the chapters on *polemika organa*. In besieged Apollonia, a Greek city on the Black Sea, Trypho of Alexandria, the architect in charge, planned, according to Vitruvius,

tunnels and, removing the soil, advanced beyond the wall the distance of a bowshot. Everywhere he hung bronze vessels. Hence in one excavation which was over against the tunnel of the enemy, the hanging vases began to vibrate in response to the blows of iron tools. Hereby it was perceived in what quarter their adversaries purposed to make an entrance with their tunnel. On learning the direction, he filled the bronze vessels with boiling water and pitch overhead where the enemy were, along with human dung and sand roasted to a fiery heat. Then in the night he pierced many openings, and suddenly flooding them, killed all the enemy who were at work there.[28]

The bronze vessels at the beginning of this account are receptive. They reverberate and thus reveal the location of the enemy, their action recalling the action of the theatrical sounding vessels of Book V. Once the location of the enemy is known, however, the bronze vessels reappear at the end of the account to turn belligerent and become agents of destruction.

TELARUM ORGANICIS ADMINISTRATIONIBUS

As cited in the epigraph for this paper, it is "by the organic assistance of looms [*telarum organicis administrationibus*]" that, according to Vitruvius, "the warp is bound to the weft, not only so that the body might be covered in order to protect it, but also so that ornament might enhance its honour."[29] The adjective *organicos*, with the related substantive *ta organica* ("organic things"), seems to have been understood as both related to, and different from, *kineticos*, or *ta kinetica* ("kinetic things"). Aristotle, for example, distinguished between the limbs of the body (*ta kinetica*) and other body parts (*ta organica*).[30] Limbs, generally speaking, move by virtue of conscious volition. They are *kinetica* (from the verb *kineo*, "I set in motion") – productive and active. Other body parts, if they move, do so independently of conscious will. *Organica*, in other words, must be passive. A body's wholeness, by implication, depends on the presence of both *ta kinetica* and *ta organica*.

What makes the assistance or "administration" of a loom "organic"? H. Ling Roth's description of weaving provides a key:

Weaving is generally considered to be the outcome of basketry and mat-making, in most cases probably it is so. It consists of the interlacing at right angles by one series of filaments or threads, known as the *weft* ... of another series, known as the *warp*, both being in the same plane.

The warp threads are stretched side by side from a *cloth*, or *breast-beam*, to another beam known as the *warp-beam* ... and the weaving is encompassed as follows: The *odd threads* (1, 3, 5, 7, 9, etc.) are raised by means of the fingers, leaving the even threads (2, 4, 6, 8, 10, etc.) in position. By raising the odd threads only, a space or opening is formed between the two sets of threads, which is called the *shed*. Through this shed the weft-thread is passed, or, as it is termed, a *pick* or *shot*, is made. This weft thread (or pick) is straightened, and pressed home into position at right angles to the warp by means of a *sword* or *beater-in*. The odd threads are then dropped back into position, and the even threads are now raised instead, whereby a new or *countershed* is produced and the pick made as before. It will be understood that, as a consequence of the lifting and dropping of the odd and even threads, these two sets of threads cross each other, but remain in their respective vertical planes.[31]

Ancient Greek looms – which are the kind Vitruvius must have had in mind since they are qualified by a word, *organicos*, that had no Latin equivalent – were vertical, with the cloth or breast-beam set over two posts planted in the ground. These vertical looms had no warp-beam at

Women weaving on an upright warp-weighted loom; Greek lekythos, c. 560 B.C.; Metropolitan Museum of Art, New York.

the bottom to keep the warp threads in place. Rather, the warp threads were kept taut by the stone, or ceramic, warp weights that were hung on them. The weft thread, once shot through, was beaten upwards, and the cloth emerged from the top down, with the textile being rolled up over the top beam as it was completed.

The two vertical posts, with the beam they supported, together made a rectangular frame – surely one of the first trabeated structures (symbolically, a house) – that defined a field of action.[32] Within this frame hung odd- and even-numbered threads, anchored by stone or ceramic weights, which recall to the architectural mind the images of Antonio Gaudí's experiments with weights and gravity.[33] Odd and even, in Pythagorean number theory, were male and female: "The even number, he [Pythagoras] says, has at its middle an empty space, capable of reception, whereas the odd number has a middle member with procreative power."[34]

Similarly, limited and unlimited (*peras* and *apeiron*) were also male and female, respectively. Looms, of course, predate Pythagoras, and yet

Interior of the funicular model by means of which Gaudí studied the structure of the church of Colonia Güell.

Pythagoras's number theory was, I would claim, already materially patent in the action that took place within the post and beam frame of the loom, where odd and even threads interpenetrated, and where the outer warp threads (necessarily odd ones) limited or defined the width of the cloth produced. Further procreative activity took place when the pick or shot, carrying the weft thread, penetrated the tunnel-like shed, under the care, as Aristophanes put it, of the "singing (or tuneful) shuttle."[35]

Roth is puzzled by the singing of this shuttle and concludes that "with regard to the low state of musical culture among the Greeks, what may have been tuneful to them is most probably not tuneful to us."[36] But as John Keats, writing on matters Greek, observed,

> Heard melodies are sweet, but those unheard
> Are sweeter
>
> (*Ode on a Grecian Urn*)

and I think that ancient looms, if they were heard to sing,[37] were heard to sing unheard melodies. *Harmonia*, after all, long before it became musical, had to do with the close fitting of a ship's joints or with the close weaving of the threads that made up a textile.

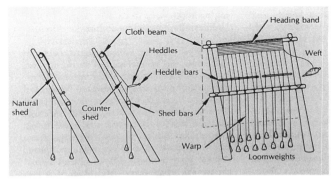

Diagrammatic reconstruction of an upright Greek loom, after E.J.W. Barber, *Prehistoric Textiles.*

All of this procreative activity was not without issue, for what emerged between the two upright posts, or *histopodes* (literally "loom feet"), was a cloth – or a tapestry, like a human life, full of stories. Such is the funeral cloth that Penelope (*Penelopeia* in Greek, "web-maker") weaves for her father-in-law Laertes in the Odyssey. "Perhaps," speculates Elizabeth Barber, "it showed his patron deity, and the exploits of himself and his ancestors ... Homer seems to have imagined it thus."[38] If so, Penelope's web would indeed have "been" her father-in-law's life.

If the cloth woven on the loom was not a tapestry, it generally became clothing that, as Vitruvius says, not only covers the body to protect it but also enhances its honour (*honestas*). In early Greece, the body itself was understood as a surface, and the word for the living body was not *soma*, which meant corpse, but *chros*, skin, from which comes *chroma*, colour. The body, like a cloth, was a surface and an appearing, and the Greek word *epiphaneia* could mean both. Clothing is a second skin, and when

Vitruvius speaks of clothing enhancing the body's honour, he means that clothing increases visibility and lets one takes one's place in the world, for the Latin word *honestas* covers a whole range of meanings: honour, reputation, character, respectability, virtue, integrity, dignity – everything, in fact, that made a Roman, properly and publicly, a Roman. Everything that allowed a Roman to *appear*. Indeed, when a Roman boy came of age, the transition became specific when he put on the *toga virilis*, the official garment of Roman manhood.

Whether metaphorically, in a tapestry woven with stories, or through the clothing it produced, the organic assistance of looms let people take their place in the ancient world. Understood in this way, the loom was not "instrumental," not an instrument of production, any more than men and women who become parents are instruments of production.

Unlike ancient children, who were believed to be the true progeny of their fathers only, today's children are known, conclusively, to have *two* parents.[39] Of all the information that has issued from a science whose roots can, in part, be traced to Francis Bacon's *Novum Organum*, this particular piece of information is possibly the most valuable. Thinking about production is rooted in thought about human reproduction, and the certain knowledge that the ejaculatory gaze is essentially sterile – that children do not come into the world "like shooting stars," the product of solitary masculine ecstasy – carries with it far-reaching implications.

Greek vase found at Chiusi in Italy, with Penelope in front of her warp-weighted loom (early fifth century B.C.); Museum of Chiusi, Italy.

Marble relief on the Ara Pacis Augustae, the altar of Augustan peace, whose construction near the end of the first century B.C. is virtually contemporaneous with the writing of Vitruvius's *De Architectura*. Although he appears in public, the half-naked child on the left does not yet "appear" publicly.

The continued appearing of human beings depends on the mitigation of instrumentality, which calls for a mitigation of the phallocracy sustained by the complicity of "seeing" males. This, in turn, demands that a truly reciprocal relation between men and women be concerned less with the power of male or female than with the place of their children. Such mutual love is perhaps, now, the only viable metaphor on which to base an organic architecture that may yet give people a place in the world.

NOTES

A shorter version of this paper was presented at the 82nd annual meeting of the ACSA in Montreal, March 1994.

1 *Attendamus enim primum inventum de necessitate, ut vestitus, quemadmodum telarum organicis administrationibus conexus staminis ad subtemen non modo corpora tegendo tueatur, sed etiam ornatus adiciat honestatem.* Vitruvius, *De Architectura*, tr. F. Granger, Loeb Classsical Library, 2 vols. (Cambridge, Mass.: Harvard University Press 1934–36), x.i.5. The translation of this extract is my own.

2 See ibid., iii.i.3.

3 On this very difficulty see, for example, Joseph Rykwert, "Uranopolis or Somapolis," *Res*, nos. 18/19 (Spring/Autumn 1989), 15–21.

4 Vitruvius, *De Architectura*, x, pref. 4.

5 Ibid., x.i.3. The "scorpion," an engine of war, was a small catapult that launched an arrow or other pointed projectile. See Claude Perrault, *Les dix livres d'architecture de Vitruve* (Paris, 1684), 296, fn. 8. On *machinae* and *organa*, see also Philippe Fleury, *La mécanique de Vitruve* (Caen: Presses universitaires de Caen 1993), 40–7; and Joseph Rykwert, "Organic and Mechanical," *Res*, no. 22 (Autumn 1992), 10–18.

6 For example, Vitruvius is indebted to Cicero for *proportio* (proportion) as the Latin equivalent of the Greek *analogia* and for *qualitas* (quality) as that of the Greek *poiotes*. It would not be appropriate to open the debate on Cicero's truncation of Greek meanings here, but it is worth noting that such truncation did occur.

7 See, for example, how Polybius (a very pro-Roman Greek historian of the second century B.C.) compares Greek and Roman methods for setting up military camps. He says that the Greeks "think it of primary importance to adapt the camp to the natural advantages of the ground, first because they shirk the labour of entrenching, and next because they think that artificial defences are not equal in value to the fortifications which nature provides unaided on the spot," whereas the Romans – as he sees it, much more efficiently – "prefer to submit to the fatigue of entrenching and other defensive work for the sake of the convenience of having a single type of camp which never varies and is familiar to all." Polybius, tr. W.R. Paton, Loeb Classical Library, 6 vols. (Cambridge, Mass.: Harvard University Press 1922–27), VI.42. For a savage indictment of the Greeks and their influence in Rome, see the third satire in *The Satires of Juvenal*, tr. W. Gifford (London: Dent 1954), lines 68 ff.

8 Vitruvius, *De Architectura*, x.x.1.

9 See Plato, *Republic*, in *Plato with an English Translation by H.N. Fowler*, Loeb Classical Library, 10 vols. (London and New York: W. Heinemann 1914–29), 374d.

10   You, Roman, remember: Govern! Rule the world!
       These are your arts! Make peace man's way of life;
       spare the humble but strike the braggart down.

    Virgil, *Aeneid*, tr. F.O. Copley (Indianapolis: Bobbs-Merrill 1965), VI, 851–3.

11 See Plato, *Timaeus*, in *Plato with an English Translation by H.N. Fowler*, 31c–32c.

12 "The organs of sense perception"; see Plato, *Republic*, 508b.

13 Plato, *Timaeus*, 45b.

14 See Jane Harrison, *Themis: A Study of the Social Origins of Greek Religion* (Cambridge, U.K.: Cambridge University Press 1912), 500ff; and Eva Keuls, *The Reign of the Phallus* (Berkeley and Los Angeles: University of California Press 1993), ch. 2.

15 See Richard B. Onians, *The Origins of European Thought* (Cambridge, U.K.: Cambridge University Press 1951), 203ff.

16 Plato, *Republic*, 508b.

17 For a recent discussion of this aspect of the significance of Oedipus's self-blinding, see Robert Jan van Pelt, *Architectural Principles in the Age of Historicism* (New Haven, Conn.: Yale University Press 1991), 220ff.

18 Anthony Vidler, *The Architectural Uncanny* (Cambridge, Mass.: MIT Press 1992), 34; and Sigmund Freud, *Art and Literature*, The Pelican Freud Library (Harmondsworth, U.K.: Penguin Books 1985), 352.

19 These drawings show the phallus in profile, hence with only one eye – presumably it was understood to have two. See Keuls, *Reign of the Phallus*, frontispiece, figures 63, 69, 76, 77, and 300, as well as figure 65, where the decorative frieze on a pottery fragment consists of stylized eyes alternating with erect phalluses.

20 Plato, *Timaeus*, 47a.

21 "*Hina gennēthēi chronos,*" *Timaeus*, 38c. The verb *gignomai*, to be born or generate, of which *gennēthēi* is the third person singular of the aorist subjunctive, is a deponent verb: although it has a passive form, it can have an active meaning. Passion and action are confounded in the deponent verbs of Greek and Latin (the deponent verb *nascor* is the Latin equivalent of *gignomai*). If language can be said to reflect the world where it is current, then the disappearance of deponent verbs in modern languages reflects a world where the fusion of activity and passivity is no longer taken for granted – perhaps not even understood.

22 Ibid., 41e, 42d.

23 Plato, *Republic*, 621b.

24 Maurice Merleau-Ponty, *The Phenomenology of Perception*, tr. C. Smith (London: Routledge & Kegan Paul 1962), 427–8.

25 That is, scaling ladders, wind-operated machines, and machines based on equilibrium. See Vitruvius, *De Architectura*, x.i.1.

26 Ibid. My reading of this rather difficult passage is based on Perrault's translation, which is more convincing than either Granger's or Morgan's. See Perrault, *Dix livres*, 295–6 and fn. 6 and 7.

27 Vitruvius, *De Architectura*, v.v.3.

28 Ibid., x.xvi.10.

29 Ibid., x.i.5.

30 Liddell and Scott, *A Greek-English Lexicon* (Oxford, Clarendon Press 1968), sv. *organikos*; and Aristotle, *De Generatione Animalium*, tr. A.L. Peek and E.S. forster, Loeb Classical Library (Cambridge, Mass.: Harvard University Press 1961), 742b10.

31 H. Ling Roth, "Studies in Primitive Looms," *Journal of the Royal Anthropological Institute* 46 (1916): 284–5. On ancient weaving see also, E.J.W. Barber's recent study, *Prehistoric Textiles: The Development of Cloth in the Neolithic and Bronze Ages* (Princeton, N.J.: Princeton University Press 1991).

32 See, especially, Vitruvius on the origins of building. The first walls, according to Vitruvius, were *woven*: "And first, with upright forked props and twigs put between, they wove [*texerunt*] their walls." *De Architectura*, ii.i.3.

33 These include the structural models that Gaudí built for the churches of Sagrada Familia and Colonia Güell.

34 Plutarch, as cited in Walter Burkert, *Lore and Science in Ancient Pythagoreanism*, tr. E.J. Minor (Cambridge, Mass.: Harvard University Press, 1972), 34.

35 *Kerkis aoida*; see Aristophanes, *Frogs* 1, 1316; cited in Roth, "Studies," 291. An *aoidos* is a bard, minstrel, or enchanter. When used as an adjective, the word means "musical" or "tuneful." The tunefulness of shuttles is referred to twice in Virgil – in the *Aeneid*, vii, 14; and in the *Georgics*, i, 143, where the Latin adjective is *argutus*, usually rendered as "rattling."

36 Roth, "Studies," 291.

37 Iphigenia, in Euripides' *Iphigenia at Tauris*, speaks of weaving on the *histois kalliphthongois* – the "lovely-sounding looms" (ii, 222–4). See Barber, *Prehistoric Textiles*, 362, fn. 4. Barber thinks the sound referred to is the sound made by the clanking of the warp weights as the warp threads were pulled back and forth.

38 Barber, ibid., 380.

39 As late as the eighteenth century, miniature people were believed to exist, fully formed, in male sperm: "After the discovery by Anthony van Leeuwenhoek (1632–1723) of the spermatozoa, Hartsoeker and Swammerdam believed themselves to see in protoplasm a tiny human being, a homunculus." Felix Cleve, *The Giants of Pre-sophistic Greek Philosophy* (The Hague: M. Nijhoff 1969), xxix.

Space and Image in Andrei Tarkovsky's *Nostalgia*:

Notes on a Phenomenology of Architecture

Juhani Pallasmaa

> In a word, the image is not a certain meaning,
> expressed by the director, but an entire world
> reflected as in a drop of water.
>
> Andrei Tarkovsky
> *Sculpting in Time*[1]

ARCHITECTURE OF IMAGERY

"Poets and painters are born phenomenologists," wrote J.H. van den Berg.[2] A phenomenological approach to the artist implies a pure looking at the essence of things, unburdened by convention or intellectualized explanation. When a writer, a painter, or a film director presents a scene, he or she must define a setting for the act. But creating a place is the primal act of architecture, and consequently these artists unknowingly perform the task of an architect. Unaware of the professional rules of the discipline, they approach the mental dimensions of architectural experience and, hence, reveal the phenomenological basis of the art of building with extraordinary directness.

Andrei Tarkovsky's films contain some of the most touching and poetic images of space and light ever created in any form of art. They touch upon the existential basis of architecture, which is saturated by memories and experiences lost in childhood. The images in his films *Mirror*, *Stalker*, and *Nostalgia*[3] exhibit the poetics of space – a poetry that does not require construction or function. Through images of space, they evoke an experience of pure existence, the poetry of being. Tarkovsky's images appear fresh and innocent, as if they had never been exposed to the human eye before.

THE RUSSIAN NOSTALGIA

Tarkovsky emphasized the importance of personal experience in art: "In the course of my work I have noticed, time and again, that if the external emotional structure of a film is based on the author's memory, when impressions of his personal life have been transmuted into screen images, then the film will have the power to move those who see it."[4] *Nostalgia* is an example of this transformation.

Nostalgia is a film about longing, the sorrow for an absent home: "I wanted to make a film about Russian nostalgia – about that state of mind peculiar to our nation which affects Russians who are far from their native land ... In Italy I made a film that was profoundly Russian in every way: morally, politically, emotionally."[5] The alienation and confused state of mind of the main character, Gorchakov, a Russian poet, is made clear at the very beginning of the film. He has driven with Eugenia, his Italian interpreter, "through half of Italy" to visit a church that had been important to the subject of his study, Pavel Shosnovski, but he does not even want to enter the church. Gorchakov carries the keys to his home in Moscow in the pocket of his overcoat and constantly fingers the keys as an unconscious indication of his homesickness. The film achieves its intensity because it expresses Tarkovsky's own yearning and nostalgia for home: "It would never have occurred to me, when I started shooting, that my own, all too specific, nostalgia was soon to take possession of my soul for ever."[6] He also wrote in his diary: "I am so homesick, so homesick."[7]

Tarkovsky suffered from the same nostalgia that countless Russian writers, musicians, and artists have endured and documented both in their correspondence and in their artistic works. More than a century earlier, Fyodor Dostoyevsky, who had escaped the wrath of his creditors by fleeing to Milan with his wife in 1868, had reported similar sentiments in a letter: "My heart is very heavy; I am homesick and I am uncertain of my situation; my debts ... make me awfully depressed. In addition I have distanced myself from Russian life to the degree that I find it difficult to write anything at all since I miss fresh Russian impressions. Just think: in six months I have not seen a single Russian newspaper."[8] In an interview, Tarkovsky defined this Russian illness further: "It is not only a feeling of homesickness. It is an illness because it robs mental strength, it takes away the ability to work and even the desire to live. It is like a handicap, the absence of something, a part of oneself. I am certain that it is a real illness of the Russian character."[9]

SYMBOL, IMAGE, AND POETRY

Tarkovsky stated explicitly that there are no symbols or metaphors in his films; water is simply water, and rain is intended to convey the experience of rain:

Whenever I declare that there are no symbols or metaphors in my films those present express incredulity. They persist in asking again and again, for instance, what rain signifies in my films; why does it figure in film after film; and why the repeated images of wind, fire, water? ... Of course rain can just be seen as bad weather whereas I use it to create a particular aesthetic setting in which to steep the action of the film. But that is not at all the same thing as bringing nature into my films as a symbol of something else.[10]

The many images present in *Nostalgia* are not intended to be symbols but rather emotional miniatures, riddles that vainly seek their own explanation. The imagery that Tarkovsky uses – water, fire, candle, dog, ruined building, and so on[11] – is inherently charged with meanings deriving from mythological and religious symbolization, but his films do not follow the logic of symbolic representation. The film director pushes the viewer off the path of convention and placid acceptance into a state of intense curiosity and yearning.

Tarkovsky considers poetry as the true language of film: "There is only one way of cinematic thinking – poetic," he writes.[12] He clarifies his point in another context: "When I speak of poetry I am not thinking of it as a genre. Poetry is an awareness of the world, a particular way of relating to reality."[13] Tarkovsky's films have an extraordinary emotional impact because they carry a pure cinematic expression that cannot be transferred to any other medium. "Poetry is untranslatable, as all art," Gorchakov tells Eugenia in *Nostalgia*.

Tarkovsky also writes emphatically about the importance of restraint in artistic expression. He quotes Paul Valéry: "Perfection is achieved only by avoiding everything that might make for conscious exaggeration." That strategy is also revealed in *Nostalgia*: "I know the great classic romances, no kisses, nothing at all, pure. That is why they are great ... feelings that are unspoken are unforgettable," says the drunken Gorchakov to a young girl in the flooded ruin.

CINEMA AND PAINTING

Tarkovsky's images frequently evoke recollections of paintings, particularly of those from the early Renaissance. "It is a miraculous painting," exclaims Eugenia about the foggy landscape in the opening scene of *Nostalgia*. Tarkovsky's frequent use of symmetrical framing is similar to Renaissance perspective representations. His manner of placing a figure

The main character of the film, Gorchakov, a Russian poet, comes to Italy to gather material on the Russian serf composer Pavel Shosnovski (alias Maximilian Beryózovsky). Gorchakov plans to write an opera libretto on the life of the composer. Shosnovski had been sent to study in Italy by his proprietor, who had noted the musical talent of his serf. Shosnovski studied composition at the Academy of Bologna, stayed nine years in Italy, and achieved some fame. Driven by the Russian longing for home, the composer decided to return to slavery, but hanged himself upon his return.

Gorchakov travels with his Italian interpreter Eugenia, a sensual and beautiful young woman. It becomes evident that Gorchakov himself is struggling with his longing, a loss of purpose and identity. He rejects Eugenia's sexual invitation, and his whole behaviour signals a loss of contact with the world. In a small town they meet an eccentric hermit, the former mathematician Domenico, who lives in a deserted and crumbling building. In his attempt to protect his family from the evil world, Domenico had kept his wife and two children locked in a house for seven years. Since the liberation of his family by police, Domenico has been drifting towards a paranoid madness. He is utterly obsessed with the demoralization of the world, which, he believes, drives humanity to its destruction. Gorchakov makes the remark that the madman Domenico is closer to the truth than others.

Domenico delivers a sermon of desperation to the citizens in Rome, standing on the equestrian statue of Marcus Aurelius: "What kind of a world is this," he cries, "if a madman has to tell you to be ashamed of yourselves?" At the end of his apocalyptic message, he douses himself with gasoline and sets himself on fire, dying by this self-immolation.

In order to fulfil Domenico's obsessive desire, Gorchakov attempts to walk across the thermal water health pool of St Catherine with a lighted candle. This would, according to Domenico's belief, save Humanity.

The film deals primarily with Gorchakov's alienation, his inability to adjust to foreign conditions, and his failure to maintain his identity, which finally pushes him to his death.

against the background of a doorway or an arched opening reminds one of the way Fra Angelico, Bellini, Botticelli, and other *quattrocento* painters placed the main figure against the background of an apse or a fictitious backdrop. Thus Tarkovsky's scenes often have the character of *sacra conversazione* paintings. And sometimes, paintings appear under strange circumstances in his films. For example, a detail of St John the

Baptist from the Ghent altarpiece, *The Adoration of the Lamb*, by the
van Eyck brothers, appears submerged in water in the pool of the "Zone"
in *Stalker*.

Surprisingly, Tarkovsky emphasizes the difference between various art
forms:

As it develops, the cinema will, I think, move further away not only from
literature but also from other adjacent art forms, and thus become more and
more autonomous ... cinema still retains some principles proper to other art
forms, on which directors often base themselves when making a film ... One
result (of this) is that cinema then loses something of its capacity for incarnating
reality by its own means, as opposed to transmuting life with the help of
literature, painting, or theatre. This can be seen for instance in the influence
brought to bear on cinema by the visual arts when attempts are made to transfer
this or that canvas to the screen ... Trying to adapt the features of other art forms
to the screen will always deprive the film of what is distinctively cinematic.[14]

Although Tarkovsky did not attempt to imitate painting, he utilized similar pictorial means of rendering space in order to achieve his intended emotional impact. We know that Tarkovsky painted for three years in his youth, and his first film to achieve worldwide attention was on the fifteenth-century icon painter Andrei Rublev. His writings refer frequently to a wealth of painters – Carpaccio, Cézanne, Dalí, van Gogh, Goya, El Greco, Picasso, Raphael, Leonardo da Vinci, Giotto, among others.

He seems to have been under the spell of Leonardo, in particular. Tarkovsky admires the artist's amazing "capacity to examine the object from outside, standing back, looking from above the world – a characteristic of artists like Bach and Tolstoy." Leonardo's portrait of *A Young Woman with a Juniper Twig* appears in *Mirror*, and in an essay Tarkovsky analyzes the strange duality of the figure – the simultaneous attractiveness and repulsiveness of the woman.[15] Still later in the same film, Aleksei, who portrays Tarkovsky as a boy, studies a book of Leonardo's drawings; his father reads Leonardo's instructions for painting a battle scene documented in the Ashbernheim manuscript.

Piero della Francesca also seems to be important for Tarkovsky: Piero's painting *Madonna del Parto* (*Madonna of Childbirth*) appears in *Nostalgia*; and, indeed, Eugenia could be a woman from one of Piero's paintings. But she could also be one of the numerous red-haired beauties of Botticelli's paintings.

As a further example of Tarkovsky's affinity for painting, *Sculpting in Time* contains illustrations of Dürer's *Apocalypse*, a painting by Hieronymus Bosch, and Pieter Bruegel's *January (Hunters in the Snow)*. A scene in *Mirror* on a snowy hill in which Aleksei takes a bird in his hand resembles the scene in Bruegel's painting so vividly that it can hardly be accidental. The closing scene, in which Gorchakov's childhood home in Russia is shown within the ruin of an Italian cathedral, bears close similarity with Caspar David Friedrich's painting *Ruins of Abbey at Eldena* (1824).

TARKOVSKY'S COMPRESSED SPACE

Tarkovsky's space is rendered as a frontal perspective with a single vanishing point. This archaism of spatial representation helps to flatten the scene into a two-dimensional image, a painting. The use of one-point perspective also results in the suppression of dynamic effect. Space is

Top right: *Nostalgia*: Eugenia, in Gorchakov's bathroom framed by the doorway and the bathroom mirror in the same manner that Renaissance painters created a focus to the main figure.

Right: Duccio di Buoninsegna, "Appearance of Christ to the Apostles at the Church Door," Maestà altar of the Siena *duomo* (1308–11); from Giulio Cattaneo, *Duccio di Buoninsegna* (Milan: Rizzoli 1972).

composed of planes parallel to the screen in the same way as the axonometric technique of Japanese *ukiyo-e*, instead of the dynamic perspective of the modern Western convention of spatial representation.

Tarkovsky diffuses edges of forms, figures, and spaces into mist, water, rain, darkness, or merely an equality of colour and tonal value, in order to abstract the image and weaken the illusion of reality. The naturalistic quality of colour is neutralized as well: "One has to attempt to neutralize colour in order to control its impact on the viewer," he writes.[16] He diffuses landscape into a silvery mist reminiscent of paintings by Camille Corot, to reduce depth and emphasize pictorial flatness. This device activates the process of unconscious peripheral vision and leads the viewer into a hypnotic state, in much the same way as the foggy mountain scenes in Chinese painting or the raked sand in a Japanese Zen garden produce a state of meditation. Figures in Tarkovsky's landscapes are frequently immobile and turned towards the camera in the manner of a still-life, further strengthening the painterly and stylized effect of the image.

Top left: *Nostalgia*: Eugenia in the Church of the Madonna of Childbirth (*Madonna del Parto*).

Left: Fra Angelico, "The Presentation in the Temple" (after 1430); from Giulio Carlo Argan, *Fra Angelico and His Times* (Paris: Skira 1955).

SPACE AND MOVEMENT

Tarkovsky's slow and prolonged camera takes move either parallel to the picture plane or along the perpendicular depth direction. As a consequence, the camera never rushes into the depicted space, and the viewer remains at the edge of the painterly image. In the opening scene of *Nostalgia*, for example, a car drives across the foggy landscape to the left of the frame. While the engine sound remains audible, the car makes a loop outside the screen and returns from the left to the front part of the scene. The movement effectively charts the space beyond the screen, just as the edges of Mondrian's squares in his diagonal paintings continue past the frame to activate our awareness of the space beyond.

In the scene in St Catherine's pool, the camera moves parallel to the pool, and an occasional vertical black bar across the screen traces the existence of the arcade columns behind which the camera is located. Towards the end of the film, the movement of Gorchakov's taxi around

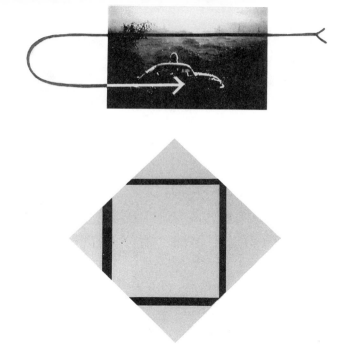

the pool carves its square shape into the space of the screen while the camera moves slowly parallel to the edge to the pool in front.

The prolonged scene in which Gorchakov attempts to leave his hotel when Eugenia unexpectedly calls him from Rome to say that Domenico is making his mad speeches, is another impressive study of architectural space through slowed motion. The camera is placed in a narrow corridor along which it moves imperceptibly to relate three courtyard spaces to one another along this depth direction. The camera carves space directly into the mind of the viewer.

FILMS IN FILM

In *Nostalgia* there are recollections of other film makers as well: people standing frontally as objects in the landscape remind the viewer of Resnais or Antonioni, while the scene with bathers in the steaming pool has a strongly Fellini-like atmosphere. The collection of objects, particularly the image of a broken doll in Domenico's house, recalls Vigo's *L'Atalante*. The frequent appearance of mirrors and the exchanged images of Gorchakov and Domenico in the mirror call forth memories of Jean Cocteau. Not surprisingly, in his diaries Tarkovsky reports having seen Cocteau's

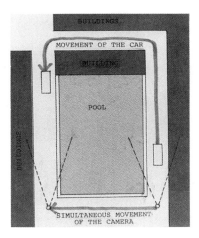

Opposite top: *Nostalgia*: Gorchakov and Eugenia's car arrives at the site of the Church of Childbirth. Movement of the car in relation to the fixed camera view (drawing by Juhani Pallasmaa).

Opposite: Piet Mondrian, "Composition 1A" (1930); from Germano Celant and Michael Govan, *Mondrian e De Stijl* (Milan: Olivetti/Electa 1990).

Above: *Nostalgia*: Gorchakov arrives at St. Catherine's pool by taxi. Movement of the car and the camera in relation to the urban space (chart JP).

The Testament of Orpheus on television during the preparatory phase of *Nostalgia*.

Snow falling slowly over the closing scene in *Nostalgia* reflects Tarkovsky's admiration of Ingmar Bergman. He writes about the disturbing scene in Bergman's *The Virgin Spring* in which snowflakes begin to fall on the face of the dying rape victim. The snowflakes in *Nostalgia* fuse the southern and northern elements of the collage into a single coherent image.

POETICS OF SPACE AND LIGHT

Windows and doors play an essential role in Tarkovsky's films: windows and doorways for looking out or into, and openings for light to enter, as much as for people to pass through. When Gorchakov first enters his hotel room, the spatial configuration of the setting is breathtakingly expressed as an abstract counterpoint of spaces, alternating in darkness and light. As the writer enters the dark room, light seeps into the darkness through the edges of shutters; he opens the shutters to reveal a tiny courtyard, and daylight floods into the room; he closes the shutters and switches on a lamp, which does not function properly; he quickly turns

Top right: *Nostalgia*: interior of Domenico's house.

Right: Gordon Matta-Clark, "Circus or the Caribbean Orange" (1978); from Mary Jane Jacob, *Gordon Matta-Clark: A Retrospective* (Chicago: Museum of Contemporary Art 1985).

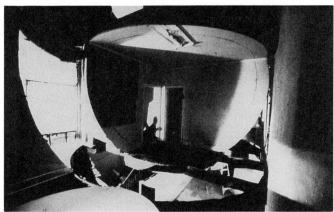

off the blinking light bulb and turns on a table lamp instead; through the open door he enters the bathroom, which reflects a blue natural light; he turns on the electric light of the bathroom and the small space is suddenly flooded by bright white light.

Tarkovsky's music of light and space creates a sequence of astonishing metaphysical beauty and power. These are images of space and light so magical and radiant with poetic essence as to compare with paintings by Fra Angelico or the mysterious light works by the contemporary artist James Turrell.

IMAGES OF MATTER AND RUINS: BUILDING AND MEMORY

In *Water and Dreams*,[17] Gaston Bachelard distinguishes between two kinds of imagination – material and formal. The imagery in Tarkovsky's films clearly belongs to the category of material imagination; his expression is based on images and dreams of matter. Spaces in *Nostalgia* are

Top left: *Nostalgia*: frame from the sequence with Gorchakov in his hotel room.

Left: James Turrell, "Raemar" (1968), fluorescent light; from Craig Adcock, *James Turrell: The Art of Light and Space* (Berkeley, Cal.: University of California Press 1982).

scenes of time and erosion, and surfaces are covered by a skin of traces and scars. The eroding surfaces feed dreams in the same way that a Rorschach figure in a personality test invites figural interpretation. The stimulating impact of eroding surfaces on imagination was observed by Leonardo. Following an ancient Chinese instruction, he advised artists to stare at a crumbling wall to reach inspiration:

When you look at a wall spotted with stains, or with a mixture of stones, if you have to devise some scene you may discover a resemblance to various landscapes ... or, again, you may see battles and figures in action, or strange faces and costumes, or an endless variety of objects, which you could reduce to complete and well-drawn forms. And these appear on such walls promiscuously, like the sound of bells in whose jangle you may find any name or word you choose to imagine.[18]

Ruins have a special hold on our emotions because they challenge us to imagine their forgotten faith. We are moved by them more readily than with new structures, because ruins have been stripped of their mask of utility and rational meaning. The ruin has ceased to play the role of a building; it represents a skeleton of memory, a sheer melancholy presence. Tarkovsky's leaking and flooded buildings recall Gordon Matta-Clark's dramatic revelations, in which he deliberately dissected buildings to expose the tragic sentiments hidden behind the utilitarian face of architecture.

Tarkovsky quotes an image from Marcel Proust – "raising the vast edifice of memories" – which he regards as the calling of film.[19] The association of buildings and memory is strong. Recall, for example, the mnemonic method of Greek orators who imagined themselves placing the individual themes of their speech within a building and, while delivering the speech, moving about in the building and picking up the themes one after another from their temporary storage places. It is clear that architecture and cities provide the most important stage of collective memory. "The house is one of the greatest powers of integration for the thoughts, memories and dreams of mankind," wrote Bachelard.[20] In similar fashion, experiencing a Tarkovsky film is an act of active remembering, discovering the immense edifice of both collective and personal memories.

MEANING OF OBJECTS AND DETAILS

In Tarkovsky's films, objects are frequently seen submerged in water as vague fragments of the tissue of memory, torn beyond recognition by time.

Typical pattern of the Rorschach personality test.

Top left: *Nostalgia*: frame from the sequence in Domenico's house.

Left: Giorgio Morandi, "Natura morta" (1958); from Marilena Pasquali, *Giorgio Morandi* (Milan: Electa 1990).

The eye struggles to identify an image washed by water – a white marble statue of an angel, discarded junk – and after the visual recognition, the mind attempts to reconstruct its history and meaning.

The surrealist still-life that is Domenico's room tends to project a specific meaning on each object present in the room. Domenico passes through a door hinged to a detached doorframe suspended in space; the scribbled "1+1=1" on the wall reminds one of Domenico, the mathematician gone mad. Every image layers meanings and recollections; the sign of a cross within a circle painted in red on the wall of the flooded ruin of Gorchakov's drunken monologue is a symbol of Christ, but it is also the Egyptian hieroglyph *nywt* for town, as well as the Roman sign for *templum*. The astonishing architectural miniature of two bottles, green and brown, on the flooded floor of Domenico's room, over which rain water sprouts while lit by bright light, has the silent monumentality and sacred radiance of a Morandi still-life. The miniaturized image is curiously contrasted by Domenico's line: "One needs bigger ideas."

Objects collected from the bottom of St Catherine's pool – the fragment of a doll, a white bicycle, a light bulb, bottles, rags – refer to lost and forgotten secrets being recovered from the bottom of repressed memory. There is an element of suspense and fear because one can never be certain what the repressed memory may reveal. "Hideousness and beauty are contained within each other," writes Tarkovsky.[21] But collecting drowned objects from the pool also makes an association with the Venetian legend of the recovery of the True Cross, depicted memorably, for instance, by Gentile Bellini.

The film contains other images that border on the surrealistic: the comb with a tangle of hair between the pages of a worn-out bible in Gorchakov's hotel room; the floor of one of the rooms of Domenico's house, turning into a landscape. But these images serve Tarkovsky's cinematic poetry and lose their conventional surrealistic tension.

The quarrel between Gorchakov and Eugenia in the hotel lobby is heightened by accidental interruptions by outsiders: an old man carrying a child; a woman and a dog; Chinese music being heard from the upper floor; the sound of distant bells. This effect bears close similarity with that created by painters who, in the depiction of a legend, included prosaic scenes of everyday life. In his monumental painting *The Presentation of the Virgin*, Titian, for instance, included a countrywoman selling eggs, a young boy playing with a dog, and a woman with a child talking with a monk. It is this fusion of meaningful and meaningless, significant and accidental, sacred and profane that reinforces the experience of truth in works of art. The interaction of deliberate design and purposeless chance keeps the viewer's entire emotional channel receptive.

ARCHITECTURE OF SOUND

Every touching experience of architecture is multi-sensory: qualities of space are measured equally by the eyes, ears, nose, tongue, skin, and muscles. Every place or space has its characteristic sound of intimacy or monumentality, rejection or invitation, hospitality or hostility. But Tarkovsky makes it clear that he rejects a naturalistic duplication of the audible world in his films: "If there is no selection then the film is tantamount to silence, since it has no sound expression of its own."[22] A subtle articulation of the sense of sound shapes the experience of space

Top left: *Nostalgia*: desire for recognition – marble statue of an angel buried in water.

Left: *Nostalgia*: fragments of memory – objects recovered from St Catherine's pool.

in his films just as much as vision does. The cavity of space is sculpted by the faint sound of a falling coin, a glass being moved casually on the stone floor by Gorchakov's dream dog, or the sudden distant whistle of a train or ship in the middle of a silent country scene. Tarkovsky's sounds activate the viewer's sense of space and scale.

Domenico's scenes, for example, are coloured by the barely audible, yet aggressive and disquieting, sound of a circular saw that shapes the space beyond the screen and makes the viewer unconsciously sense the blade cutting into the innocence of wood. The music that accompanies the image of Domenico on fire suddenly slows down as if the tape had caught in the tape recorder. The effect both adds an extra element of terror and brings a welcome dimension of distance from the emotionally unbearable scene. In Domenico's house the arhythmic beating of rain drops creates an impressive sense of dense volume. A distant telephone ringing in the hotel scenes hints at the reality outside the screened image.

IMAGES OF WATER AND FIRE

In his films Tarkovsky frequently uses images that have the highest charge for our imagination – fire and water. Flame has a dramatic role in *Nostalgia*, and it appears in various forms, from a candle to a burning book, and finally, a man set on fire. A scene in which a flock of birds miraculously bursts into flight from the belly of the *Madonna of Child-birth* is also related to the image of a flame. The altar itself in the scene is flooded with candles as an introduction to the Purgatory at the end of the film. The images of fire and water have, of course, a multitude of symbolic meanings, but Tarkovsky rejects explicit psychological as well as religious symbols, as we have seen.

Bachelard, who devoted the latter half of his life to a penetrating phenomenological analysis of the elements and imagination, wrote two books on images of fire[23] and one on images of water. His views throw light on the experiential dimensions of Tarkovsky's scenes. Bachelard speaks of "a poetics of water" and "water poets."[24] "Perhaps more than any other element," he writes, "water is a complete poetic reality."[25] He goes on to state: "One cannot dream profoundly with *objects*. To dream profoundly, one must dream with *substances*. A poet who begins with a *mirror* must end with the *water of a fountain* if he wants to present a *complete poetic experience*."[26]

The most essential poetic tension in *Nostalgia* between the contradictory images of fire and water is explained by Bachelard: "In the realm of matters, no two can be found which are more opposed than water and fire. Water and fire give what is perhaps the only really substantial contradiction."[27] Balzac's cryptic declaration, "Water is a burned body," and Novalis's sentence, "Water is a dampened flame,"[28] further explain the power and strange unity of Tarkovsky's fused imageries of water and flame.

In his fascinating book on Marcel Duchamp's *The Large Glass (The Bride Stripped Bare by Her Bachelors, Even)*, Octavio Paz also discusses the imageries of water and fire.[29] He refers to the common ritual of throwing torches or candles into rivers or lakes, and the Catholic ritual of blessing the baptismal bowl by dropping a burning candle into the water. Paz also recalls that the neo-Platonists associated fire and water.

The perfect visual and mental congruence of the scenes at St Catherine's thermal bath in *Nostalgia* and the significance of flames is explained by

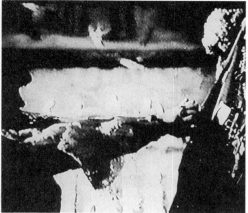

Above left: Piero della Francesca, "Madonna del Parto" (about 1640); Cappella del Cimiterio, Monterchi (Arezzo); from Oreste del Buono, *Piero della Francesca* (Milan: Rizzoli 1967).

Above right: *Nostalgia*: a flock of birds bursts into flight from the belly of the Madonna of Childbirth. Piero's painting behind the sea of candles which serves as an introduction to the theme of flames in the film.

Bachelard's observation: "Thermal water ... is imagined first of all as the immediate composition of water and fire."[30] As well, after his apocalyptic sermon, Domenico burns himself with gasoline while standing on the equestrian statue of Marcus Aurelius. The saviour scene has stunning mythical power. Paz's observation that "the mixture of water and fire is explosive"[31] gives a hint at the psychological logic of Domenico's violent end. His suicide by fire arouses recollections of the wall of fire in Dante's Purgatory, a symbolic baptism through which all who seek salvation must pass. In his desperate deed, the former mathematics teacher and private philosopher also re-enacts the fate of the pre-Socratic philosopher Empedocles, who threw himself into the flames of Mount Etna. But he also repeats the fate of sixteenth- and seventeenth-century Russian religious dissidents who often burned themselves to death.

Domenico represents the image of a holy madman – a well-known one in the orthodox religious tradition in Russia and, consequently, a popular motif in Russian art and literature. In the sixteenth century, holy madmen – a figure exemplified by the character of Prince Myshkin in Dostoyevsky's *Idiot* – even had an influence on the Czar.[32]

After Domenico's death, Gorchakov fulfils the madman's desire to transport a burning candle across St Catherine's pool. The sequence of Gorchakov's successive attempts and failures is almost painful in its prolonged duration. As soon as Gorchakov reaches the opposite side of the pool with the barely burning candle, he collapses from a heart attack.

(In earlier scenes he had taken pills from his pocket, thereby suggesting he had heart problems.)

Throughout this scene, Tarkovsky makes the viewer experience time as a dense and heavy material presence. The extraordinary power of the sequence of the transportation of the feeble candle flame across the emptied pool is explained by the wealth of meanings that the image of flame suggests. "Of all images, images of flame ... bear the mark of the poetic. Whoever dreams of a flame is a potential poet,"[33] writes Gaston Bachelard. The curious sense of empathy felt by the viewer in the scenes with Gorchakov and the candle becomes understandable through the association of flame and life. As Bachelard notes, "the flame is an image of life ... a living substance, a poeticizing substance ... an image of life which consumes but surprisingly rejuvenates itself."[34] His statement, "where a lamp once reigned, now reigns memory,"[35] serves to explain the strength with which Tarkovsky's scene invites personal memories. And the experience of extreme solitude is understandable through Bachelard's observation: "The flame of a candle is, for many dreamers, an image of solitude."[36]

THE FINAL SCENE

An image of home appears throughout the film in the dual image of Gorchakov's and Domenico's dog. But it is significant that Tarkovsky uses a wolfhound, a breed combining contradictory images of safety and threat (dog *and* wolf), fidelity and savageness. In the final scene, Gorchakov is seen sitting with his dog in front of his house in Russia, which is, however, viewed within the ruin of an Italian cathedral. The scene is a deliberate collage, which strikes one as being somewhat too literal and fabricated, given the context of the film and Tarkovsky's general intent. The film maker himself acknowledges: "I would concede that the final shot of *Nostalgia* has an element of metaphor, when I bring the Russian house inside the Italian cathedral. It is a constructed image which smacks of literariness (and hence it is against my own principles) ... All the same, even if the scene lacks cinematic purity, I trust that it is free of vulgar symbolism.[37]

Tarkovsky goes on to explain the relation of theoretical principles and creative work: "Clearly I could be accused of being inconsistent. However, it is for the artist both to devise principles and to break them ... artistic

Top left: *Nostalgia*:
Domenico on fire after his
mad speech.

Left: *Nostalgia*: Gorchakov
transports a candle across
St Catherine's pool.

texture is always richer than anything that can be fitted into a theoretical schema."[38] In another context, he elaborates: "A film is bigger than it is – at least, if it is a real film. And it always turns out to have more thought, more ideas, than were consciously put there by its author."[39] Here, Tarkovsky shares Milan Kundera's view that a great novel is always wiser that its writer.

TARKOVSKY'S LESSON IN ARCHITECTURE

In architecture we are rarely confronted with rooms through which rain pours or rooms that are flooded with water. In Tarkovsky's films, however, these images have a dramatic power. That impact is based on the fusion of the exclusive imageries of building and water, protection and exposure, shape and shapelessness, definite and infinite. In this connection, Tarkovsky recalls Paul Valéry's view that "the real is expressed most immanently through the absurd,"[40] and he also quotes Goethe: "The less accessible a work is to the intellect, the greater it is."[41]

Nostalgia: collage of Gorchakov's home in Russia fused within Italian cathedral.

Nostalgia's images of Domenico's rooms with rain pouring through the roof, along with similar scenes in *Stalker*, are among the most fascinating architectural images ever created. Although they are scenes of erosion, they radiate an astonishing beauty and purity of feeling. They possess an almost sacred or ecclesiastical presence. The wealth of details, images, and associations, and the fusion of figure and ground in these images bring to mind Balthazar Neumann's Baroque church of Vierzehnheiligen.

Architecture today rarely seems to enter the realm of poetry or to awaken the world of unconscious imagery. The sheer poetic radiance of Tarkovsky's architectural images brings into relief the contemporary language of architecture, which is one-dimensional in terms of the scope of emotions evoked by its imagery. Architecture tends to be engaged with visual effects, and it lacks the tragic, the melancholy, the nostalgic, as well as the ecstatic and transcendental tones of the spectrum of emotions. As a consequence, our buildings tend to leave us as outsiders and spectators without being able to pull us into full emotional participation.

Architecture must again question its functionality and existence on the level of materiality and practicalities in order to touch the deeper levels of consciousness, dream, and feeling, as revealed by Andrei Tarkovsky's *Nostalgia*. Ingmar Bergman has aptly chosen architectural metaphors – room, door, keys – to describe Tarkovsky's contribution in creating an authentic cinematic language that is new and ageless at the same time:

Tarkovsky's first film was as a miracle to me. Suddenly I stood at a door, the keys to which had never before been given to me. I had always wanted to enter that room and there he was, moving about freely and unaffectedly. I was encouraged and excited. Someone gave an expression to what I had wanted to say, not

Caspar David Friedrich, "Ruins of the Abbey at Eldena" (1824); from Helmut Börsch-Supan, *Friedrich* (Milan: Rizzoli 1976).

knowing how. For me, Tarkovsky is the greatest. He created a new, authentically cinematic language. It catches the reflection of life, the dream of life.[42]

NOTES

1 Andrei Tarkovsky, *Sculpting in Time: Reflections on the Cinema*, tr. K. Hunter-Blair (London: Bodley Head 1986), 110.

2 J.H. van den Berg, *The Phenomenological Approach in Psychology* (Springfield, Ill.: C.C. Thomas 1955), 61; quoted in Gaston Bachelard, *The Poetics of Space*, tr. M. Jolas (Boston: Beacon Press 1969), xxiv.

3 *Nostalgia*, Tarkovsky's first film made abroad, was completed in 1983. His last, *The Sacrifice*, was shot in Sweden and completed in May 1986. He died of cancer later that year at the age of fifty-four.

4 Tarkovsky, *Sculpting in Time*, 182–3.

5 Ibid., 202.

6 Ibid., 216.

7 Andrei Tarkovsky, *Martyrologia: Diaries 1970–1981* (Joensuu, Finland: Kustannus Oy Mabuse 1989), 342.

8 Anders Olofsson, "Nostalgia," in *Tanken på en Hemkomst*, ed. M. Bergh and B. Munkhammar (Stockholm: Alfa Beta Bokförlag 1986), 150.

9 Ibid., 152.

10 Tarkovsky, *Sculpting in Time*, 212.

11 See, for example, George Ferguson, *Signs and Symbols in Christian Art* (London: Oxford University Press 1961); and James Hall, *Dictionary of Subjects and Symbols in Art* (New York: Harper & Row 1974).

12 Tarkovsky, *Sculpting in Time*, 150.

13 Ibid., 21.

14 Ibid., 22.

15 Ibid., 108.

16 Ibid., 138.

17 Gaston Bachelard, *Water and Dreams: An Essay on the Imagination of Matter*, tr. E.R. Farrell (Dallas: Dallas Institute 1983).

18 Quoted in Robert Hughes, *The Shock of the New: Art and the Century of Change* (London: Thames & Hudson 1980), 225.

19 Tarkovsky, *Sculpting in Time*, 59.

20 Bachelard, *Poetics of Space*, 6.

21 Tarkovsky, *Sculpting in Time*, 38.

22 Ibid., 161–2.

23 Gaston Bachelard, *The Psychoanalysis of Fire*, tr. A.C.M. Ross (London: Quartet Books 1987); and *The Flame of a Candle*, tr. J. Coldwell (Dallas: Dallas Institute 1988).

24 Bachelard, *Water and Dreams*, 5.

25 Ibid., 15.

26 Ibid., 22.

27 Ibid., 98.

28 Quoted in ibid., 97.

29 Octavio Paz, *Suuri lasi* [The Large Glass] (Hämeenlinna, Finland: Karisto, 1991); and *Marcel Duchamp, Appearance Stripped Bare*, tr. R. Phillips and D. Gardner (New York: Seaver Books 1973).

30 Bachelard, *Water and Dreams*, 97.

31 Paz, *Suuri lasi*, 155.

32 Olofsson, "Nostalgia," 161.

33 Bachelard, *Flame of a Candle*, 45.

34 Ibid., 45.

35 Ibid., 11.

36 Ibid., 9.

37 Tarkovsky, *Sculpting in Time*, 213–14.

38 Ibid., 216.

39 Ibid., 118.

40 Ibid., 152.

41 Ibid., 47.

42 Peter von Bagh, *Elämää suuremmat elokuvat* (Helsinki: Otava 1989), 611.

The Momentary Modern Magic of the Panorama

Stephen Parcell

Chora

The sun is one foot wide.

Heraclitus[1]

REPRESENTATION PRESUMES AN ANALOGY between two things –
between *this* and *that*. Sometimes, *this* is near and *that* is far. Sometimes,
this is drawn and *that* is built. In *Notre Dame de Paris*, Victor Hugo
warned, retrospectively, *this* will kill *that*.

Since the Renaissance, perspective has been dedicated to making *this*
appear to be *that*. A perspective offers a virtual space that one can imagine
inhabiting, while the edges of the perspectival image mark a boundary
that continues to distinguish *this* from *that*. However, the nineteenth-
century panorama (known as "cyclorama" in the United States) sought
to disguise that boundary and to immerse observers as fully as possible
into a represented world, using a variety of theatrical techniques to try
to convince them momentarily that this *was* that; that here-and-now *was*
there-and-then. Consequently, the panorama is an important historical
benchmark. Its foibles and idiosyncrasies also illuminate some basic characteristics of architectural representation that tend to be taken for
granted.

BACKGROUND

A panorama is a 360-degree view of a vast landscape, or a picture that
represents that view on the interior surface of a cylindrical building.[2]
Panoramic representations were extremely popular in nineteenth-century
Europe and America, and about twenty still exist.[3] Each consists of an
enormous landscape painting,[4] a central platform from which observers
survey the vista, and a building that contains everything and choreographs
the passage of observers and light. Together, these efforts attempt to
produce a credible illusion – to make us believe that we are looking out
at a vast landscape, not just a big painting, and to encourage us to mistake
representation for reality.[5]

Although the panorama has been identified retrospectively as a socio-
political symbol,[6] originally it was promoted merely as an entertaining
diversion or a minor educational device. Panorama paintings faithfully
depicted exotic places and historical events such as battles and crucifix-
ions. In some languages, the word "panorama" has come to mean a

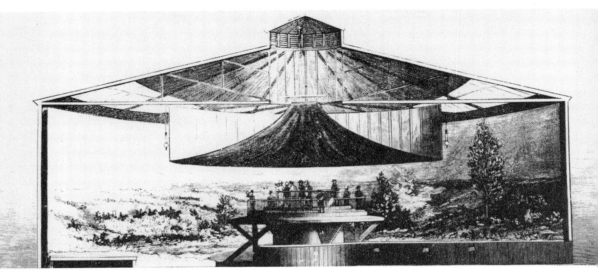

Cross-section through the interior of a panorama rotunda, with "The Battle of Gettysburg," painted by Paul Philippoteaux (1883); from *Scientific American* 55, no. 19 (November 6, 1886).

historical or geographical survey. Illustrated booklets were sometimes handed out to visitors, pointing out specific features in the manner of a guided tour. Revived panoramas often employ a narrator to fill the empty silence of the rotunda with information about the invention of the panorama and the making of the painting, underlined with frequent reminders about its lifelike appearance.

Upon entering a panorama building, one proceeds down a dark, narrow passageway, ascends a helical stairway, and finally arrives at the centre of a circular platform surrounded by a vista. With this simple choreography, the darkened corridor acts as a contrasting bottleneck, connecting and implicitly comparing two "exterior" worlds. The experience is similar to diving underwater and re-surfacing inside a large, bright cave. Unlike a conventional painting, it is impossible to behold an entire panorama at once. At least half of it is always hidden beyond the limits of peripheral vision, regardless of how quickly one turns around. Experientially, the horizon inside closely resembles the horizon outside. The representational *mode* of the panorama – its represented spatial experience – is clearly the primary fascination; the particular painting on display is a secondary (but necessary) means of sustaining the fundamental impact of the panorama.

While a section drawing clearly shows how a panorama building is constructed and how one's experience is choreographed, interior perspec-

Interior view of "Panorama of Constantinople," painted by J. Garnier (1883), shown in the Vondelpark in Amsterdam; Københavns Bymuseum, Copenhagen.

tives begin to suggest the magnitude of the illusion. The panorama's potency is based on an apparent paradox: the interior has a large vista while the exterior is only a small, cylindrical mass. External adornments, added to attract customers and promote a frivolous air, cannot successfully disguise the silent, monolithic quality of the building. The opacity of the exterior and the elemental quality of its cylindrical shape suggest that the building contains a singular institution of some kind. If one imagines interior sight-lines emanating from the central platform ("ground zero") and projecting out to the horizon, yet forcibly contained within a round exterior shell, the basic geometry of the panorama building curiously resembles a bomb. If this building were not innocently housing a painting, one could imagine with some trepidation what else might be going on inside.

Writers have introduced the panorama into a variety of cultural contexts, suggesting that it be conceived as an aerial depiction of cities and landscapes, a theatre and stage set, a perspectival *trompe-l'œil* illusion, a museum and art gallery, a diversion for tourists, an observation device, a descendant of the panopticon, and an ancestor of cinema, television, and

Panorama rotunda on the Leidscheplein in Amsterdam; drawing by J. Saffrie (1816); Gemeentearchief, Amsterdam.

the planetarium. Although the panorama formally resembles other centralized buildings (such as the Pantheon), its intentions, operations, and centrifugal focus are unique. However, certain architectural works demonstrate a deeper resemblance – for example, Boullée's *Cenotaph for Newton*, which preceded the invention of the panorama by a mere three years:

The monument is shaped in its interior like a vast sphere, with access to its centre of gravity through an opening cut in its base, on which I have placed the tomb. This shape has one unique advantage; whichever way you direct your gaze (the same is true in nature) you see nothing but a continuous surface with neither beginning nor end, and the more you look, the further this surface reaches out. This shape, never before put to use, and which is alone suited to this monument, is such, by reason of its curve, that the spectator can never draw near to what he looks upon; as though overpowered by a hundred circumstances, he is forced to remain in his allotted place which, fixed as it is at the centre, keeps him at a distance favourable to illusory effects. These delight him, but unable to satisfy his curiosity by a closer approach, his pleasure remains unclouded. Isolated on all sides, his gaze can but reach out to the boundless heavens. Only the tomb has material form.[7]

As a device with which humans conceive the world as a visual landscape, the panorama also recalls Petrarch's observations upon climbing Mont Ventoux in 1336.[8] When he looked out at the world surrounding him and saw not only a display of God's work but also an echo of the human soul, nature was first conceived as a reflected reality, a new means of human expression, vividly conveyed by Ernst Cassirer: "Nature cannot be understood, felt, and enjoyed *per se,* but only as a dark or light background for the Ego."[9] This modern concept is echoed in Rilke's description of the landscape painted by Leonardo da Vinci behind Mona Lisa: "This landscape ... is not the judgment of a man on things at rest; it is nature coming into being ... unknown to man as the jungle of an unknown island ... far and strange, remote, without love, as something living a life within itself ... completely unlike us ... a redeeming likeliness of our fate. It had to be almost hostile in its exalted indifference, if, with its objects, it was to give a new meaning to our existence."[10]

In our own century, Le Corbusier's obsession with promontories and vistas seems to continue this line of thought.[11] One may refer to the "Arc de Triomphe fireplace" and the "horizon wall" in the de Beistegui penthouse, the window opening at the very top of the ramp in Villa Savoye, and the roof garden of the Marseilles Unité complex, each with its own rhetorical trajectory between the ground on which one stands and the distant horizon that one can contemplate but not reach. Regardless of how actively one pursues the horizon, it always maintains its distance.

TOWARDS A CONVINCING ILLUSION

In Robert Barker's 1787 patent application, the panorama was originally called *la nature à coup d'œil* or "nature at a glance."[12] Sir Joshua Reynolds, at first sceptical of Barker's invention, was eventually convinced by a panoramic painting of London exhibited in 1792: "I was in error in supposing your invention could never succeed, for the present exhibition proves it is capable of producing effects and representing nature in a manner far superior to the limited scale of pictures in general."[13]

By adapting principles of perspective to a large cylindrical surface, Barker was participating in a long tradition. His method for recording the landscape around Edinburgh in the late 1780s[14] was replicated by Hendrik Willem Mesdag, who made a 360-degree perspective drawing of the Dutch seashore at Scheveningen in 1881. Mesdag reconfigured Albrecht Dürer's transparent perspective screen into the shape of a drum, climbed inside it and, as he rotated, traced the outlines of the landscape onto the inside of the glass. The drum was later positioned at the centre of a new cylindrical building in The Hague, and the outlines of the image were projected back onto a large, cylindrical canvas suspended around the perimeter of the building.[15]

Perspective attempts to create an illusion of uniform space and mass, encouraging the observer to mistake representation for reality. When all of the conditions are right, the illusion works. When the object and the observer's station point are both fixed, when the object's orthogonal lines recede towards a single vanishing point, and when receding rhythms become logarithmically smaller, the surface of the canvas seems to disappear. In one sense, it is a magic trick.

Perspective demands a willingness not to ask too many questions. A perspectival image is credible from only one general direction; from an oblique viewpoint, its proportions become distorted and unbelievable.[16]

Mesdag's glass cylinder (1881); Foundation for the Preservation of the Centenarian Mesdag Panorama, Den Haag, The Netherlands.

To contemplate a perspective, one remains stationary, without reaching out and touching its surface to see why one's eyes do not fully perceive depth.[17] This "gentleman's agreement" then enables us to talk about the image as if it were real.

The panorama avoids some perspectival shortcomings by distancing the painting from the observer. Sometimes there is also a *faux terrain* ("false ground") – a horizontal stage set, with real, volumetric objects in the foreground. The *faux terrain* blends seamlessly into the painting, heightening the illusion of reality and depth. Intuitive reactions to panoramas attest to this lifelike appearance:

I actually put on my hat, imagining myself to be in the open air ... I could form no idea how far the canvas was from my eye, in one spot it appears thirty miles off and in another not so many feet.[18]

The king, queen, and princesses came to see the picture [of Portsmouth harbour in 1794] ... Queen Charlotte is reported to have said that the sight of this picture made her feel sea-sick.[19]

An incident is related of a Newfoundland dog, which had been brought to the panorama [of Malta in 1810] and was so deceived by the natural appearance of the water in the harbour, that he leapt into the picture to enjoy a bath in the briny element.[20]

Whether or not these accounts are factual, the obvious pride they exude indicates that panoramas were striving for such a confusion. These intuitive reactions suggest a faithful belief in a real presence, while expressions such as "My, how real it looks!" presume that one is still confronting a representation. One observer even claimed that "there are aspects of soil and climate which ... in great panoramas ... are conveyed to the mind with a completeness and truthfulness not always to be gained from a visit to the scene itself."[21] The power of a representation can be most evident when it is suddenly disrupted. For example, when "Cairo and the Banks of the Nile" collapsed in 1971, it revealed the interior of a rather claustrophobic brick building in Brussels.

For a panorama to be convincing, the painting must be done systematically. The horizon line must coincide with the eye level of the observer standing on the central platform. The image must be consistent with real

Transition from *faux terrain* to painting; from *Scientific American*, 55, no. 19 (November 6, 1886).

landscape views; everything must be recognizable or at least conceivable. Because the painting is inherently still and silent, it must avoid depicting things that move and things that are noisy: no galloping horses.[22] The painting's inherent materiality should be suppressed: no seams or folds in the canvas, no brush strokes. Fortunately, the observer is restricted to a platform about ten metres away from the painting, so details need not be overly realistic. The tonality and colour saturation of the landscape should diminish with distance, suggesting atmospheric depth. Despite occasional promotions as works of art, panoramas are more convincing if they are not subject to painterly idiosyncrasies.[23]

The painting must also be "framed" properly, to hide the edges where representation ends and reality begins. Seeing the edge of the painting would diminish the apparent depth of the vista. Vertical edges are avoided automatically because of the painting's cylindrical shape. The upper horizontal edge is masked by a canopy above the central platform, which also hides the fact that the light pervading the panorama is not the ambient light of the painted sky. The lower edge of the painting is masked by a foreground plane or a *faux terrain*. Foreground objects and surfaces in a *faux terrain* must be real or at least credible representations; planar

"Cairo and the Banks of the Nile," painted by Émile Wauters (1882), after its collapse in 1971; Institut Royal du Patrimoine Artistique, copyright A.C.L., Bruxelles.

cut-out figures and artificial ground surfaces would undermine the overall illusion.[24] Indirect access via the passageway below and the central stairway avoids the comical alternative of a doorway puncturing the vista.

When some of these techniques are not followed, the observer must try to mask out the offending portions for the panoramic illusion to become convincing. The painting's horizon is usually the most reliable reference because it resembles a real horizon so closely. When we survey an outdoor

Detail of "Jerusalem on the day of the Crucifixion," painted by Paul Philippoteaux (1882); *cyclorama de Jérusalem*, Ste-Anne-de-Beaupré, Québec.

landscape and mask out the foreground, the horizon could very well be a giant cylindrical painting (or even hemispherical, if one were to include the dome of the sky); our senses have no way to distinguish between the two. The horizon's stillness, silence, and apparent flatness coincide exactly with the mode of a painting. An enormous panorama, with a habitable *faux terrain* and a translucent dome, might be indistinguishable from the real world as it appears from where we stand.

FICTIONS FOR THE PANORAMA

Having been superseded by movies, television, and tourism, the panorama has been relegated to the status of a historical curiosity protected by preservation societies. Nonetheless, it remains the most dogged attempt to represent the spatial experience of being immersed in the world.[25] Techniques from painting, sculpture, optics, theatre, and architecture have been invoked to help blur the apparent threshold between representation and reality. To pursue this perceptual "twilight zone," one cannot rely solely on organizational analyses of the panorama but must also consider the experience of an observer, perhaps best described within the age-old domain of storytelling.

We are outside in the open air. The sky is clear and there is not much wind today. A familiar song blares from a passing Honda. The last few panes of mirrored glass are being installed in a new office building across the street. When the hoarding comes down we will be able to see our reflections. Beyond this building, the land rolls down to the river and up again to become the far shore, with its blanket of houses disappearing into a line of hills in the distance.

The other building nearby is a blank, cylindrical structure, probably about three or four storeys high. A single entrance faces the street. We proceed through the entrance, into a vestibule (some money may have changed hands here), and quickly into a dark corridor. At the end, we ascend a steep stairway towards a brighter area above. Now we are standing on a circular platform, slowly scanning the view. Having surveyed its magnitude, we move to the edge of the platform to see what the territory contains. It is a biblical scene with people in flowing garb scattered across a rocky plateau, with what must be the old city of Jerusalem in the background.

As the representation seduces our imagination, various things could now happen:

a) A kid with a backpack and a mischievous expression strolls up to the edge of the platform and fires a spitball at an opening in the clouds. It sticks for a moment and then drops out of sight into the faux *terrain. He immediately sends a paper airplane off in the same direction. It soars horizontally and after about a minute it is no more than a speck in the distance. With a small pair of rented binoculars, we follow it until it disappears once again into the textureless sky.*

b) We bump into another observer, apologize to her, and continue walking around the edge of the platform. In the middle ground of the painting is a figure, gesturing awkwardly. This figure looks just like the bumped observer. We scan the platform for her, to point out the resemblance, but only three men and some children are present. Puzzled, we peer more closely at the other faces in the painting, only to find that each of them resembles a relative or a friend. After turning around and shading our eyes against a sudden brightness from the skylight above, we look back across the faux terrain *at the unfamiliar faces of the observers leaning out over the railing.*

c) The city wall is situated just below the portion of the horizon where the sky is vividly rendered in purple and orange. The fine details of the wall demonstrate extreme painterly precision. Along the top edge of the wall is a row of tiny figures, little more than a series of dots, moving almost imperceptibly past others proceeding in the opposite direction. Over to the right, on a darker portion of the wall, a sack or a body is pushed over the edge, disappearing into a grove of trees with a muffled thud, just loud enough to be heard.

d) Suspecting a single, linear narrative in the circular panorama, we move clockwise around the platform, surveying one portion at a time. A sequential plot is indeed evident, culminating in the crucifixion. The three crosses and their figures are elevated slightly above the horizon. Roman soldiers are on their way down from the hill, near the edge of the plateau. Farther on, in a field to the south of the city, General Lee and his troops watch and wait as the Union forces pause during their forward rush. General Armistead lies mortally wounded. Smoke from cannons lingers above the battlefield. Several men are being carried on stretchers across the sand dunes to a waiting ship. A storm is brewing out at sea. To the left and right, large waves approach the fishing boats along the beach. Inland, on the opposite side of the platform, clouds are building up over the rooftops of houses in The Hague.

e) Having tired of the panorama, we descend via the central stairway, out through the darkened corridor and into the vestibule. Upon leaving the building, we stride out onto the top of the dunes overlooking the North Sea. The fishing boats are

still scattered along the beach and the clouds continue to build up over the city.
A horse-drawn cart full of nets moves silently along the waterfront. A large man
nearby disassembles a cylindrical contraption made of glass and wood, muttering
to himself in Dutch that this crummy thing will never work.

Representation and reality are easily confused when the panorama's illusion is subtly extended. In this fictional zone, the order of things is
unstable and the observer's situation is questioned, as if a small, virtual
crack were opening up between one's feet, and for a moment it is not
clear which foot is on the stable mainland and which is on the receding
vessel.[26] This momentary state of confused equilibrium indicates a chaotic
gap between conventional categories of thought – between presence and
representation. The fictional passages above certainly can be dismissed as
paradoxical or simply erroneous, but that would disregard the panorama's primary intention – to produce a convincing illusion. The panorama does not seek a stable ground.

The representational capacity of verbal language (one imagines things
elsewhere as one reads the words on a page) is well-suited to documenting
experiential ambiguities.[27] The smooth flow of words disguises complex
transitions among stable situations. The intended "transparency" of the
panorama (one sees a distant landscape "through" the canvas) tries to
achieve the same fluid ambiguity. With a little imagination or a perceptual
error, the panoramic illusion is consummated. This moment of unstable
equilibrium, when the panorama hovers treacherously between picture
and world, is also evident in works by painters such as René Magritte.[28]

MAGIC

Although the panorama was promoted as a glorified educational display,
it recalls Roland Barthes's remark about the Eiffel Tower, that "the naive
utilitarianism of the enterprise is not separate from the oneiric, infinitely
powerful function which, actually, inspired its creation."[29] One may then
wonder if the panorama's enormous popularity in nineteenth-century
Europe and America was based on something other than a voracious
desire to learn about foreign landmarks. The inclusion of the panorama
in nineteenth-century books on magic suggests a possibility.[30] Because of
obvious similarities between theatrical stage sets and nineteenth-century
stage illusions, this connection between panorama and magic is not unex-

René Magritte, "La belle captive" (1949); copyright 1992 C. Herscovici/ARS, New York.

pected. Both involve an audience and a display of illusion, whether through an active performance of magic tricks or a more contemplative presentation.

To investigate this interpretation further, the panorama may be subjected to a confrontation with the institution of magic in non-modern cultures before the nineteenth century or in other parts of the world.[31] In these cultures, a magical rite was believed to have a real influence on worldly things. This belief would eventually lead magic into an encounter with modern science, which assumed that both had laid claim to the same territory. In the court of modern scientific laws, archaic magic understandably has little credibility, yet its presence in so many vital cultures (including those of our cultural ancestors in ancient Greece and Rome) suggests that it need not be dismissed automatically because it does not meet modern scientific expectations; that it be acknowledged at least as a semi-religious conciliation between humans and the world.

Archaic magic indeed demonstrates some surprising similarities to the operation of a panorama. A magic rite is performed by a skilled magician (medicine man/shaman) on behalf of his community or a specific individual. As explained by Mauss, the aim is to change something out in the

René Magritte, "L'univers démasqué"; copyright 1992 C. Herscovici/ARS, New York.

world – to make rain arrive, illness depart, etc. A sympathetic connection is presumed to exist between the magician's esoteric actions/materials/tools and the distant object of attention.[32] Such connections are made by performing an act on a local representation – a fragment of the distant object (e.g., hair, teeth) or a related object with which it has made physical contact (e.g., clothing, a footprint, a personal possession). Connections may also be made by performing an act on a mimetic representation (e.g., a doll, a picture, even a name). Magical potential can be stored in physical objects and images for later use (e.g., amulets), when the magician is no longer present.[33]

Magic is performed in a specific place distinct from the everyday – a permanent sanctuary, or a temporary circle or square that the magician has drawn around himself. A magical event may be introduced by an entry rite and concluded by an exit rite (e.g., applause). Sometimes observers are expected to play an active role in reinforcing the rite.[34] During a magical episode, the magician is typically in a state of ecstasy,[35] either naturally induced or faithfully feigned.

Despite all of these operational similarities between archaic magic and the panorama, an important difference returns the panorama to the nineteenth century, when magic referred to stage illusions and tricks.[36] This difference is based on the fundamental intentions of archaic magic as opposed to stage illusion. In performing a rain dance, an archaic magician promotes a particular effect on something in the world.[37] In stage illusion, modern magic is appreciated not for its ultimate effect on something external, but for the audacious yet casual impression it makes on the observer. The question of belief is crucial to this difference. Archaic magicians and their faithful followers believe in real effects; they believe that the everyday operation of the world can be suspended when special rites are performed. For them, make-believe is an *active* form of belief, analogous to myth-making. With our modern preference for *passive* belief, make-believe seems more like delusion or even hypocrisy. In modern magic, neither the magician nor the observer wholeheartedly believes that natural laws can be suspended; the magician merely pretends that this is so, and the audience is impressed that the magician and his apparatus can make the illusion appear so real. Although an observer may

Samoyed shaman; from *Mythologie des peuples lointains et barbares*, courtesy Larousse.

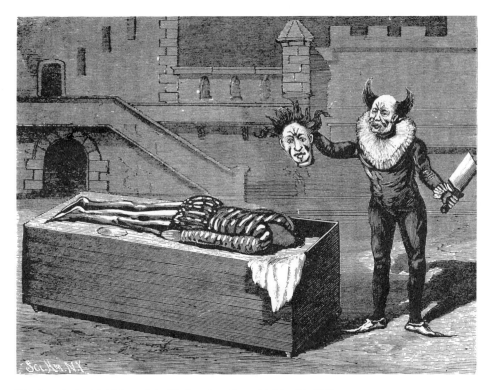

"The Decapitation Trick"; from *Scientific American* 62, no. 21 (May 24, 1890).

be forever puzzled about how a certain illusion is achieved, to believe for more than a moment that the illusion is real is contrary to the premises of modern thought. A persistent declaration of belief is sure to prompt the magician to show how the trick was done, to provide reassurance that the world is indeed rational, despite appearances. The modern magician is ultimately a human just like everyone else. Considerable skill may be demonstrated, but unless the magician is famous (which opens up another discussion), no one really suspects any special, semi-divine status.

Observing magical performances and panoramas – or more recent versions of them[38] – need not be regarded as a proclamation of amazement over someone else's technical skill. In language, and perhaps also in experience, it is not far from the *expression* of wonder (amazement) to the *question* of wonder (to wonder if ...). As a magical illusion reaches its climax, modern observers are momentarily suspended between belief and disbelief, wondering if the illusion could indeed be real. For a brief instant, we savour the possibility that a small gap has opened up in the midst of the patterns of thought with which we have tamed both the

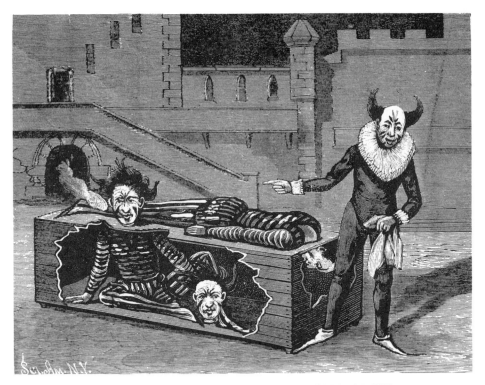

"Explanation of the Decapitation Trick"; from *Scientific American* 62, no. 21 (May 24, 1890).

natural world and ourselves. This anticipation of non-rational possibilities occurs despite the tacit modern belief that magic is merely a representation, with no bearing on reality. Unlike its archaic counterpart, however, modern magic can endure for only a moment. Like ecstatic events and poisonous substances, its vitality is possible only in short bursts and small doses.

NOTES

1 Guy Davenport, *Herakleitos and Diogenes* (Bolinas, Cal.: Grey Fox Press 1979), 17.

2 Following European usage, "panorama" here is defined by its cylindrical format. In North America, this came to be known as "cyclorama," while the "panorama" imitated a journey by reeling a very long painting past a window opening.

3 In North America, panoramas can be found in Atlanta, Gettysburg, and Ste-Anne-de-Beaupré, near the city of Québec. Other full-size cylindrical panora-

mas are located in Australia (Alice Springs), Austria (Innsbruck and Salzburg), Belgium (Eigenbrakel), Bulgaria (Pleven), the Czech Republic (Prague), Egypt (Heliopolis), Germany (Altötting and Bad Frankenhausen), Iraq (Al-Mada'in), the Netherlands (The Hague), North Korea (Pyongyang), Poland (Wrocaw), Russia (Moscow and Volgograd), Switzerland (Einsiedeln, Lucerne, and Thun), and Ukraine (Sevastopol).

4 Standard panorama paintings circulating throughout Europe and North America during the nineteenth century were approximately fifteen metres high and 120 metres in circumference.

5 A discussion of the reverse tendency – to mistake reality for representation, to treat the world like a picture – is beyond the scope of this paper. See Donald Horne, *The Great Museum: The Re-presentation of History* (London: Pluto 1984); and Erwin Panofsky, *Perspective as Symbolic Form*, tr. C.S. Wood (New York: Zone Books 1991).

6 See Roland Barthes, *The Eiffel Tower and Other Mythologies*, tr. R. Howard (New York: Hill & Wang 1979), 12–14.

7 Étienne-Louis Boullée, *Treatise on Architecture*, in *A Documentary History of Art*, ed. E. Holt (Garden City, N.J.: Doubleday 1966), vol. 3, 270. See also Adolf Max Vogt, "Die Newtonischen 'Opticks' und die Optik des Panoramas," *Zeitschrift für Schweizerische Archäologie und Kunstgeschichte* 42, no. 4 (1985): 251–6.

8 Francesco Petrarca, "The Ascent of Mont Ventoux," in Ernst Cassirer et al, *The Renaissance Philosophy of Man* (Chicago: University of Chicago Press 1948), 36–46.

9 Ernst Cassirer, *The Individual and the Cosmos in Renaissance Philosophy*, tr. M. Domandi (New York: Harper & Row 1963), 145. See also Jacob Burckhardt's discussion of "the discovery of the beauty of landscape" in *The Civilization of the Renaissance in Italy*, tr. S.G.C. Middlemore (New York: New American Library 1960), 218–25.

10 Rainer Maria Rilke, "Von der Landschaft"; quoted in J.H. van den Berg, *The Changing Nature of Man* (New York: Norton 1983), 231.

11 Sylvain Malfroy, "Extensions de l'illusionisme du panorama dans l'architecture privée," *Zeitschrift für Schweizerische Archäologie und Kunstgeschichte* 42, no. 4 (1985): 331–8.

12 *Repertory of Arts and Manufactures* 4 (1796), 165–7; quoted in Scott B. Wilcox, "Unlimiting the Bounds of Painting," in *Panoramania! The Art and Entertainment of the "All-Embracing" View*, ed. R. Hyde (London: Trefoil 1988), 17.

13 George R. Corner, *The Panorama, With Memoirs of its Inventor, Robert Barker, and his Son, the Late Henry Aston Barker* (London 1857), 6.

14 Ibid., 4.

15 *The Panorama Phenomenon*, ed. E.J. Fruitema and P.A. Zoetmulder (The Hague: Foundation for the Preservation of the Centenarian Mesdag Panorama 1981), 103.

16 For an anamorphic image, the reverse is true: the image is recognizable *only* from an oblique angle. See Jurgis Baltrušaitis, *Anamorphic Art*, tr. W. Strachan (New York: Abrams 1977).

17 Perspective drawings ignore two of our optical capacities for perceiving depth – binocular parallax and focal accommodation.

18 Charles Robert Leslie, letter to Thomas J. Leslie, 2 December 1812 (Yale Center for British Art); quoted in Wilcox, "Unlimiting the Bounds of Painting," 28.

19 Corner, *Panorama*, 7.

20 Ibid., 11.

21 *The Times*, 27 December 1861; quoted in Wilcox, "Unlimiting the Bounds of Painting," 38.

22 Daguerre later devised "dioramas" that added sound, lighting effects, moving objects, and even atmospheric changes. See Helmut and Alison Gernsheim, *L.J.M. Daguerre: The History of the Diorama and the Daguerreotype* (New York: Dover 1968), ch. 2.

23 The panorama thus anticipates the anonymity and apparent reality of photography.

24 At the Mesdag Panorama in The Hague, the panoramic illusion benefits from a *faux terrain* with real anchors and nets lying in real sand that one can almost touch. A "ha-ha" technique (by which the receding ground dips out of sight and reappears farther on) assists the transition between *faux terrain* and painting. Ironically, Mesdag's painterly gestures (which contribute to its status in Dutch landscape art) diminish the overall panoramic illusion.

25 Recent developments in computerized virtual-reality devices (flight simulators, computerized helmets and gloves, etc.) may be seen as descendants of the panorama.

26 Ambiguous fusions of reality and representation in literature are discussed in Kendall L. Walton, "How Remote are Fictional Worlds from the Real World?" *Journal of Aesthetics and Art Criticism* 37, no. 1 (Fall 1978): 11–23.

27 Foucault's discussion of "heterotopia" in the preface to *The Order of Things* (New York: Vintage Books 1973) notes the privileged position of language

for representing enigmatic gaps among our conventional patterns of thought. His subsequent writing about heterotopia, however, defines it in a less radical way – as real sites for human institutions exiled from mainstream culture. See Michel Foucault, "Of Other Spaces," tr. J. Miskowiec, *Diacritics* 16, no. 1 (Spring 1986): 22–7.

28 Such ambiguities are savoured in other modern works connected only remotely to the panorama. Here, one could cite writers (Jorge Luis Borges, Alain Robbe-Grillet), painters (Giorgio de Chirico, Juan Gris), film makers (Alain Resnais, Jacques Rivette), and even architects (Peter Eisenman, Hiromi Fujii).

29 Barthes, *The Eiffel Tower*, 7. Barthes also describes the Eiffel Tower's capacity to transform the city of Paris below into a panorama.

30 See, for example, Albert A. Hopkins, *Magic: Stage Illusions and Scientific Diversions* [1897] (New York: Arno 1977), 354–61.

31 See Marcel Mauss, *A General Theory of Magic*, tr. R. Brain (London: Routledge & Kegan Paul 1972).

32 Ibid., 47–8.

33 Ibid., 64–71, 76.

34 Ibid., 46, 49, 134.

35 From the Greek *ekstasis*, "to put out of place."

36 See Henry Ridgely Evans, "The Mysteries of Modern Magic," in Hopkins, *Magic*, 1–26.

37 The transcendent, conciliatory intention of archaic magic distinguishes it from instrumental techniques concerned solely with cause and effect.

38 In *The Magician and the Cinema* (New York: Oxford University Press 1981), Eric Barnouw describes the relation between the decline of magical stage illusion and the simultaneous rise of cinema. Perhaps the decline of the panorama is paralleled by a similar metamorphosis.

The Building of a Horizon

Louise Pelletier

Chora

Mexico City, 11 July 1991

A TOTAL ECLIPSE OF THE SUN had been predicted in Mexico City, and I awaited the event with childish excitement. The previous day, I had climbed the Pyramid of the Sun at Teotihuacan to watch a descendant of the Aztecs re-enact an ancient ritual, and that seemed a fitting prelude to what must have seemed, five centuries earlier, a portentous event. A few minutes before daylight began to fade, I climbed to the roof to watch the transformation of the city. The sky was obscured by clouds and by a thick smog that bleached out everything. Imperceptibly, the light grew dim, and even though I could not witness the actual overlapping of the moon and the sun and could experience only the disappearance of light, I was truly overcome by an apocalyptic feeling.

The whole cycle of transition between day and night and day again occurred in a short lapse of time. The city became very quiet – a nightmarish feeling. The darkness lasted only a few minutes, and gradually but this time more rapidly, light reappeared behind clouds. Roosters sang, children were exalted, screaming and shouting in the artificially quiet afternoon. It seemed as though time had stopped, for a night, for a day.

Words can barely describe the intensity of an event that lasted no more than half an hour. When the light had almost completely returned, I went back inside and was amazed to find people watching the event on television. Scientific descriptions of the event were transmitted on every television screen, showing graphics of the moon's orbit passing between the sun and the earth, and representing the whole event beyond the clouds as it happened successively at different geographic points. The apocalyptic feeling created by the disappearance of light was described in terms of the overlapping of celestial bodies in the solar system, while the incredible elasticity of the temporal sequence experienced during the eclipse was reduced to milliseconds. Everybody pretended to know exactly what an eclipse was, yet they had no idea of what had really happened during that afternoon, beyond their television screen.

Television images are so deeply ingrained in our experience of everyday life that this realistic depiction of the world gives the illusion that one can fully grasp the truth of a place or an event through visual objectification. Yet the experience of a natural phenomenon goes far beyond its reduction to an image. It is impossible to separate the actual phenomenon from our perception of it without leaving aside the essence of the phenomenon itself. We may never escape the realm of representation, for it is firmly rooted in our cultural understanding of the world. We can only seek alternative forms of representation that may enable us to engage the event through a participatory experience – images that recreate the lapse of time experienced during an eclipse without losing the horizon, even when looking at the zenith.

● ▲ ■

If one decided to look at depictions of the transforming sky throughout history, one would find a great variety of representations, expressing an almost infinite range of ideologies. Each image is a potential unfolding of an entire world. Every representation, even the most primitive drawing ignorant of perspectival conventions, is more than the depiction of a single theme. The place given to the observer, his presence in the image or the intentional denial of a unique point of view, the very nature of what is shown or hidden from the frame – all of these considerations express the

Between the zenith and the horizon: frame from Andrei Tarkovsky's *The Sacrifice* (1986); from *Le Sacrifice* (Munich/Paris: Schirmer/Mosel 1987); Sven Nykvist and Swedish Film Institute, Stockholm.

spirit of the time and ultimately determine the production of architectural space.

Today, in the realm of architectural representation, we usually assume that the sky is an infinite and immaterial void above the earth. In some specific cases, its conceptual vault is postulated to be 100 kilometres high in order to meet the requirements of computer-generated images. The meeting of the sky and the earth at the horizon is reduced to a fine thread that divides the picture plane at infinity, inaccessible to the embodied observer. The horizon also collapses in the tracing of an architectural section, where the skyline is assimilated to the earth in a dark line; the liminal condition is deprived of its potential thickness. In order to frame the very dilemma of a world of representation that tends to ignore the crucial involvement of the spectator in a space either built or represented, the paradigmatic architectural task of the building of the Tower of Babel links various experiences of the horizon in the meeting of the sky and the earth.

The biblical allegory of the Tower of Babel is not, as has often been claimed, only about the arrogant dream of man to conquer heaven. The texts of Genesis (11:1–9) describe the necessity of naming a bounded place, of defining the limits of the world, and of delineating a horizon. The new translation by David Rosenberg of the first part of the Old Testament, *The Book of J*, emphasizes precisely the importance of the Tower of Babel in fulfilling this need for unity and boundness. Rosenberg goes back to "what scholars agree is the oldest strand in the Pentateuch."[1] His translation proposes an entirely new dimension to the dogmatic interpretations of the Bible, suggesting some hypotheses that substantially transform the reading of the holy texts. According to Harold Bloom in his introduction to *The Book of J*, this very first version of the text that initiates the Old Testament was written by a woman.[2] In *The Book of J*, Yahweh is not the absolute and terrifying God of the Old Testament, but rather a "literary character" often subjected to humanly passions, who gets mad at crowds and threatens to murder Moses.

When these texts of the Old Testament appeared in the "Authorised Version of the Bible" (the "King James Holy Bible," 1611), which is considered to be the culmination of English style, it had been revised many times, and the composite result had homogenized it into one absolute voice. Rosenberg's translation of the Tower of Babel episode, on the other hand, reveals the profound subtlety of the ancient text:

Now listen: all the earth uses one tongue, one and the same words. Watch: they journey from the east, arrive at a valley in the land of Sumer, settle there.

"We can bring ourselves together," they said, "like stone on stone, use brick for stone: bake it until hard." For mortar they heated bitumen.

"If we bring ourselves together," they said, "we can build a city and tower, its top touching the sky – to arrive at fame. Without a name we're unbound, scattered over the face of the earth."

Yahweh came down to watch the city and tower the sons of man were bound to build. "They are one people, with the same tongue," said Yahweh. "They conceive this between them, and it leads up until no boundary exists to what they will touch. Between us, let's descend, baffle their tongue until each is scatterbrain to his friend."

From there Yahweh scattered them over the whole face of earth; the city there came unbound.

That is why they named the place Bavel: their tongues were baffled there by Yahweh. Scattered by Yahweh from there, they arrived at the ends of the earth.[3]

Bab-ili ("Gate of God"), the Assyrian name given to the city of Babylon, is also related to the Hebrew *balal* ("to confuse"); thus the Tower of Babel, symbol of Bavel, is also the confusion of languages.[4] The translation of "baffle their tongues" plays on the similarity between *balal* and Babel, so as to assimilate Babylon to a "universe of bafflement."[5] Rosenberg's translation also emphasizes the "boundness" of the enterprise, in which "the sons of man were bound to build" and brought themselves together "like stone on stone," using "brick for stone," while their boundness gave them a name and protected them from being scattered.

It would be inappropriate in the present context to argue about the authenticity of Rosenberg's translation or the plausibility of Bloom's interpretation. The controversy introduced by an unusual reading of the Old Testament, however, certainly raises questions about the absoluteness and dogmatism surrounding the writings that make up the Bible. The perennial attempt to retrieve the "original" meaning from the biblical texts has led to passionate polemics and a great diversity in graphic representations of the Tower of Babel from the early medieval and Byzantine periods to the archaeological reconstructions of the nineteenth and twentieth centuries. Every artefact attempts to redefine the meaning and relevance of the tower in a given world. The juxtaposition of a multitude of representations of the Tower of Babel may indeed disclose a world of new interpretations free from the shackles of dogmatism.

The early Western representations of the Tower of Babel's construction do not describe primarily an existing space or structure. In fact, they provide few details about the appearance of this archetypal building. The unfolding of the story takes precedence over a formal rendering of the tower (namely the eight storeys of Herodotus's description),[6] putting the emphasis on the narrative structure of the event – that is, the building of the tower, followed by God's punishment. In the Middle Ages, the bound-ness and unity of workers is indeed the main theme of representation, and importance is clearly given to the collective and anonymous labour devoted to the building of the tower – to the building enterprise rather than to the tower as an architectural product. The orthogonal tower of the Romanesque bas-relief in Salerno (1050–80), for example, serves as a scaffolding for the workers' endeavour. The earth meets the infinity of

The building enterprise, Romanesque bas-relief in ivory, from the sacristy of the cathedral of Salerno (1050–80).

The temporal unfolding of the Tower of Babel, from a mosaic in the Basilica of San Marco, Venice (1220–30); Alinari/Art Resource, New York.

heaven in the actual labour of the workers, inviting God Himself to come down to earth. There is no need to define the boundary between sky and earth, for the horizon is embodied in the physical work of the builders.

Similarly, a mosaic in the Basilica of San Marco in Venice (1220–30) represents the building of the Tower of Babel as a temporal unfolding of the biblical story. The tower itself is nothing more than a rectangular facade without depth or modulation. Yet the whole mosaic embodies the arrogant action of man against God in a sequential story. On the left side of the image, the tireless workers join their efforts to erect the highest construction ever built by mankind. The tower is surrounded by scaffolding, still in the process of being built. From an opening in the sky above, three angels are pointing down at the tower, bringing this insolent construction to God's attention. The tower is duplicated on the right, this time dominated by God's presence, with His angels dispersing workers "to the four cardinal points."[7] In the Middle Ages, the image of an event

The omnipresence of God in the medieval representation of the building of the Tower of Babel, Romanesque wall-painting, St-Savarin-sur-Gartempe (early twelfth century).

cannot be dissociated from its temporality. The complete mosaic suggests a discontinuous space that unfolds as the viewer enters the image and follows the story.

God is often present among men in medieval and Byzantine representations of the Tower of Babel, as in the Romanesque wall painting at St-Savarin-sur-Gartempe (early twelfth century). The tower is represented for the first time as a volume, emphasizing the pictorial depth. Yet the realm inhabited by God is not subject to the rules of linear perspective. Not only is the tower distorted, it is seen from the top – a vantage point inaccessible to human vision. Its structure, as well as the parallel sides of stones carried by the workers, converge towards the foreground. In the Middle Ages, human vision was understood in terms of *perspectiva naturalis*, the science of optics, in which visual rays are believed to converge towards the seeing eye; but contrary to the Renaissance notion of the image as a frozen section of the cone of vision, the medieval image establishes a different relationship between the picture plane and the actual perception of the world.

In *De Visione Dei* (1453), Nicholas of Cusa (or Cusanus) explains to a group of monks the "wonders which are revealed beyond all sensible, rational, and intellectual sight"[8] through an icon of God. Cusanus describes the sacred image as an all-seeing presence that "beholds everything around it."[9] From the realm of God, never violated by human sight, the divine gaze is turned towards us. God's face can be seen only in a veiled and symbolic manner, between the "most sacred darkness" and the "presence of Inaccessible Light," as His realm is protected by the "Wall of Paradise."[10] Exceptionally, God's face can be seen unveiled when the seeker enters "into a certain secret and hidden silence wherein there is no

The tower becomes a volumetric entity in the Chronicle of Rudolph von Ems (c. 1383); Landesbibliothek, Stuttgart.

knowledge or concept of a face."[11] In other words, God's face becomes accessible to the faithful who enters the vision of God and beholds himself through God's eye.[12] In medieval painting and religion, there is a clear distinction between sight, which is the internal vision, and optics, which is the science of the eye. The sacred image is *not* a construction of the world as it is presented to the eye, but an all-encompassing mirror image of the world, made accessible by the vision of God. The icon is not the representation of God, but rather His sight; the divine rays of vision converge towards us, in the space beheld by Him. This inversion of viewer and "viewed" may cast some light on the unexpected inversion of perspective in Byzantine images.[13]

In the chronicle of Rudolph von Ems (c. 1383), the tower is represented as a volumetric entity in an undulating landscape. The materiality of the tower is clearly expressed by the thickness of its walls, and the centre wheel, activated by two men, is the ultimate mechanism that enables its construction. Yet the very shape of the tower is moulded by God's projective vision from beyond the opaque background; parallel sides of the portal converge towards the foreground, and stones on the ground are foreshortened for a divine observer beyond the golden screen. The horizon line as we conceive it today simply did not exist in the Middle Ages.

197

Instead, the conceptual boundary between the earthly world and the sky was transposed, as in icons or mosaics, in the collapse of planes onto the golden screen.

With the transformation of pictorial depth during the Renaissance came a fundamental change in the configuration of the Babel theme. Although labour remained a crucial subject of representation, the vertical proportion and the size of the tower increased, and space gradually became more hierarchical in the depiction of depth and the distinction between the internal space and the exterior of the tower. The opaque background of the Middle Ages, however, was first transformed into a concrete landscape or urban context only during the first half of the fifteenth century. In painting, the "urbanization" of the Tower of Babel coincides with the first attempt to represent the world in linear perspective. In 1420, Brunelleschi developed a method to flatten the image of the world through reflection in a mirror. This method, further described by Leon Battista Alberti in *Della Pictura* (1435–36), also involved the reduction of human binocular vision to the view from one fixed eye at the apex of the cone of vision. By looking with only one eye, says Alberti, we can observe *de visu* the deformation that is revealed through the mirror. The extension of the world, however, is not blurred in the distance as in seventeenth-century paintings. The sharpness of depth reveals instead the finiteness of the world. The very idea of infinity is foreign to Renaissance man, who still lives in an ordered universe, and the hierarchy of the image is to be found in a collapse of the entire event onto the picture plane, its background and foreground flattened onto the section through the cone of vision. The coincidence of the layers of events and the accumulation of geometric ordering are precisely what make the depth of fifteenth-century paintings so fascinating.

Gozzoli's tower of Campo Santo in Pisa is part of an urban context, and the visual structure of the city converges towards the centre of the tower's gate. Workmen have become a minority in the whole picture, and Nimrod and the Medici court passively observe the building of the tower. Their gaze is unified by a common horizon, but in the fresco the sky meets the earth above the multitude, just below the highest level of the construction. The accelerated landscape around the city fills the space of an extended horizon between the crowd and the end of the earth with numerous and tortuous paths ascending towards a higher horizon. The sky itself continues this progression through a layering of clouds, with

A multi-layered horizon surrounds the tower depicted by Benozzo Gozzoli
(c. 1470); detail, Campo Santo, Pisa (destroyed during the war).

the final layer unifying the top of the tower and the summit of the
mountains. The dominating view remains confined to the realm of God.
In His celestial medallion, however, the divine gaze is now challenged by
a group of workers on top of the construction. While the multitude
surrounding the tower is passively looking at the enterprise, the viewer
of the fresco himself is now involved in the building of the tower's
horizon. The geometric construction is ordered around him, with a reciprocity between the centre of the tower and the viewer's eye. As a result,
the external observer is engaged in the pictorial depth between the earthly
and celestial horizons.

The shape of the tower also becomes more sophisticated in the fifteenth
century. In "The Book of Hours" of the Duke of Bedford (1424–30), the
volume of the tower seems to stand out from a receding background, and
the ascension of the ramp corresponds to a gradual unfolding of the
horizon. There is no homogeneity of space in the image. The whole
picture is presented frontally, like a stage set, but the tower diminishes in
scale towards the top, as if seen from the ground. The geometric ordering
of stars shows an acceleration of perspective towards the zenith, while

The Tower of Babel stands on a layered background in a miniature from the Duke of Bedford's *Book of Hours* (1424-30); by permission of the British Library, London.

the receding ground overlaps with the sky as if they belonged to the continuous surface of a cylindrical space. The dense blue of the sky confirms the closing of the celestial vault, and it also constitutes the liminal space where the divine intervenes in the action of man. The tower is about to touch the veil of the sky when two angels interrupt man's project, introducing confusion between the workers.

In sixteenth-century engravings, the horizon also encompasses the whole space between the earth that grounds the tower, and the sky that limits its apex. The space surrounding the tower is still finite, invariably framed by natural reliefs or clouds. The tower is more of a hinge revealing the order of heaven on earth, perhaps echoing the classical tradition recently recovered in architecture. The spectator is again involved directly in the discontinuous space "in between" two worlds, as the thickness of the skyline is mysteriously disclosed to him. The image of the tower provides the viewer with a privileged higher horizon that still belongs to God, and yet enables a human observer to behold the world from a vantage point that had always been reserved for the divine gaze.

In many copper engravings of the sixteenth century, workmen are busy building the tower in the foreground, while behind it the landscape recedes in a layering of natural and man-made artifacts. The image often

The extended horizon of Tobias Stimmer's engraving encompasses the entire structure of the tower, from its foundation to the summit of the construction; from Stimmer, *Neue kunstliche Figuren biblischer Historien* (Basel 1576).

presents distinct levels of horizon – one in the foreground (the workers' view line) and the other at the top level of the tower. The extended horizon links the ground of the workers to the top of the tower, giving unexpected access to the landscape visible from the top of the tower. The eye of the artist indeed seems to be looking simultaneously from the workmen's vantage point towards the top of the tower, and from the top of the tower to the extended landscape, creating a strange distortion of the tower's verticality. The basic rules of perspective usually determine the structure of the engravings, yet the depicted space is far from homogeneous, preserving instead the hierarchical structure of an unshaken cosmology. Tobias Stimmer emphasizes the role of the architect in his engraving of the Tower of Babel (1576), but the issues are similar. The mast of Nimrod's ship seems to separate the act of creation on the left side, with Nimrod and the architect united through their gaze, from the right side, where the actual building of the tower is taking place. The horizon between the sea and the sky then relates Nimrod's gaze to the tower's centre of convergence, the point that in fact governs the distorted construction. The horizon is thus a geometric symbol of the transcendental order that regulates both the built world and human hierarchy.

The horizon of Cornelis Anthonisz's etching dissolves on the right into obscurity (1547).

The tower in Cornelis Anthonisz's etching (1547) has attained completion and is now being subjected to God's hurling thunders. People are scattered around the crumbling tower, dispersed in a dismantled space. The tower occupies a geometrical axis (the *axis mundi*) that divides the world between night and day. Dramatically, God's reproving sight casts darkness upon the tower, dissolving its horizon into the night. The geometric order of the tower, its essential verticality, epitomizes the hyphen that simultaneously unites and divides earth and heaven.

Many of the woodcuts and engravings of the sixteenth century were produced as illustrations for the Bible. The paintings of the same period, however, exhibit a different concern with space and horizon. Rather than a geometric ordering of space, painters seemed more concerned with the massive volume of the tower and the potential boundlessness of its ground. While fifteenth-century paintings of the tower still reveal a mysterious depth, depictions of the tower in the late sixteenth century provide the viewer with a dominating, all-encompassing view.

The tower of Pieter Bruegel the Elder (1563) is built on a single horizon;
Museum Boymans-van Beuningen, Rotterdam.

Among the numerous painters concerned with the Tower of Babel between the sixteenth and early seventeenth centuries, Pieter Bruegel the Elder (1520–69) is the most prominent. His representations of the tower embody a truly novel interpretation of the biblical theme. The tower and the landscape now share a single horizon. From an elevated position, the viewer's eye embraces at once King Nimrod in the foreground, the landscape receding towards the skyline, and the entire tower now built as a homogeneous structure. Whereas in previous examples the summit of the tower never extended beyond the surrounding mountains, or else was subjected to the gaze of God, here it clearly dominates its natural surroundings. The tower stands on a boundless space where the horizon continues beyond the frame, unlimited by natural landscape. The foundation of Bruegel's tower is also quite unusual. It stands directly on the edge of the water and is pierced with orifices that lead to the centre of the construction. The unstable foundation, combined with the deviated vertical axis of the tower, already alludes to the predestined failure of man's construction.

The horizon of Hendrick van Cleve's Tower of Babel is reduced
to a line, painting on wood; private collection, Frankfurt.

The concern with foundation appears again in Hendrick van Cleve's
painting (1525–89) of the Tower of Babel. Two great avenues frame the
base of the tower and provide direct access to a complex urban development. They converge brutally towards a horizon clearly defined by the
sky and the sea – the geometric horizon of a perspectival construction.
The tower, distorted by the accelerated perspective, no longer stands on
a natural landscape but on a man-made structure, confident of reaching
the sky. The axis of convergence clearly corresponds to the eye of the
viewer, and the edge between the ground and the sky is reduced to a line.
The realm of God is hidden beyond thick clouds whence a mysterious
light emanates. The sight of God opens up a gap in the sky and swallows
up the tower. The essential geometry of the tower becomes solely responsible for translating the infinitude of God into sensuous finite experience.
In contrast with the geometrically constructed engravings of the same
period, this proto-Baroque representation identifies the geometric horizon
with the geometric essence of the tower – that is, with its vertical axis.
The point of reconciliation, previously occupied by God, is now the
vertical *homo sapiens* himself.

In the sixteenth century, vision was no longer understood as the classical, tactile perception of visual rays. In Vignola's treatise on perspective,
the traditional section of the cone of vision becomes a geometrical
abstraction, and foreshortening of depth is determined scientifically.[14] The
complexity of Vignola's method may have had a direct impact on the

painters of the time. Nevertheless, it is clear that the artists of the sixteenth century had the insight to determine mathematically the foreshortening of depth in relation to a fixed observer. Space would soon become a homogeneous continuum determined by a unique and universal point of view. Van Cleve's volumetric presentation of the tower is already affected by an exaggerated accelerated perspective resulting from the extreme proximity of the observer. This vantage point is gradually fixed to one predetermined position, and the viewer's involvement in the scene accordingly disappears in this perspectival world. Sixteenth-century paintings offer the viewer an almost objectified picture. The scene is presented to an all-seeing spectator, cancelling out the fascinating depth of earlier depictions, along with the viewer's involvement in the rebuilding of the liminal space.

In the last quarter of the seventeenth century, Athanasius Kircher, in a major exegetical work that summarizes his life-long concern for retrieving a universal language for post-Reformation Christianity, identifies the pitfalls of the Tower of Babel. The paradigmatic building is ultimately a sign of the fallen nature of humanity, the unsacred architecture at odds with that of the Temple of Jerusalem and its genealogy. The Jesuit polymath qualifies the biblical allegory with a kind of "theoretical" demonstration about the existence of the tower. *Turris Babel* (1679) is indeed a scientific refutation of the tower that makes its destruction unnecessary.[15] It seems to be at once an admonition against arrogant human action and a sanctioning of the constructed nature of human culture, the "historical" world of the seventeenth century. The biblical text is obviously the point of departure for the text and illustrations, yet Kircher adds a new discursive meaning to the biblical event. Kircher's illustration of the Tower of Babel cantilevered from the earth is based on a complex mathematical calculation that aims to prove the foolishness of Nimrod's ambition. Kircher calculated that "in order to reach even the lowest heaven, that of the moon, the tower would have had to be 178,682 miles high, necessitating some three million tons of substance. Beside its economic impossibility, it would have had the effect of pulling the very earth from its place in the centre of the universe, causing cosmic ruin."[16] Kircher's interpretation of the Tower of Babel demonstrates the rationality and mathematical spirit of the time. His religious concern for keeping the traditional place of the earth "in the centre of the universe" also reflects the growing power of man to control and transform his world. The entire earth is given to

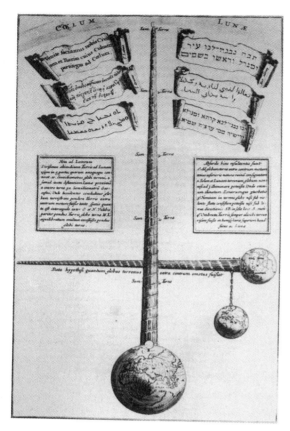

"Demonstration of the impossibility to build a tower as high as the moon's sky"; plate from Athanasius Kircher, *Turris Babel* (Amsterdam 1679).

human vision, while man occupies God's place and becomes responsible for the destiny of the earth.

Once the tower had become an objectified concern of science, and the impossibility of its construction was finally proven, it ceased to be the preferred allegory of man's ambition to attain heaven. It was instead relegated to the background, as a stage set in front of which King Nimrod and the architect, as actors, took over the narrative dimension of the scene, plotting the future of the empire. In a number of large-format illustrated bibles of the eighteenth century, the building fades into the background, framed out of the picture, while the dramatic features of the characters dominate the image. The tower's massive presence and abundant details, characteristic of sixteenth-century depictions, are replaced in the eighteenth century by an indistinct volume with little relief. Fischer von Erlach's engraving on the same theme,[17] on the other hand, emphasizes the objectified architectural artefact. No characters enact the political roles, but a text under the engraving tells of a completed archetypal building, comprising all of the eight storeys mentioned by Herodotus.

In early eighteenth-century engravings, the tower is relegated to the background;
Georg David Nessenthaler, copper engraving from the "Cotta" bible (1730).

While previous depictions of the Babylonian event demonstrated a cosmological concern for the rendition of the tower, Fischer von Erlach introduces a historical approach, the *mythe-histoire*, in which history is created through the artist's imagination and historical fragments.

●　▲　■

Johann Bernhard Fisher von Erlach described the archetypal building
in *Entwurf einer historischen Architektur* (Leipzig 1725).

Various archaeological excavations have uncovered thirty-five "Towers of Babel" in the land of Mesopotamia.[18] Many of them have been considered from time to time as *the* original tower described in Genesis. Since the late eighteenth century, the location of the "real" tower has been scientifically debated and "proven" or rejected by archaeological evidence. Have these discoveries brought us any closer to the archetypal Tower of Babel, the "door to the sky," reconstruction of the "primordial broken axis"?

While archaeology developed as an adjunct to history during the nineteenth century, describing the Tower of Babel with ever-greater scientific precision, the gap between the tower as symbol or paradigm and as architectural artefact widened further. Biblical illustrations reduced the tower to only a shape, often a dark silhouette, that served as a background for the tragedy taking place in front of it. The tower disappeared from the scene of artistic representation, becoming no more than the dark backdrop of technological exploitation. The explorers of Babylon were no longer interested in the allegorical meaning of the biblical event or in its mysterious construction. They tried, instead, to discover the tower's utilitarian function and to establish its most realistic and consistent typology. They found a number of artifacts, such as ziggurats and ancient illustrations on vases and funeral cylinders, that seemed to correspond to the paradigmatic building. The unveiling of cuneiform writing also marked a new turn in the study of the Tower of Babel. Even though the interpretation of the old tablets remains a matter for discussion and disagreement among scholars, some proportional measurements of width and height have been found and have been used in isometric and axonometric reconstructions of the tower.[19] For nineteenth-century archaeologists, however, such measurements revealed nothing but the enormity of size, a far cry from the symbolic geometry disclosed by traditional representations. Indeed, the apparent precision of the scientific method has drawn us further away from the meaning of the paradigmatic tower. The reconstruction of fragments provides evidence of a mysterious tower, but no absolute truth can be drawn from these discoveries because the information never completely fulfils the expectations of three thousand years of allegories.[20]

The tower, together with the horizon of axonometric projection, has actually disappeared, leaving behind only a few fragments of evidence. These scientific fragments, however, do not enable us to reconstruct the

Above left: The tower disappears into a dark backdrop in Gustave Doré's engraving for the "Illustrated Bible" (1880).

Above right: The horizon has disappeared in the isometric archaeological reconstruction of the Tower of Babel; from Chipiez, *Histoire générale de l'art dans l'Antiquité* (Paris 1882).

tower from an implicit narrative, as was the case with earlier representations – the sequential story told by the Byzantine mosaic in the Basilica of San Marco, for example, or the fourteenth- and fifteenth-century paintings and engravings that created a new horizon for the viewer. Instead, archaeological reconstructions and the sets of orthogonal projections that are used to represent them leave us with pieces of an irreconcilable totality. The irrevocability of every piece of evidence cancels out any further story, and therefore limits our possibility to access the ultimate ground of the architectural artefact.

● ▲ ■

Modern literature has produced a few attempts to re-invent the story of Babel and to create a narrative that articulates fragments without reducing us to silence. A story by Franz Kafka, for example, displaces the foundations of the tower to retrieve its meaning. In "The Great Wall of China," Kafka relates how, when the wall was built, a scholar had written a book in which he demonstrated that "the Tower of Babel had failed to reach its goal ... because of the weakness of the foundation" and maintained that "the Great Wall alone would provide for the first time in the history of mankind a secure foundation for a new Tower of Babel."[21] China appeared to be a boundless country where time was extended in such a way that the present of Peking was the "historical past" of the south. The building of the wall was therefore the ideal opportunity for the king to establish a link that would enable him to traverse "the souls of almost all the provinces"[22] – a boundary that would unite the country under a common name – making the half-circle of the wall a spiritual foundation for the tower. Thus for Kafka the dream of a universal language symbolized by the building of the Tower of Babel is attained by the technological achievements of universal communication.

Kafka provoked a "change of role" of the original artefact and thus created a new place from a historical setting. By bringing together realities of two distant worlds, he created a new entity from a "succession of *latencies*."[23] The fragments do not cancel each other out from their inherent memory, but their juxtaposition evokes the tower potentially present in the telling of the story. The narrative therefore has the power to redefine a new horizon in an existing world.

Other artistic disciplines offer a similar potential for displacing the fragments of our environment and for inducing a new role in known artifacts. Cinematographic montage extends another possibility for creating a space to be rediscovered by the spectator, a space whose horizon may not be given, but is nonetheless present. The building of the Tower of Babel has also been invoked in film. One of the most explicit and remarkable example is *Metropolis* by Fritz Lang. As Lang wrote, "in the year 2000, Freder, the son of the Master of Metropolis, rebels against the way his half of the city – the idle 'aristocracy' – has dehumanised the labourers."[24] The duality of body and mind becomes a social division in the building of Metropolis, a perennial conflict that has to be mediated through love and emotion. The Tower of Babel unfolds as the tension builds up among the workers, until the final revolt and the ultimate destruction of the city.

A strange inversion of the original Babel story characterizes the destiny of Metropolis. The workers, led by a technological idol, destroy the construction that was first initiated by the dominant class, the industrial society. Through montage, the duplication of the heroine is made possible.

Maria, the peacekeeper among the workers, is used as a model for a demonic machine that will arouse anger among the workers and eventually persuade them to rebel and lead Metropolis to its destruction. The hierarchy of the city is also expressed through the montage of images. The repetition of corners and stairways transforms a simple stage set into an impossible labyrinth that leads to "the great machines, far underground, yet above the workers' city."[25] The juxtaposition of views of the city framed at different scales disorients the viewer and provokes the overgrowth of Metropolis. The cinematographic representation exceeds a reduction of existing space; it is the creation of a new temporal place that unfolds along the narrative path determined by the author. The artist who traces this path through familiar objects is a real discoverer who is not limited to the explicit, but who shows what was potentially present in the individual object and yet unseen.[26]

The photographic realism of cinema makes it possible to isolate an object from the world, preserving the precision that makes it palpable. Every fragment can then be removed from its context, preserving the memory of the surrounding world. The extreme precision of every detail taken out of context capitalizes on the scientific objectivity of archaeological research. While the latter's objective is to retrieve every existing fact, film represents only certain fragments of the story, and the overall scene has to be re-created by the spectator. The assemblage of fragments provokes a disruption of the spatial and temporal perspective, while its narrative confounds the linear structure of mechanical time into a re-enacted time. The represented depth of the world is not extended as a geometrized space behind the screen. Rather, space is perceived as a movement through time, and its real dimension is projected in front of the screen, in the temporal world of the spectator. In doing so, it inverts the traditional system of linear perspective.

Film montage, especially in surrealist films, enables the seeing subject to distance himself from the seen object and makes him conscious of his position as observer. The sudden inversion of these two terms bridges for a moment the gap between the spectator and the filmic space. This transgression of the imaginary space temporarily transcends the Cartesian paradigm of dualism between man and the world. The whole notion of image in surrealist discourse is indeed partly derived from this desire to retrieve a non-dualistic order, a coincidence of the seeing and the seen, the touching and the touched, that gives access to a united and embodied

Collapse of the horizon in Tarkovsky's *The Sacrifice*;
Sven Nykvist and Swedish Film Institute, Stockholm.

presence. The film frame is opened to the depth of the screen, beyond the single-sided view of the perspective window. It reveals the invisible side of what was hidden by the perspective frontality and redefines the limits inherent in each fragment. Ultimately, it delineates and frames the realm of experience in a world now unlimited and unbound. The montage of fragments is indeed similar to the original description of the Tower of Babel in *The Book of J*: it is the naming of a new order in a world that would otherwise be boundless.

In *The Sacrifice* by Andrei Tarkovsky, we also find a thematic connection to Babel. The continuity of movement is interrupted during specific moments by fragments of another reality. The oneiric, black and white fragments of the devastated city after a nuclear catastrophe are the consequences of arrogant action, of logocentric domination and control. It is the collapse of Babel. The camera glides on the surface of the world, avoiding a direct penetration of space, emphasizing the opacity of the image and reflecting to the spectator his own immobility. The movement of the camera follows the action, envelops it with extreme restraint and subtlety, as if to disappear and let the filmed space reveal itself with all

The absence of sky defines a new potential horizon in *The Sacrifice*,
Sven Nykvist and Swedish Film Institute, Stockholm.

the complexity of its composition. The consciousness of movement is not
that of the camera through space, but rather that of the transforming
space; the immobile frame confronts the spectator with its internal movement. The sky is almost completely absent from the frame. If we can
perceive a glimpse of it, it is pushed to the upper limit of the screen so as
to prevent our gaze from becoming lost in a wide, transparent space. The
horizon is dissolved into the bleached, non-existent sea that emphasizes
only the "contour" of the beach, the earth. In periods of catastrophe, the
sky comes down to earth and collapses the horizon. The cycle is closed
and redemption may be at hand – a new beginning of history.

●　▲　■

As we can see, the Tower of Babel is more than a single theme or a
paradigmatic building that can be described in absolute terms. The very
means of representation disclose the relevance of the archetypal construction in a historical period, and thus every tower is determined by the tools

of its pictorial construction. The construction of Babel demonstrates very clearly the impact of the representational tool on the architectural space created by the artist.

In the late twentieth century, if our objective is to find an appropriate form of architectural representation grounded in the context of a post-modern imagination, we must acknowledge the various steps in the transformation of the pictorial space of our Western tradition. And as architects, we have much to learn from the spatiality of film. Through its recovery of embodied motion and the reconstruction of tactile space from the perspective frame, film opens a possibility of transcending the limitations of the technological "enframed" vision. We may conclude with Kafka that, had it been possible for man to build the tower without climbing it, its construction might have been permitted.

NOTES

1 *The Book of J*, also known as the Five Books of Moses or the Torah, is believed to have been "composed at Jerusalem in the tenth century B.C.E. (before the common era)." Harold Bloom, introduction to *The Book of J*, tr. D. Rosenberg (New York: Vintage Books 1991), 3–5.

2 Ibid., 16. Bloom praises the literary quality of J's writings, "unmatched among Western writers until Shakespeare"; he also describes the ironic playfulness and sense of humour of the biblical author.

3 Ibid., 73–4.

4 Helmut Minkowski, "Turris Babel: A Thousand Years of Representation," *Rassegna* 16 (1983): 8.

5 *The Book of J*, 53.

6 "In the middle of the sacred enclosure (zeus-Belos), there is a massive tower, its base a stadion long and a stadion wide. Another tower stands on it, and one more upon this, and so on: on the whole eight towers over each other. One can climb up by stairways winding around the outside of each tower: half-way there is a platform with seats where those who are climbing can rest. Finally, in the top tower there is a large temple with a golden bed and splendid blankets and beside it a golden table. But there is no statue of the god. No human being can spend the night there except a woman of the country, chosen among the others by the god – or so the Chaldeans say, who are the priests of Bel Zeus." Herodotus, *Histories*, tr. G. Rawlinson, ed. E.H. Blakeney (London: Dent 1964), 1, CLXXXI.

7 Minkowski, "Turris Babel," 15.

8 Nicholas of Cusa, *De Visione Dei*, tr. E.G. Salter (New York: Ungar 1960), ch. 1.

9 Ibid.

10 "God's seeing is His being seen by us." Ibid., ch. 5.

11 Ibid., ch. 6.

12 Nicholas of Cusa compares this seeking of God's unveiled face to the sunlight. The eye must pass "beyond all visible light, because all such light is less than the light it seeks." The eye will therefore reach darkness.

13 Jean Paris develops this notion of inverted perspective in an analysis of the depiction of the Virgin Mary. See *Paintings and Linguistics* (Pittsburgh: Carnegie-Mellon University 1975).

14 Jacomo Barozzi da Vignola, *Le due regole della prospettiva pratica* (Rome 1583). There is no corollary in Vignola's method that may explicitly involve an infinite space or a vanishing point at infinity, but the potential of parallel lines intersecting in a receding background was already present. In his first "rule" of perspective, he claims that according to Euclidean geometry, parallel lines never converge, but the eye of the observer remains the point of convergence of the rays of vision. This convergence of visual lines is transposed in the second rule into converging lines in a perspective.

15 Massimo Scolari, "Form and Representation of the Tower of Babel," *Rassegna* 16 (1983): 10.

16 Joscelyn Godwin, *Athanasius Kircher: A Renaissance Man and the Quest for Lost Knowledge* (London: Thames & Hudson 1979), 35.

17 Johann Bernhard Fischer von Erlach, *Entwurf einer historischen Architektur* (Vienna 1721).

18 Scolari, "Form and Representation," 10.

19 For more about the dimensions of ziggurats, see André Parrot, *Ziggurats et Tour de Babel* (Paris: Michel 1949), ch. 2.

20 The actual site of what might have been the authentic Tower of Babel, for example, is somewhat distant from the historical site of ancient Babylon; the ornamentation of another potential Tower of Babel is more Assyrian than Babylonian; the shape of a third ziggurat differs from Herodotus's description, and so on. For a detailed account of the archaeological debate concerning the coordinates of the Tower of Babel, see ibid., ch. 2.

21 Franz Kafka, "The Great Wall of China," tr. W. and E. Muir, in *The Complete Stories and Parables*, ed. N.N. Glatzer (New York: Quality Paperback Book Club 1983), 238–9.

22 Ibid., 247.

23 This expression is borrowed from André Breton, "Crisis of the Object," *Surrealism and Painting* (New York: Harper & Row 1972), 275–80.

24 Fritz Lang, *Metropolis*, intr. Paul M. Jensen (London: Villiers 1926), 6.

25 Ibid., 29.

26 Hans-Georg Gadamer, *The Relevance of the Beautiful and Other Essays*, tr. N. Walker (Cambridge, U.K.: Cambridge University Press 1977), 91.

Anaesthetic Induction: An Excursion into

the World of Visual Indifference

Natalija Subotincic

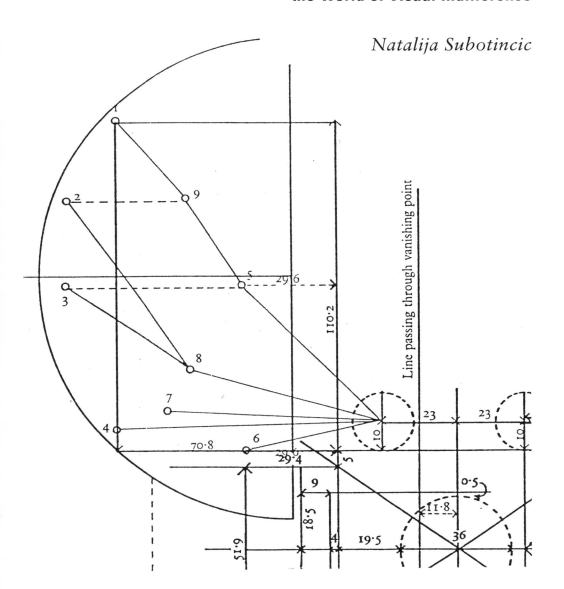

Rrose Selavy; from *Marcel Duchamp*, ed. A. d'Harnoncourt and K. McShine (Philadelphia: The Museum of Modern Art and Philadelphia Museum of Art 1973).

Marcel Duchamp; from Fundación Caja de Pensiones and Fundació Joan Miró, *Duchamp*, catalogue for an exhibition at the Sala de Exposiciones de la Caja de Pensiones, Madrid (1984).

THIS PROJECT is primarily an interpretation of Marcel Duchamp's works. More specifically, my investigations engage his writings on perspective and the fourth dimension through an examination of his two major projects. The first is *The Bride Stripped Bare By Her Bachelors, Even ...*, also known as *The Large Glass*. This piece, begun in 1915, was intentionally left incomplete in 1923. To accompany it, Duchamp wrote a text called *The Green Box*, dated 1934.[1] The second project is *Étant Donnés: 1º La chute d'eau, 2º Le gas d'éclairage ...* (translated as *Given: 1º The waterfall, 2º The illuminating gas ...*). Duchamp worked on this final piece in secret from 1946 to 1966, a time when he claimed he had given up art for chess. He subtitled it a "demountable approximation" and in 1966 proceeded to compile a *Manual* illustrating fifteen operations for reassembling the construction.

Duchamp died on 2 October 1968, at the age of 81. Before his death, his final construction, *Étant Donnés*, was acquired by the Cassandra Foundation and presented to the Philadelphia Museum of Art, where it joined the largest collection of his work in the world. Although the piece was assembled by 7 July 1969, the terms of the agreement specified that no photographs of the interior of the construction or the notebook of instructions were to be published for at least fifteen years. Consequently, it was not until 1987 that the museum published a photographic reproduction of Duchamp's *Manual of Instructions*,[2] exposing the construction twenty-one years after its completion.

Because of the "delicate nature" of the subject matter, this project has been restricted to speculation.[3] Certain propositions "given" by Marcel Duchamp lead to extrapolations and discoveries that can be *made*. From this exploratory vivisection, the most that we may hope for is to discover, by "slightly distending the laws of physics and chemistry," as well as history, medicine, and architecture, the nature of what is *inside*.

Most of the elements of my investigation were not evident at the point of departure.[4] As the project proceeded, it took on a life of its own and emerged as a tapestry in which language, thought, and vision came to act upon one another. This tapestry may propose larger implications for the perceptions that we consider in the making of architecture. The main intention of this project is to engage in an exploration of the "unseen of architecture – its unconscious [possibly] offering us a glimpse of the actual,"[5] where the actual may be understood as pre-categorical founded space or that which exists before consciousness.

CONDITION OF THE PATIENT

A fatigue as old as the world, the sense of having to carry one's body around, a feeling of incredible fragility which becomes a shattering pain, a state of painful numbness, a kind of numbness localized in the skin which does not inhibit any movement but which changes the internal sensation of a limb … Probably localized in the skin, but felt as the radical elimination of a limb, and presenting to the brain only images of limbs that are threadlike and woolly, images of limbs that are far away and not where they should be. A sort of internal fracturing

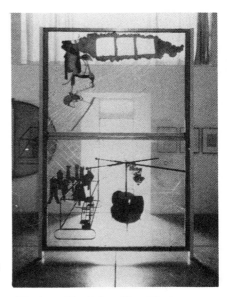

"The Large Glass"; from *Marcel Duchamp*, 1994/Vis*Art Copyright Inc.

"Given: 1° The waterfall, 2° The illuminating gas…"; from *Marcel Duchamp*, 1994/Vis*Art

219

"Nude Descending a Staircase" (1912); 1994/Vis*Art Copyright Inc., *Duchamp.*

of the whole nervous system ... One must speak now of the disembodiment of reality, of that sort of rupture that seems determined to multiply itself between things and the feeling they produce in our mind the place they should take. This instantaneous classification of things in the cells of the mind, not so much in their logical order as in their emotional or affective order (which no longer holds): things have no more odour, no more sex. But their logical order is also sometimes broken precisely because of their lack of emotional aroma. Words rot at the unconscious summons of the brain, all the words for any kind of mental operation, and especially those operations which affect the most habitual, most active responses of the mind.[6]

In pursuing this experiment, I take my instructions from Marcel Duchamp: "I have forced myself to contradict myself in order to avoid conforming to my own taste ... Any idea that came to me, the thing would be, to turn it around, and try to see it with another set of senses."[7] Or, as Merleau-Ponty put it, "a reversibility of the seeing and the visible, and as at the point where the two metaphorically cross what we call perception is born."[8]

Perception involves an experiential embodiment within which "questioning and response" reveal multiple ambiguities. A danger exists, however, when this seeing or vision ceases to reveal. This "condition" reaches a critical state, presently observed in our patient, once the "arbitrary nature" of experiences becomes the possession of unquestionable habit. The *perceptual field* is therefore relegated to this *container of habit*.

PROPOSED EXPLORATORY VIVISECTION

The proposed operation adheres to the following simple theory, which has become the basis for the medical procedure of vaccination: it is hoped that by treating like with like, by treating the disease with a small dose of itself, the patient will become somewhat immune to any recurring tendencies of his/her present *condition.*

The purpose of this pseudo-scientific surgical procedure is to "rid perception of its habitual baggage" by attempting to induce a "state of indeterminacy."[9] Exploratory surgery hopefully will uncover the extent of the damage already incurred and perhaps stimulate the patient's facilities for reaching "the Impossibility of sufficient *visual* memory, to transfer from one like object to another the *memory* imprint,"[10] subsequently altering his/her "actual" perception.

The procedure will begin by inducing anaesthetic[11] unconsciousness. It is believed that the undue stresses and tensions caused by the obtrusive condition may be alleviated by inducing a slow and progressive detachment from perception and aesthetic habit. Depending on the condition of the patient, current medical practice considers this procedure to be the safest and most discerning means of radically eliminating "transferable memory imprints." The hope is to release the patient eventually from obstacles of logic and taste, extending his/her horizon into this state of indeterminacy.

To achieve the degree of aesthetic unconsciousness necessary to reach a state of indif-

"Bride" (1912); 1994/Vis*Art Copyright Inc., *Duchamp.*

ference, an anaesthetic[12] will be administered. Inhalation of anaesthetic gas eventually causes a total loss of consciousness. Under general anaesthesia, a patient is temporarily rendered unconscious and insensitive to the pain of a surgical operation.

Ether[13] has been selected as the anaesthetic vapour for inhalation, as it exhibits slow induction and has a relatively high index of anaesthesia, allowing greater margins for misjudgment or inexperience. It has proven to be safe, reliable, and also relatively inexpensive.

Like a sorcerer, the anaesthetist seems to be endowed with magical powers that control the capacity of an individual "to speak, move and have their being."[14] For an-aesthetic induction to proceed without complications, the anaesthetist's senses of sight, hearing, touch, and smell must be highly developed and the powers of observation cultivated to the utmost.

PREPARATION OF THE PATIENT

> One hour before the operation: Pre-anaesthetic medication allays the fear of the operation, producing a calm and well-rested patient, which minimizes the hazards of anaesthesia and surgery. The medicine replaces anxiety with a carefree, euphoric state of mind.

Ether and light were considered to be capable of mutual interaction. Ether was suggested as the intermediary between light and "ponderable matter": "Primordial Being was not only compared with Light, but identified with it. True light is intelligible light; from the latter the visible springs as an emanation, not according to the substance, but in a dynamic sense, i.e. as a radiation of force ... Light is the *corporeitas*, i.e. the first form which, combining with the *prima materia*, forms bodies to be perceived by the senses."[15]

In seventeenth-century physics, material bodies were widely believed to absorb light. A luminous body would become visible to the eye by means of vibrations that it excited in this hypothetical medium that pervaded all space, known as the ether. These vibrations would travel through the ether, causing heat to be generated and finally, by affecting the retina of the eye, give rise to sensations of brightness. The velocity of propagation of the vibrations was affected by the nature of the material. Variations in their transmission produced the three elements of the visible world – luminosity, transparency, and opacity.

By illuminating an obstacle of finite dimensions with a very small source of light, and by following the geometrical projection of its shadow, light was found to travel in straight lines. *Perspectiva naturalis* was concerned precisely with optics, with examining "how one sees" and giving mathematical formulations to these natural operations of sight. The very *act of seeing* constituted a *present* condition for perceiving.

Perspectiva artificialis was concerned with "elaborating a practically useful construction of the surface of a picture," systematically reproducing what one "has seen" by making a sectional cut through the cone of vision. Perspective "presupposes that things unfold in a predestined order, the sense of which lies beyond ... in an infinite, unchanging and

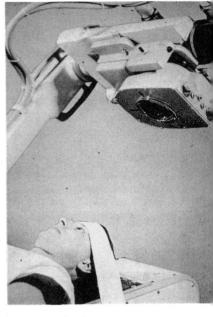

Preparation of patient.

Durer's perspective "window."

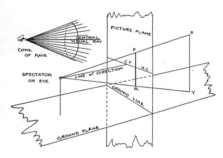

Perspective construction.

homogeneous space,"[16] thereby providing a "representation" (a "picture" or "appearance") that denies direct bodily experience.

The word perspective (in reference to *perspectiva artificialis*) means "to see through." Objects represented in perspective are supposed to be seen through a transparent plane (for example, a sheet of glass) standing vertically in front of the spectator. The lines forming the object are drawn on a piece of paper exactly as they would appear if drawn on this transparent plane. For this reason the vertical, transparent section has come to be called the picture plane.

Perspectiva artificialis, however, has been extended imperceptibly into our present perceptions of space. It has become an overwhelming and practically habitual organizing system, condemning "true being" to the appearance of things seen. The camera is today's perspective machine. As a result, "the free and, as it were, spiritual intuition of form is now bound to the appearance of *things* seen."[17] Perspective has become an aesthetic that detaches us from our bodily senses.

Katherine Dreier, the second owner of *The Large Glass*, points out: "The essential principle of human consciousness cannot be grasped until we abandon the psychological attitude of conceiving the image as a petrified thing or object ... the result of emphasis, the external vision, which is rarely related to perception."[18] Now we may think about Duchamp's exhortation to "turn it around and try to see it with another set of senses."

Anamorphosis,[19] initially developed as a means of verifying perspective, ultimately carries perspective to an extreme. A reversal of the principles of perspective construction is required to reconcile the "hidden" image within the construction. This reconciliation only emerges if the spectator willingly shifts his/her viewing position, relative to the plane of representation. By locating oneself at the vanishing point (or "centre of gravity") on the horizon of the image, a recognizable appearance finally materializes from the unrecognizable "distortion." At this point of reconciliation the image, or more correctly its "figure," is released from the confines of the flat picture plane. The images are now intricately woven within this crossing or cancel-

Top and bottom: From *Anamorphic Art*, ed. J. Baltruaitis (Cambridge 1977).

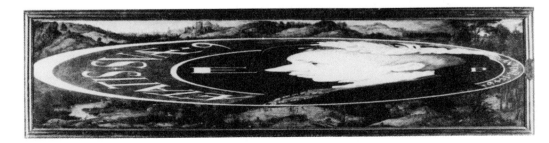

ling of perspective by its reversal, provoking a perplexing fusion of figure and space. Figure and space become distended, revealing an "apparition" from within the "appearance." The apparition is revealed through this extended (or perhaps distracted) "experience of seeing."

An anamorphic projection inherently speculates on the divergences between appearance and apparition or between the palpable realities revealed by geometry and the proposition of distortions as possible realities. Fluid-like landscapes perpetually appear as lateral suspensions of space, filling the empty space left by cutting sectional, perspectival picture planes. The curiosity that these images provoke is just a reminder of the unstable and uncertain state of appearances.

Inhalation anaesthesia involves the inhalation of vapours from a liquid anaesthesia or an anaesthetic gas. Although safe and reliable, it is unpleasant for a patient who resents a mask being put over his/her face.

The following operation involves a rotation rather than a cut:

FINAL PREPARATION

1. Ensuring that the patient's stomach is empty.
2. Obtaining his/her signature on a form of consent for the anaesthesia and operation.
3. Removing dentures, jewellery, and other aesthetic valuables.
4. Preparing the patient for surgery, including removal of any hair in the surgical region.

Face mask: the dotted lines indicate the position of the expiration valve when turned aside for the admission of unvaporized air.

5. Checking, administrating, and recording of pre-anaesthetic medication.
6. Assembling patient's notes and x-rays.

The following propositions are *Given* by Marcel Duchamp in his notes on perspective and the fourth dimension:[20]

Given a linear perspective in the third dimension, we can establish that a direction right/left is equivalent to a two-dimensional plane and top/bottom is equivalent to three-dimensional space.

Gravity and centre of gravity relate to three-dimensional space, whereas in a two-dimensional plane the vanishing point corresponds to the centre of gravity.

A perspective cannot be tested by touch because vision is the sense of perspective. A gravity experience, real or imagined, or attraction towards a centre of gravity, is registered inside the spectator. Duchamp emphasizes that this registration occurs in the region of the stomach.

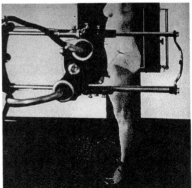

And finally, to perceive a perspective in the fourth dimension, we must distinguish clearly between our flat eye^2 and our eye^3. The eye^2 can see only a two-dimensional perspective.

The eye^2 and eye^3 are physically the same eye. But there are differences in perception, depending on how one chooses to "see" with the eye, a single sense with distending potentials. If our eye^2 sees the two-dimensional perspective or an "appearance," then perhaps our eye^3 sees an "apparition." *The Large Glass*, for example, seems to contain simultaneous representations of all dimensions:

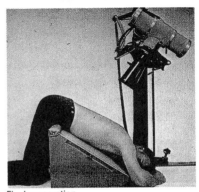

Final preparation.

The first is the centre of gravity or point of

"The Large Glass," back view; from *Marcel Duchamp*, 1994/Vis*Art Copyright Inc.

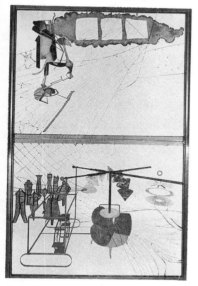

"The Large Glass," front view; from *Marcel Duchamp*, 1994/Vis*Art Copyright Inc.

attraction, the vanishing point of the perspective.

The second is the horizontal horizon line and the vertical glass plane.

The third, as a two-dimensional perspective appearance, is located in the lower realm of the Bachelor.

The fourth proposes a three-dimensional perspective appearance of a four-dimensional apparition located in the upper realm of the Bride.

Since these views are physically restrained, literally sealed within the transparent, two-dimensional vertical glass planes, then perhaps they are meant to be seen only by our eye[2]. Duchamp also states that the eye[3] has a view of the whole (yet the whole is not presented: recall that Duchamp purposely left *The Large Glass* incomplete in 1923). The eye[3] is able to perceive a three-dimensional perspective of a four-dimensional object, in a three-dimensional medium.

Bear with me and I will attempt to clarify this.

The two-dimensional perspective is a representation or appearance on a flat plane and relies on the laws of perspective for its construction.

A three-dimensional perspective is a built perspective representation or appearance, relying on perspective principles and seen only by the eye[2].

A four-dimensional perspective, then, proposes a built apparition that reveals a construction which both relies on and is then released from the constraints of perspective. This cancellation results in the presentation of a construction which we may "see" with the eye[3] in a three-dimensional medium. A perception yet to be realized ...

The lower space or perspective representation of the Bachelor (the zone of our attraction) and the top space or four-dimensional representation of the Bride (the zone of our desires) remain trapped in the flat two-dimensional space of the vertical glass planes and do not engage space outside the glass. *The Large Glass* is vertical in orientation, and space seems only to pass through its transparency. Therefore, for the spectator there is no internal fusion, experience, or gravity – simply the representation of a "delay," an appearance that is intended to be seen only by the eye[2]. Unsettled and unfinished, the zone of our desires (a four-dimensional presentation) remains unattainable, as does the Bride by her Bachelor. This is literally a sectional cut that suspends or delays a registration within the body of the spectator.

This x-ray presents only the appearance of potential perceptions ...

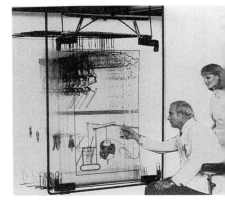

Inspecting the x-rays.

7. Checking on availability of blood for transfusion.
8. Communicating with the operating theatre, ensuring that the patient goes to the correct theatre.

However, if we consider the *Étant Donnés* or *Given* as the other half of the whole, intended to be seen through the two eye holes in the Door, then a shift in orientation will horizontally engage the spectator and three-dimensional space ...

Anamorphic representations also require a shift of up to 180 degrees in orientation, in order to assemble the "recognizable" image.

"The Large Glass – Given."

Erhard Schon, picture puzzle: "Out, you old fool" (perspective), 1535; from Baltrusaitis, *Anamorphic Art*.

This latent presence not only reveals the vanity of appearance but also acknowledges the constant transmutation of things or the "apparition."

The anaesthesia room is a small room located between the operating theatre and the main corridor of the suite. It provides:

1. A place where the patient can be taken on arrival at the operating suite and be spared the sight and sounds of the preparation for the operation.
2. An atmosphere which remains undisturbed by the noise and movement of the rest of the surgical team.
3. A storage place for apparatus and equipment.

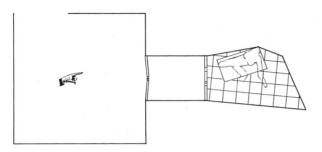

YOU ARE HERE: plan of "Given" in the Philadelphia Museum of Art.

The wooden "mirror-door"; from *Marcel Duchamp*, 1994/Vis*Art Copyright Inc.

... resting on the dark burlap surface of a dimly lit room, with two eyes, close to, for almost an hour ... I've noticed that few people have "even" approached the door, most think that what they first see is the entire piece – an old door in a wall ...

> Decoration of the room differs from the rest of the suite in an attempt to conceal its clinical purpose. Diffuse lighting spares the eyes of the patient lying on the trolley. Soft pastel colours on the walls and a decorated ceiling, painted with a pleasing picture, represent an attempt to deflect the thoughts of the conscious patient from the business at hand, inducing a tranquil state of mind.

... unfortunately, we no longer "see," we only "look," and we are so seduced by the appearance of things ... Very few people even notice the haunting hands and mask that survive as greasy imprints, desperately grasping the wrinkles of this wooden "mirror." Their presence, suspended above a horizontal batten or the horizon, acknowledges our desire to remain if only for those scarce moments – these are the marks left by the few who were curious enough to approach the door ...

OBSERVATION OF THE PATIENT

What, then, is the difference between appearance and apparition?

> The "art" of the anaesthetist is to carry the patient from complete consciousness to a condition of surgical anaesthesia by a gradual process. For purposes of description it is convenient to divide the induction period into a number of stages, with each stage passing imperceptibly into the next, with no line of demarcation. The anaesthetist estimates the depth of anaesthesia by observing changes in respiratory rhythm and reflex activity as follows.

An appearance is a representation of a thing. It is both familiar and recognizable, relying on visual memory imprints. An appearance is deceivingly orienting and therefore seductive, tending to become second nature, even habitual.

An apparition is a presentation, constantly in the action of becoming visible. It is a becoming-visible of being: in a sense, a mould, found only in a field of disorientation – a state not generally enjoyed for very long, for it quickly becomes painfully disruptive.

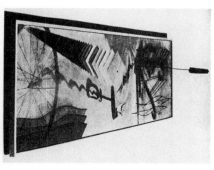

> 1. Automatic respiration coincides with loss of consciousness.

2. Eyelid reflex, swallow reflex, and conjuncti-
val reflexes disappear, in that order.
3. Progressive depression of reflex activity of
the intercostal and abdominal muscles, necessary for relaxation, is evident by reversal
of normal respiration rhythm. When this
rhythm is dependent only on the diaphragm,
the patient assumes a gasping character
with pauses after inspiration instead of after
expiration. Reflex movements following a
cutting of the skin do not necessarily indicate consciousness or ability to feel pain.

Anamorphosis upsets the stable orientation of
order, releasing elements from their visible
limits or appearances and throwing all into
disorientation. The representation of an image
is questioned by distending the boundaries
constraining the figure. Anamorphosis releases
the figure and its representation by a "non-
sensical" reversal. These ultra-rapid exposures
reveal all forms as permutations, modulations,
or distorted images of other forms. Only
when viewed from a certain point are they
returned to their familiar, systematic constraints.

Opposite and above: *Tu m'* (1918); 1994/Vis*Art Copyright Inc.,
Duchamp.

INDUCTION WITH ETHER

There must be two people – the anaesthetist and an assistant – to make the patient insensible with ether. The identity of the patient, a "confirmed bachelor," as well as the proposed operation and pre-operation injection should be checked before the induction of anaesthesia. Absolute silence is essential. The four approximate stages of anaesthesia can be identified as:

1. Analgesia/disordered consciousness
2. Delirium/excitement
3. Surgical anaesthesia
4. Respiratory paralysis

... approaching the door, my hands unconsciously duplicate the position of the reflecting greasy imprints. My arms bare the shifting weight of my body as it comes to rest along the horizontal batten, or the horizon ...

The face mask is flat, or curved to the contours of his face to ensure a "gas tight fit."

Induction with Ether.

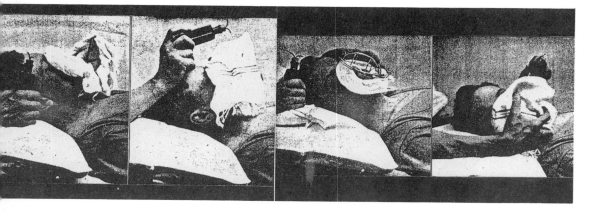

There are four stages or degrees of ether anaesthetic that are, in some measure, arbitrary. These different degrees run gradually into each other, not always remaining clearly distinguished.

... my advancing facial features compress the infra-thin gap, forming a mask, completed by the inspiration of a vaporous stench emanating from the musty wooden crevasse ... Ether is a colourless, volatile liquid with a pungent, unpleasant odour ...

He should be restrained, if necessary, gently but firmly during the struggling stage that marks the transition from the conscious to the unconscious state.

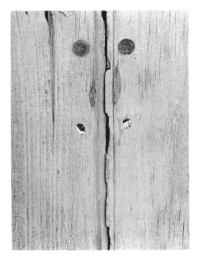

Eye holes "given" in the door; 1994/Vis*Art Copyright Inc., *Duchamp.*

Many questions surrounded the relation between the medium that filled the interstellar void and the condensations of matter scattered throughout it. Ether was suggested as the vehicle for the conveyance and transformation of energy around and between heavenly bodies. The discovery of a universal law of gravitation gave rise to the dilemma of assuming either that bodies had an occult property to attract at a distance or that a gaseous medium caused such attractions by its pressure.[21]

OPERATIONS FOR DETERMINING
THE FOUNDATIONS FOR
THE CONSTRUCTION OF
A FOUR-DIMENSIONAL FIGURE

Marcel Duchamp (M.D.) says that a perspective in the fourth dimension can be explored

Dr Liston's operating table and knives, used for the first operation under ether anaesthetic in Europe (1846).

with the help of transparent glass and a mirror.

With the introduction of mirrors to resolve anamorphic images, the visual angle was replaced by the angle of reflection. However, many of these mirrors were used not for anamorphic purposes but for projecting figures into space. "The image appears in the air, outside the mirror, and cannot be seen elsewhere."[22]

Stage One: Analgesia/Disordered Consciousness

Analgesia is an altered state of consciousness brought about by drugs, obtunding minor pain sensations. It is accompanied by sedation, euphoria, and amnesia. This state exists between complete consciousness and the excitement stage preceding surgical anaesthesia.

From this point onward, we must be aware that formation is not the projection of line or plane to define the figure. Instead, a sort of "negative" relies on space to constrain and thus cause the "cohesion" of a figure.

Sedation – Begins about twelve seconds after the first inhalation of ether.

... my readjusting gaze reveals the phosphorescent blue, fading to a pallid incandescence, conceding an unyielding arm bracing the illuminating gas ...

Causes warmness, dizziness, and calm. The patient still has full muscular control and can voluntarily hold his breath or breathe faster or slower.

... the ethereal nakedness is slowly unveiled through the descent of our gaze, lying outstretched on a bed of branches before the seductively serene and disturbing landscape. A waterfall glistens softly in the distance ...

> Thoughts become unbalanced, disproportionate, and muddled. Senses are active and even abnormally acute, so remarks made will be remembered and their importance perhaps greatly exaggerated. For this reason, all talking and noises of any kind should be avoided. The patient still retains consciousness of where he is and what is occuring around him, and has the capacity to direct his voluntary movements. Generally anything that is remembered is from this stage, and tends to be an agreeable feeling.

Several anamorphic projections were constructed by projecting the light of a lamp through an "ectype."[23] Duchamp adapted a similar method for his construction of the nude figure in the *Given*. Perhaps "[an] apparition is the mould [or ectype] of an appearance."[24]

Duchamp, 1994/Vis*Art Copyright Inc.

A three-dimensional perspective implies that lines are present in the world and that the figures are "in" space, "separate" from space, or even "containing" space. However, the four-dimensional figure reveals space as present. Space seems to constrain the *Given*, moulding the "flesh" in an integral collapse or merging of Attraction and Desire.

Preparatory "Study for the Nude Figure" in "Given" (1950); transparent perforated plexiglass used to mould the figure (an ectype?); from *Marcel Duchamp*, 1994/ Vis*Art Copyright Inc.

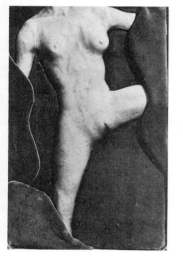

Preparatory study of "Given" (1948–49); pigment and graphite on vellum over gesso, mounted on velvet; from *Marcel Duchamp*, 1994/Vis*Art Copyright Inc.

As a substance, ether was believed to pervade the pores of all material bodies, thus causing their "cohesion." By projecting light rays through a vacuum, it was determined that the medium of ether was composed of very tiny particles that were hard and exceedingly elastic. Just as air contains "aqueous vapour," ether was believed to contain various "aethereal spirits" that produced phenomena such as electricity, magnetism, and gravitation.[25]

From the sketches for the completion of *The Large Glass*, one may see that the forces that drive the mechanisms of the Bachelor and Bride are also electricity, magnetism, and gravity. These forces, curiously enough, are the elements of *The Large Glass* that were left intentionally incomplete in 1923. These invisible or incomplete phenomena will now be further examined through the construction of the subtle and supple details of X-rated rays.

First, we must look at the general laws of reflection and refraction. When a ray of light falls on a surface, its angle with respect to a line, which is 90 degrees to the surface (the "Normal"), is called the angle of incidence. Part of this ray will be reflected (bounce off the surface) and part of it will be refracted (pass through the surface). The relative proportion depends on factors such as the reflecting power of the surface and the angle of the incident ray. Under normal circumstances, if a ray of light approaching a pane of glass has an angle of incidence between 37 and 42 degrees, then all the light will be reflected and none will be refracted. This phenomenon

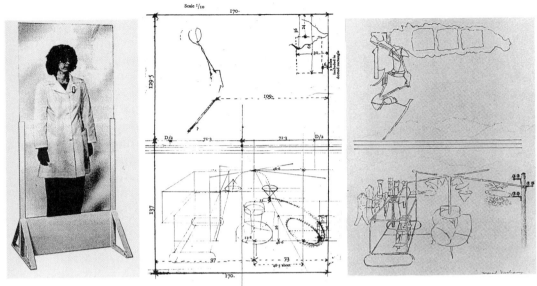

"Bride."

Sketch for the "completion" of "The Large Glass"; from Marcel Duchamp, *The Bride Stripped Bare by Her Bachelors, Even: A Typographic Version of the Green Box*, 1994/Vis*Art Copyright Inc.

Sketches for the "completion" of "The Large Glass"; from *Marcel Duchamp*, 1994/Vis*Art Copyright Inc.

causes glass to act as a mirror and is called the limiting angle or critical angle.

If we look now at the plan and elevation of *The Large Glass*, constructed by Duchamp himself, we see the curious placement of the edges of the glass. This placement effectively excludes the first four malic moulds, which are clearly presented "outside" the confines of the glass frame. Our "Normal" view is re-constructed by drawing the elevation of each element of *The Large Glass* onto a separate sheet of acetate, and then placing each of these sheets according to the location of each element in the plan view.

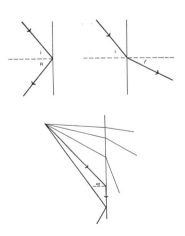

Laws of reflection and refraction.

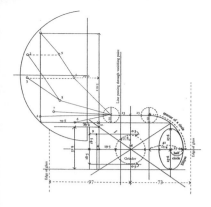

"Bachelor Apparatus – Plan" (1913); from Duchamp, *The Bride Stripped Bare*, 1994/Vis*Art Copyright Inc.

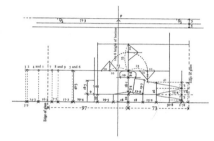

"Bachelor Apparatus – Elevation" (1913); from Duchamp, *The Bride Stripped Bare*, 1994/Vis*Art Copyright Inc.

"Bachelor Apparatus."

The Large Glass, as seen in the Museum, appears as a one-sided transparent representation with no apparent reversibility. For the spectator who stands in front, "looking," it is a two-dimensional plane, to be viewed from one side but perhaps not from the Normal view located directly in front, as our X-rays are revealing. If we undertake a directional movement right/left, implied by this two-dimensional plane with its vertical orientation (remember Duchamp's *Givens* mentioned earlier), a closer inspection of the X-rated rays reveals the critical angle of an assembled "view" of *The Large Glass* appearing approximately 42 degrees to the right of the Normal view. However, at this point the glass loses its transparency and becomes a mirror.

The released malic moulds direct the polygon of sex, the spangles of invisible gas, and the spectator to a new "optical orientation" aligned with both this 42-degree critical angle and, more importantly, with the Oculist Witnesses. The spectator is no longer located in front of the frame, at the predetermined, perpendicular, fixed location of the single-point perspective representation. The spectator has, in effect, been displaced and has even been denied his apparent place in front of the glass. He now stands to the side of this alleged mirror (a marginal position), seeing only its newly found reflective surface, concealing the previous "image" of Attraction.

The "mirrorical return" of this oblique view has been used before by both Niceron, who wrote the first treatise on anamorphosis in 1638, and Duchamp, in the *Green Box* of

1934. Perhaps *The Large Glass* is a disguised mirror, waiting to reflect:

The function of the Oculist Witnesses, despite their marginal position, is central: they receive the spray from the Illuminating Gas, now converted into Sculpture of Drops, and transform it into a mirror image that they throw into the Bride's domain, in the zone of the Nine Shots. The Oculist Witnesses refine (sublimate) the Illuminating Gas, turned Spray of explosive drops: they change the drops into a look – that is, into the most immediate manifestation of desire. The look passes through the obstructed passages (cols alités) of the Bride and reaches her. It arrives thus far not as reality, but as the image of desire.[26]

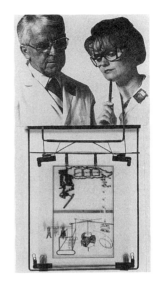

A "normal" view of the x-rated rays by the Oculist Witnesses (1989).

The Large Glass seems to disclose the limited perception of remaining within a perspective projection by providing an "appearance" or image of the continuum that masks the latent possibilities of a fourth dimension or direction.

A fracture has been revealed in the X-rated rays. *The Large Glass* was also smashed in transit in 1926, as it returned from its first public appearance at the International Exhibition of Modern Art in the Brooklyn Museum. Ten years later, Duchamp spent several months repairing and securing it between two even heavier panes of glass and a new metal frame.

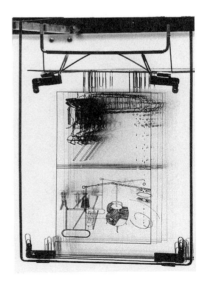

> Euphoria and Amnesia with Minor Pain Obtundation – Patient starts to perspire, response to conversation is delayed, and with semi-sleep his eyes close and pain threshold is raised. Voice changes to a deep-

A mirrorical return.

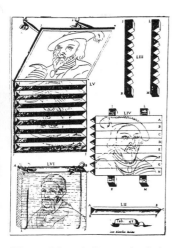

"Niceron," from *La Perspective Curieuse* (1653).

Mirrorical return—Each drop
will pass the 3 planes at the horizon
between the perspective and the geometrical drawing of 2 figures which will be
indicated on these 3 planes by the Wilson-Lincoln system (i.e.
like the portraits which seen from the left show
Wilson seen from the right show Lincoln —)

seen from the right the figure may give a square for example
from the front and seen from the right it could give the same
square seen in perspective —
The mirrorical drops not the drops themselves
but their image pass between these 2 states
of the same figure (square in this example)
(Perhaps use prisms stuck behind the glass.)
to obtain the desired effect)

Duchamp's "mirrorical return" and the Wilson-Lincoln system; from Duchamp, *The Bride Stripped Bare.*

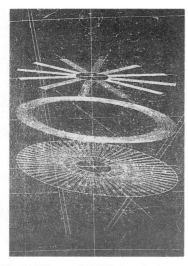

"Oculist Witnesses" (1920); from Duchamp, *The Bride Stripped Bare,* 1994/Vis*Art Copyright Inc.

ening tone. The consciousness is so disordered, the patient no longer knows where he is and frequently dreams he is elsewhere. The mental functions may be exercised and the voluntary actions performed, but in a disordered manner. The patient passes quickly and quietly through this degree (it is difficult to detect this level).

... a change in position sometimes provokes a change in perception ...

Anamorphic pictures integrated both fragmented and fluid landscapes. Natural, that is, easily recognizable and therefore familiar images appeared simultaneously with anamorphic images. On viewing these images, the natural became anamorphic and vice versa. Through their reversal, the images not only illuminated the elusiveness of defining a figure but also revealed the instabilities, or plurality of states and resonances, inherent in all figures. Perhaps anamorphosis proposes the certainty of uncertainty. An inverted paradox disclosing the continuation of appearance and apparition in all figures ... Forms gives birth to latent forms.

As Duchamp has suggested, the fourth dimension – the fourth "direction" of the continuum – does not involve movement but rather sustains that which results from movement. Front, back, reverse, and side have no consequence, now implying that direction has no orienting points.

The *Given*, on the other hand, appears to involve a continuous reversibility, invertibility,

Emmanuel Maignan, anamorphic fresco from Saint Francis of Paola (1642); monastery of Santa Trinità dei Monti, Rome.

and traversal of the appearance of *The Large Glass*. This illuminated apparition suggests a four-dimensional figure that seems to be extended in the direction of the "reflection" of the spectator's body, which is held transfixed by the two eye holes in the door.

Duchamp continues: "A perspective three starts in an initial frontal plane, without deformation, where the plane is true and the projection beyond is distorted. A perspective-four has a three-dimensional medium as a starting point."[27]

In the *Given*, the initial frontal plane of the three-dimensional perspective construction is the closed door. As a perspective-four, however, the initial three-dimensional medium that is its starting point is the spectator who embraces the frontal plane or door. The spectator's position is therefore integral to the realization of the perspective-four. The coincidence of experiencing what the spectator "sees" has been subtly registered within his/her body. The spectator is now implicated.

Niceron's "Door"; from Baltrusaitis, *Anamorphic Art*.

As a perspective-four, the *Given* begins to offer a perceptual opening of the door, whereas in three-dimensional reality it remains closed. Access to this work requires an illuminated perception. A registration occurs only when the body also is able to engage in seeing.

Many anamorphic projections were constructed on the walls of rooms, with the viewpoint for their elongations located at the entrance of the room. A painting in the cloister at Place Royale was arranged to be seen through a hole in the entrance door.

Possible distended levels of viewing:

... the spectator enters the dimly lit room, looks at an old wooden door in the far wall, and then leaves bewildered by the apparent simplicity of this purported "work of art." This rather unengaging appearance is its disguise: the door is like a mirror, but if one does not step in front of it and examine it, one may see only a door.

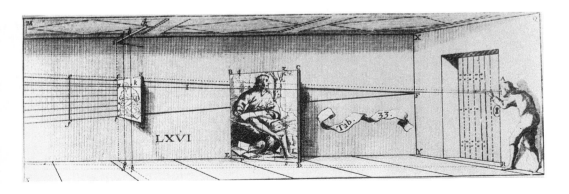

... the eye[2] subsequently watches someone else approaching the door, to discover the two viewing holes in the upper realm (zone of the Bride). Intrigued, we duplicate our predecessor's position and "look through" (similar to perspective). Taken aback, perhaps even shocked, this look holds us in the three-dimensional direction of the continuum ... ah! ... but only momentarily. The dismay of the shock disturbs us the most ... we've been taken ... we saw something we didn't expect. How could Duchamp do this? What is this all about? "Looking" at the *Given* may reveal only an appearance. Is she the Bride and are we the Bachelors? ... Perhaps this is a three-dimensional representation of *The Large Glass* ... but that's too simple, for he spent twenty years of his life working on this piece! ... If one stands in front of the mirror/door, one sees a "reflection" of oneself. But this time, the mirror reveals a disturbing image, instead of the familiar, unengaged vanity glance we are so used to ...

Attraction exists in three-dimensional space.

Curiosity prevailing, the eye[3], bored with recognizing the familiar, is now haunted and gently loosens the constraints, divulging other, more potent possibilities. "Seeing" beyond the appearance of the eye[2] – "visibility sometimes wandering and sometimes reassembled ... the seer and the visible reciprocate one another and we no longer know which sees and which is seen."[28]

... refusing to be always the recipient, one may now become the vehicle for an actual reg-

istration. The apparition has been registered
deep within us. Our foundations, the "familiar," are not only disturbed but quietly
shaken. What seems to be presented is a "seeing" of what one's "reflection" itself sees – a
perceptual passing across the mirror, merging
with our own reflection. Perhaps the *Given*
involves an illuminated seeing that requires
more than our simple "retinal" response. This
illumination reveals latent possibilities. When
the door is understood as a mirror, a perceptual crossing of the threshold occurs and one's
perceptions are inherently reversed. The spectator now sees from the eyes of their own
reflection.

> The concern of the anaesthetist at this
> stage is to keep the mask firmly on the
> patient's face. After one or two breaths of
> air, consciousness will return and induction
> must begin all over again.

... accessing Desire through Attraction ...
trapped in the paradox of the visible, my eyes
succumb to the initial unfaltering curiosity,
returning me to the captivity of the mask and
my reflection ...

The attraction of the earth for a falling body was
due to a circulating ether, condensed when it con-
verged upon the earth, it bore down upon any
objects in its path with a force proportional to the
areas of their parts, descended to the centre of the
earth for replenishment by a process like fermentation or coagulation, turned into atmosphere as it
rose out of the earth, and eventually receded into
outer space, whence it returned again as the gravi-
tational ether.[29]

... the attraction of the centre of gravity ...

Stage Two: Delirium/Excitement

The second stage is a limbo between the
start of analgesia and the beginning of complete muscle relaxation. If the vapour produces coughing, it is diluted and
occasionally gesticulation, words, or
attempts to move are made. In some hysteri-
cal individuals, sobbing, laughing or screaming may occur. The patient also tries to lift
his hands or move his head to remove the
inhalation mask because it interferes with
normal respiration. These are voluntary
endeavours, guided by instinct rather than
reason. The patient can often be quieted by
words, and will do as he is told.

Once upon a time
Eight Years later
Towards three in the morning
Sixteen Years before
In the spring[30]

"The belly evokes surgery and the Morgue,
the construction yard, the public square, and
the operating table. The body of the belly
seems made of granite or marble or plaster,
but a plaster that has set."[31]

He is unaware of where he is, as his
answers will show. The patient will also
move his eyes around, even directing them
to objects. He talks in his dreams about subjects totally unconnected with pain, referring
to early periods in his life. Many patients
dream that they are travelling.

Driving.

Prolonged etherization causes post-operative depression and vomiting ... in which the existence of animal spirits in the human body are of an ethereal nature and 'subtle enough to pervade the animal juices as freely as the electric, and perhaps magnetic, effluvia do glass' ... These animal spirits are generated in the heart by fermentation and conducted thence to the brain. 'All the motions we see in animals' are produced by the soul impelling this ethereal spirit into the motor nerves and moving the muscles by its inspiration.[32]

... gasping, my entire body heaves ...

> Those who have experienced the adult in full excitement realize that any word description is inadequate. It is a violent, uncontrollable, unreasonable patient that seeks, and many times accomplishes, injury to the doctor, the equipment and to himself.

But of beauty ... coming to earth we find her here too, shining in clearness through the clearest aperture of sense. For sight is the most piercing of our bodily senses; though not by that is wisdom seen ... But this is the privilege of beauty, that being the loveliest she is also the most palpable to sight.

Now he who is not newly initiated or who has become corrupted, does not easily rise out of this world to the sight of true beauty in the other; he looks only at her earthly namesake, and instead of being awed at the sight of her, he is given over to pleasure, and like a brutish beast he rushes on to enjoy and beget; he consorts with wantonness, and is not afraid or ashamed of pursuing pleasure in violation of nature.

But he whose initiation is recent, and who has been the spectator of many glories in the other world, is amazed when he sees any one having a god-like face or form, which is the expression of divine beauty; and at first a shudder runs through him, and again the old awe steals over him ... then while he gazes on him there is a sort of reaction, and the shudder passes into an unusual heat and perspiration.[33]

> The baser elements of being are released and the patient kicks, screams and fights. The patient retains all muscular reflexes (exaggerated reflexes) and has the strength of a bull. Breathing and pulse are both fast and jerky. This stage has no value and attempts to shorten it to a bare minimum should be made.

... for, as he receives the effluence of beauty through the eyes, the wing moistens and he warms. And as he warms, the parts out of which the wing grew, and which had been hitherto closed and rigid, and had prevented the wing from shooting forth, and melted, and as nourishment streams upon him, the lower end of the wings begins to swell and grow from the root upwards; and the growth extends under the whole soul – for once the whole was winged. During this process the whole soul is all in a state of ebullition and effervescence ... bubbles up and has a feeling of uneasiness and tickling; but when in like manner the soul is beginning to grow wings ...[34]

> If prolonged, these dreams are apt to produce movements such as struggling, trying to sit up, loud talking and singing.

"He who sees cannot possess the visible unless he is possessed by it, unless he is of it [flesh], unless, by principle, according to what is required by the articulation of the look with the things, he is one of the visibles, capable, by a singular reversal, of seeing them – he who is one of them."[35]

The patient also tries to raise his head from the pillow or a limb from the table.

From Marcel Duchamp, *Manual of Instructions for Étant Donnés: 1° La chute d'eau 2° Le gaz d'éclairage* …1994/Vis*Art Copyright Inc.

From *Duchamp*, 1994/Vis*Art Copyright Inc.

... the beauty of the beloved meets her eye and she receives the sensible warm motion of particles which flow towards her, therefore called emotion, and is refreshed and warmed by them, and then she ceases from her pain with joy. But when she is parted from her beloved and her moisture fails, then the orifices of the passage out of which the wing shoots dry up and close, and intercept the germ of the wing; which, being shut up with the emotion, throbbing as with the pulsations of an artery, pricks the aperture which is nearest, until at length the entire soul is pierced and maddened and pained, and at the recollection of beauty is again delighted ...

And this state, my dear imaginary youth to whom I am talking, is by men called love, and among the gods has a name at which you may be inclined to mock[36] ... Desire ...

> The patient is fully relaxed and there is no need to strap him down, except during induction. The patient's colour is pink and there is a complete loss of consciousness, sight, feeling, and pain. Muscular depression prevents any movement of the limbs or response to stimuli; the muscles become paralyzed.

The patient is in a state of rest, an inward expansion. A fusion has now taken place between the bachelor and the mechanical bride, and between the spectator/patient and his reflection.

> When the anaesthetist gives the signal to move, theatre porters move the patient, making sure that the anaesthetic machine does not become separated from the patient.

The spectator is gently transferred to the operating table, a horizontal batten.

OPERATING TABLE AND ROOM

The merging of the reflection and the spectator about the operating table involves a physical operation.

General rules for positioning the patient on the table (or, points of impact when fixing the nude in place):

1. The patient should always be covered, as far as possible, particularly at the end of the operation.
2. An unconscious patient is insensitive to pain. For this reason, constant care is needed to avoid injury during movement and positioning. Joints may be injured if they are forced and nerves may be damaged from pressure or stretching. Pressure on the nerve at the outer side of the knee or the nerve that winds round the back of the arm (radial) can cause paralysis of the ankle or wrist joints (foot drop or wrist drop). Stretching the nerve can cause paralysis of the arm or shoulder, a risk much increased when the arm is put at right angles to the body in the "head down" position.
The skin should be protected from heat and abrasion. When diathermy is being used no skin should come into contact with the metal of the operating table, since burns may result from the diathermy current, shorting to the earth through the table.

Ether is flammable when mixed with air, and explosive when mixed with oxygen. An over-

From Duchamp, *Manual of Instructions*, 1994/Vis*Art Copyright Inc.

253

From Duchamp, *Manual of Instructions*, 1994/Vis*Art Copyright Inc.

heated electrical connection will burst into flames in an oxygen enriched atmosphere ... Ether is two and a half times heavier than air. Therefore in a room it tends to flow toward the floor ...

Precautions are taken in all operating suites to ensure static electric charges pass immediately to the earth and are rendered harmless. The floors of the anaesthetic room and operating theatres should be anti-static. Sometimes water is poured on the floor. Soaking the anaesthetic hoses in water before use will raise humidity sufficiently to avoid the generation of static charges.

... and to remain for sometime, unmixed with the general atmosphere ... "Radiation of influence from celestial bodies is no longer believed to be distinct and superior to the elemental world. Instead a new 'ethereal matter' is determined as the 'insensible effluvia' radiating from all sorts of objects."[37] The medium

From Duchamp, *Manual of Instructions*, 1994/Vis*Art Copyright Inc.

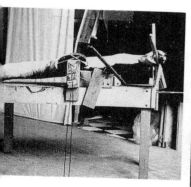

of ether has finally been brought to the elementary world ...

Stage Three: Surgical

The onset of this stage is marked by regular, deeper, and more audible automatic respiration. Automatic respiration is more easily appreciated from experience than from description. Breathing becomes quite rhythmic and somewhat rapid, proceeding with the regularity of a pump driven by mechanical power.

... as we undertake a crossing from the eye[2] to the eye[3] ...

"If only one could taste one's void, if one could really rest in one's void, and this void were not a certain kind of being but not quite death either. It is so hard to no longer exist, to no longer be in something ..."[38]

Should the automatic quality cease, owing possibly to a slight overdose of anaesthesia, lengthening pauses will be noticed between successive expirations and inspirations. These are equal in magnitude and at a rate of 12–16 per minute. There is a progressive loss of eyelid reflex. If this state is achieved as slowly and deliberately as our theory insists, we need never concern ourselves with depth.

" ... the real pain is to feel one's thoughts shift within oneself. But thought as a fixed point is certainly not painful. I have reached the point where I am no longer in touch with

From Duchamp, *Manual of Instructions*, 1994/Vis*Art Copyright Inc.

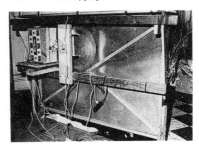

From Duchamp, *Manual of Instructions*, 1994/Vis*Art Copyright Inc.

From Duchamp, *Manual of Instructions*, 1994/Vis*Art Copyright Inc.

life, but still have all the appetites and the insistent titillation of being. I have only one occupation left: to remake myself."[39]

... presence gently slips across the surface. An illuminated perception of the situation ... seeing, is a continuous condition ... a duration ...

The patient may moan but never with articulated sounds, only groans and flinches. The patient is incapable of being influenced by external impressions. Muscles are completely relaxed and will rest in any position in which they are supported. By the end of this stage the patient is devoid of any facial expression and the lower jaw has a tendency to droop, as in a state of helpless drunkenness.

Fermentation, whether natural or artificial, proceeds from the inflow of an ethereal spirit or sub-

From *Marcel Duchamp*, 1994/Vis*Art Copyright Inc.

stance related to primitive light, which concurs with implanted spirits of the same essence. From their concurrence arise in water and air universal ferments on which all particular ones depend, and a basic salt of nature is formed ... The fiery ferment can invade all three kingdoms, but there are two others for vegetables and animals, vinous and putrefactive. The acid abounding in them is fixed by the ethereal spirit into oil and attenuate into ardent spirit: when destitute of acid, they lose their ether, so that they are resolved into putridity, and, if any oil remains, it becomes alkali.[40]

Plane One

There is a progressive decrease in the range of excursion of movements of the eye and in the rapidity of these movements. Finally, at the end of this plane, the eye comes to rest in the central position. Mechanical breathing begins and the jaw is not relaxed but the other muscles are.

Perhaps a revelation of the whole is, itself, in a continual process of becoming. The mirror simplifies the passage and traversal of possible and potential perceptions resulting from reversibility. It encourages the simultaneity of reflecting on, and being completely bound to, the three-dimensional world.

Plane Two

The eye is in a central position, and there is complete function of the intercostal muscles and the diaphragm.

Both *The Large Glass* and the *Given* can be regarded as a hinge with a space on each side. In *The Large Glass* the two spaces are vertical in orientation, whereas in the *Given* they are horizontal. In the *Given*, however, there is also a rotation that results in a convergence, transference, and continual reversibility. The mirror/door, as hinge, is the plane where a reflection and a three-dimensional figure coincide.

The spectator (now speculator) and the Bride are now in perceptual rotation in the three-dimensional continuum about the door: the merging of figure and space on an operating table.

The spectator may remain unengaged with the *Given*, as noted earlier, merely acknowledging the appearance of the Door in a plaster wall. However, to register the apparition there must be an illuminated perceptual rotation about the door (understood as a hinge). Remember, this registration occurs within the "stomach region" of the body of the speculator. The speculator now feels the perceptual experience of the *Given*, because the *Given* is experiencing a passage into desire and conceiving in the illuminating light of the continuum.

... Penetrating the barrier, the brick wall,
the hymen ...
Revealing the duration of a moment of ecstacy
in the intertwining of "illuminating gases" and
"falling water" ...
Given: ... the virgin silently passes as a bride ...
Enveloped by the dark, cool void of the womb
desire is now registered within the body ...

She is the natural recipient of all impressions, and is stirred and informed by them, taking different appearances at a given time ... Wherefore, that which is to receive all forms should have no form itself ... Therefore the mother and receptacle of all created and visible and sensible things is not to be termed either earth or air or fire or water ... but an invisible and still undetermined thing ... which, while in a mysterious way it partakes

Assembled by author.

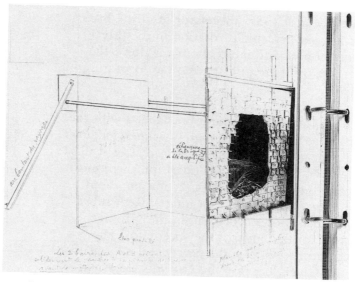

From Duchamp, *Manual of Instructions*, 1994/Vis*Art Copyright Inc.

of the intelligible, is yet most incomprehensible. [Of this] receptacle and nurse of all generation ... we have only this dreamlike sense, being unable to cast off sleep and determine the truth about it [because it exists] only as an ever-fleeting shadow even though out of it all tangible things are generated.[41]

If the vision and the body are tangled up in one another; if, correlatively, the surface of the visible, is doubled up over its whole extension with an invisible reverse; and if finally, in our flesh as in the flesh of things, the actual, empirical, ontic visible, by a sort of folding back, invagination, or padding, exhibits a visibility, a possibility that is not the shadow of the actual but is its principle.[42]

Ether is a liquid which gives off vapour at room temperature. This is achieved by the pas-

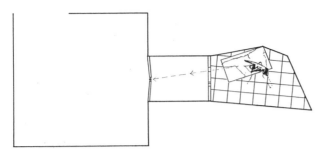

YOU ARE HERE: Plan of "Given" in the Philadelphia Museum of Art.

sage of air or oxygen through the liquid enclosed in a glass jar or metal container, known as a vaporizer ... The "concept" of a material ether was developed when it was demonstrated that the velocity of light was seven hundred thousand times that of sound, so it became necessary to regard the ether as a fluid which was seven hundred thousand times more rigid than air but with only one seven hundred thousandth of the density of air[43] ... Since it is highly explosive it constitutes a danger if any naked light, electric sparks or open flame are present.

Glass is placed between lights and the Nude figure for protection from the heat; from Duchamp, *Manual of Instructions*, 1994/Vis*Art Copyright Inc.

Plane Three

A progressive decrease in thoracic respiration commences, ultimately leaving only the
diaphragm to carry on the respiration at the
commencement of ...

Attraction exists in space, as with gravity,
establishing the confines of the shape of a figure. Distraction exists in the continuum.

– *A Total of One Ounce of Ether Has Been Inhaled* –

This perceptual awakening is what separates
our familiar reality from an actual reality.
Flesh is the continuity of the world and the
appearing of its cohesion – a cohesion that is
continually forming through a rotation, resulting in a left/right and inside/outside reversal.
Beginning and end are left dangling, and the
fourth-dimensional figure resides in the passage from one state to another, in a field of
distraction.

An infinite state of gestation, not in-finite
state.

If the three-dimensional figure determines its
finite state through restrictive habitual perceptions, perhaps the fourth dimension is a horizon of duration where the field of perception
can be opened.

One might actually "see," without appeal to
memory or the recognizable ... Perhaps this is
the actual space of consciousness ... A transmutation of appearance to apparition ...
Awakened perception necessitates a continu-

ously changing consciousness ... The beauty
of aesthetic indifference allows one "to reach
the impossibility of sufficient *visual* memory,
to transfer from one like object to another the
memory imprint.[44]

Plane Four

At the end of this plane and at the commencement of stage four, respiration effort
is absent.

[In] a work of art the umbilical cord linking it
with the totality of our concerns has not yet been
severed, the blood of the mystery still circulates:
the ends of the blood vessels vanish into the surrounding night, and return from it full of dark
fluid ... it offers a certain recipe for reality, posits a
certain special kind of substance. The substance of
that reality exists in a state of constant fermentation, germination, and hidden life. It contains no
dead, hard, limited objects. Everything diffuses
beyond its borders, remains in a given shape only
momentarily, leaving this shape behind at the first
opportunity. A principle of sorts appears in the
habits, the modes of existence of this reality: a universal masquerade. Reality takes on certain shapes
merely for the sake of appearance, as a joke or
form of play ... shape does not penetrate essence,
it is only a role adopted for the moment, an outer
skin soon to be shed. A certain extreme monism of
the life substance is assumed here, for which specific objects are nothing more than masks. The life
of the substance consists in the assuming and con-
suming of numberless masks. This migration of
forms is the essence of life. Thus an all pervading
aura of irony emanates from this substance ...
What the meaning of this universal disillusioning

reality is I am not able to say. I maintain only that it would be unbearable unless it was compensated for in some other dimension. In some sense we derive a profound satisfaction from the loosening of the web of reality: we feel an interest in witnessing the bankruptcy of reality ... The róle of art is to be a probe sunk into the nameless. The artist is an apparatus for registering processes in that deep stratum where value is formed ...[45]

Arousal can cause one to return to the previous degree of etherization.

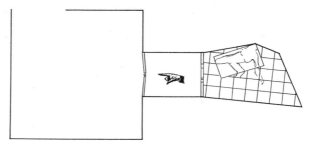

YOU ARE HERE: Plan of "Given" in the Philadelphia Museum of Art.

A distension, release, swelling out and dilation by pressure from within ... The conception of an illuminated perception ...

Duration is the speed of gestation and perhaps speed is the situation of perception.

The mould gives birth ... "The road will begin in the chief of the 5 nudes, and will not end in the headlight child."[46]

"The sage is by definition one who has captured the structural network on which appearances move, the deep grate on which phenomena dance, one who has an all-encompassing vision, even if crawling within the hard stuff of things."[47]

If *The Large Glass* remains a two-dimensional construction or sectional cut ... then perhaps the *Given* has offered a glimpse or "spatial section" of a "reflection" ... Attraction and Desire reveal the possibilities of physically releasing figure and space from pre-determined constraints established by familiarity.

The *Given* is in gestation – an apparition of a direction yet to be realized. Vision and visible are crossed in an anamorphic operation.

Ether inhalation is Given with plenty of air in abdominal surgery for it delays the onset of the next uterine contraction and thus prolongs labour.

Stage Four: Respiratory Paralysis

The patient's respiration is irregular, feeble and laborious, and only artificial respiration and oxygen will restore the patient to consciousness. This stage produces deep narcosis through over-dosage and there is a real danger of death. The heart still beats but the patient stays alive only by artificial respiration. The patient is motionless and flaccid. This stage immediately precedes death and is to be avoided. Death has been observed only in animals.

"[F]or the first time I appear to myself completely turned inside out under my own eyes

... the body ... floats in its Being with another life, of making itself the outside of its inside and the inside of its outside."[48]

Speculation *made inside* ... The flame of becoming dies only when the gas is shut off.

Establish a society
in which the individual
has to pay for the air he breathes
(air meters; imprisonment
and rarefied air, in
case of non-payment
simple asphyxiation if
necessary (**cut off the air**)

on condition that (?)
Ordinary brick satiates the knot.
to be tired of

From Duchamp, *The Bride Stripped Bare,*
1994/Vis*Art Copyright Inc.

If discontinued
1 to 2 minutes, patient returns to third stage
3 to 4 minutes, patient returns to second stage
5 minutes, patient returns to first stage and finally 10 to 15 minutes intoxication/ exhilaration entirely subsides

... turning to the conscious space I left ... or was that right?

RECOVERY ROOM

The patient is usually kept here until the effects of anaesthesia have passed. There should be continuous observation during the recovery. This room should be located between the sterile and unsterile sections of the operating suite.

The patient progresses through recovery in three phases:

1. reception and positioning
2. observation
3. return to the ward

For normal recovery, progress can be said to occur if there is a progressive return of consciousness, pulse, and respiration rates.

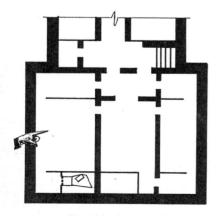

YOU ARE HERE: Plan of the Arensberg Collection in the Philadelphia Museum of Art.

266

There is also a steady return to the pre-operative figure.

"This is possible as soon as we no longer make belongingness to one same 'consciousness' the primordial definition of sensibility, and as soon as we rather understand it as the return of the visible upon itself, a carnal adherence of the sentient to the sensed and of the sensed to the sentient ..."[49]

> Recovery of consciousness is complete when response to the spoken word is shown by re-opening the eyes and attempting to speak. Speed of recovery depends on many factors, and can vary from a few minutes to half an hour or more. Rapid recovery should occur after short operations and those in which the anaesthetist has maintained a light plane of anaesthesia with inhalation agents. More prolonged recovery may follow very long procedures on debilitated patients.

" ... for, as overlapping and fission, identity and difference, it brings to birth a ray of natural light that illuminates all flesh and not only my own."[50]

From *Marcel Duchamp*, 1994/Vis*Art Copyright Inc.

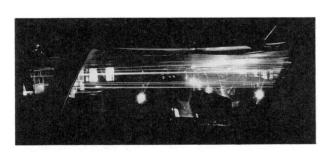

Waiting for a green light.

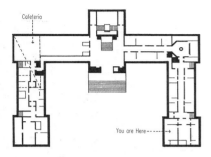

The cafeteria is located on the basement level of the Philadelphia Museum of Art.

... oh! ... the insistence of this pain in my stomach. There must be a cafeteria in this museum somewhere? ...

If he talks in an excited way, a word or two may calm him.

Marcel Duchamp once said that the life of a work of art is approximately twenty years.

RETURN TO THE WARD

Patient is ready to return to the ward when:

1. Consciousness has returned and patient has shown response to pain and the spoken word.
2. Blood pressure, pulse, and respiration rates are stable, indicating absence of complications.
3. The wound dressing is dry, drainage tubes are in place, and suction is operating correctly.

Next time you go on a trip, make sure you wash the windshield and check the gas ... and keep your eyes on the illuminations of the "headlight child."

Coasting.

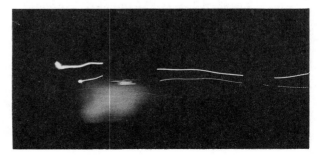

LAST WORD

You are probably now too frightened to approach an anaesthetic machine. If so, this pamphlet has not failed in its objective, for a knowledge of the possible dangers associated with anaesthesia is essential to ensure a safe administration. The emergencies of the subject have been treated with emphasis, but none should arise in a thoughtful and careful administration. Remember the best way to get out of trouble is to avoid it, and at all times observe safety first. Common sense is the basis of good anaesthesia, but then so is it the foundation of many things.

And finally, remember .... At most speeds, in a rear view mirror "objects in mirror are closer, [then] they appear."[51]

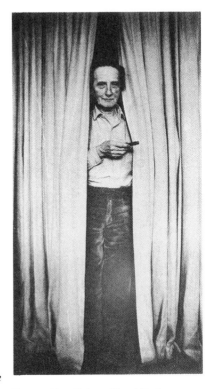

The M.D. himself; from *Marcel Duchamp*, 1994/Vis*Art Copyright Inc.

NOTES

1 In 1976, Marcel Duchamp published *The Bride Stripped Bare by Her Bachelors, Even: A Typographic Version of the Green Box*, tr. R. Hamilton (New York: Jaap Rietman).

2 Marcel Duchamp, *Manual of Instructions for Étant Donnés: 1° la chute d'eau, 2° le gas d'éclairage* ... (Philadelphia: Philadelphia Museum of Art 1987).

3 The verb "speculate" derives from *speculum*, Latin for "mirror."

4 Of initial importance were observations in *Salt Seller: The Writings of Marcel Duchamp (Marchand du Sel)*, ed. M. Duchamp, M. Sanouillet, and E. Peterson (New York: Oxford University Press 1973).

5 Jerzy Rozenberg, "Ce n'est pas la colle," *Dichotomy* (1986): 91.

6 Antonin Artaud, "Description of a Physical State from Umbilicus Limbo," *Selected Writings*, tr. H. Weaver, ed. S. Sontag (New York: Farrar, Straus & Giroux 1976), 64–5.

7 *Étant Donnés 1° la chute d'eau; 2° le gaz d'éclairage: Reflections on a New Work by Marcel Duchamp*, ed. A. d'Harnoncourt and W. Hopps (Philadelphia: Philadelphia Museum of Art 1987).

8 Maurice Merleau-Ponty, "The Intertwining: The Chiasm," *The Visible and the Invisible*, tr. A. Lingis, ed. C. Lefort (Evanston, Ill.: Northwestern University Press 1968), 154.

9 Harriett A. Watts, *Chance: A Perspective on Dada*, Studies in the Fine Arts (Ann Arbor, Mich.: UMI Research Press 1980), 33.

10 Duchamp, *The Bride Stripped Bare*.

11 "An-aesthetic" comes from the Greek root *an-*, "without," and *aesthetic*, "pertaining to the appreciation or criticism of taste or the beautiful; Having or showing refined taste, in accordance with good taste; The science of the conditions of sensuous perception; The philosophy of taste, or the perception of the beautiful." See *The Oxford Universal Dictionary on Historical Principles* (Oxford: Oxford University Press, 1955).

12 "Anaesthesia" comes from the Greek root *an-*, "without," and *aisthesis*, "feeling." General anaesthesia is a medical procedure resulting in the total loss of sensation, especially tactile sensitivity. It is an artifically induced unconsciousness causing general insensitivity to pain, leaving a patient devoid of feeling.

13 *Ether* comes from the Greek root *aither*, referring to "the upper air, clear sky" and also to "burn brightly." Therefore, the term was adopted, imaginatively, by science for both the liquid and the

anaesthetic ... In 1911, Marcel Duchamp's sister Suzanne married a pharmacist from Rouen.

14 William Webster, *The Science and Art of Anaesthesia* (St Louis, Missouri: Mosley 1924).

15 Robert Grosseteste (1175–1253), "Metaphysics of Light," quoted in "Thirteenth-Century Optics," ed. E.J. Dijksterhuis, tr. C. Dikshoorn *The Mechanization of the World Picture* (Princeton, N.J.: Princeton University Press 1986), 150–2.

16 Erwin Panofsky, *Perspective as Symbolic Form*, tr. C.S. Wood (New York: Zone Books 1991), 1, 4.

17 Ibid., 18.

18 Katherine Dreier and Matta Echaurren, *Duchamp's Glass: An Analytical Reflection* (New York: Société Anonyme 1944).

19 "Anamorphosis" comes from the Greek root *ana-*, "back," indicating a return towards *morph*, "form."

20 All *Givens* are appropriated from Marcel Duchamp's notes in *Salt Seller*, 86–101.

21 Newton's theories in *A History of Magic and Experimental Science*, vol. 8, "The Seventeenth Century," ed. L. Thorndike (New York: Columbia University Press 1958).

22 Vitellion described catoptics in 1270; see *Anamorphic Art*, ed. J. Baltruaitis, tr. W.J. Strachan (New York: Harry Abrams 1977).

23 From *ek*, "out of," and *typos*, "imprint."

24 Duchamp, *The Bride Stripped Bare*.

25 Theories of Huygens and Newton's *Principia* (1713), in *History of Magic*.

26 Octavio Paz, *Marcel Duchamp, Appearance Stripped Bare*, tr. R. Phillips and D. Gardner (New York: Seaver Books 1981), 116.

27 All *Givens* are appropriated from Marcel Duchamp's notes in *Salt Seller*, 86–101.

28 Merleau-Ponty, "Intertwining," 137–9.

29 Newton (1665), see *History of Magic*.

30 Luis Buñuel, from the film *Un Chien Andalou.*

31 Description of a painting by André Masson in Artaud, "Description of a Physical State," 67.

32 Newton, *History of Magic.*

33 Plato, "Phaedrus," in *Philosophies of Art and Beauty: Selected Readings in Aesthetics from Plato to Heidegger,* ed. A. Hofstadter (Chicago: University of Chicago Press 1964), 61–2.

34 Ibid., 62.

35 Merleau-Ponty, "Intertwining," 134–5.

36 Plato, "Phaedrus," 62–3.

37 Beliefs at the end of the seventeenth century; see *History of Magic.*

38 Artaud, "The Nerve Meter 1925," *Selected Readings,* 84.

39 Ibid., 84.

40 Definition of chemistry (1688) by Justus Vesti in *History of Magic.*

41 "Mother" in Greek is also synonymous with "womb." These lines are quoted from Plato's *Timaeus* in Ivan Illich, *H₂O and the Waters of Forgetfulness* (Berkeley, Cal.: Heyday Books 1985), 17.

42 Merleau-Ponty, "Intertwining," 152.

43 Attributed to Olaus Roemer (1676); see *History of Magic.*

44 Duchamp, *The Bride Stripped Bare*

45 Bruno Shulz, *Letters and Drawings, with Selected Prose,* tr. W. Arndt, ed. J. Ficowski (New York: Harper & Row 1987), 112–14.

46 Duchamp, *The Bride Stripped Bare.*

47 A. B. Oliva, *Vita di Marcel Duchamp,* tr. L. Gane and T. Eijndhaven (Rome: Marani 1976), 45.

48 Merleau-Ponty, "Intertwining," 143.

49 Ibid., 142.

50 Ibid., 142.

51 Adapted from the label on the rear view mirror of a car.

About the Authors

Jean-François Bédard

Jean-François Bédard is currently curatorial assistant in the Department of Prints and Drawings at the Canadian Centre for Architecture (CCA) in Montreal. He received a bachelor of architecture degree from McGill University in 1987 and a master's degree in architectural history and theory from the same institution in 1992. Mr Bédard is an editor for the magazine *Architecture Québec*. He recently curated a retrospective exhibition of the work of the American architect Peter Eisenman, "Cities of Artificial Excavation: The Work of Peter Eisenman, 1978–1988," for the CCA.

Indra Kagis McEwen

Indra Kagis McEwen holds an Honours B.A. in English and philosophy from Queen's University, a professional degree in architecture from McGill University, and a master's degree in architectural history and theory, also from McGill. She is the author of *Socrates' Ancestor: An Essay on Architectural Beginnings* (MIT Press 1993) and of a translation of Claude Perrault, *Ordonnance des cinq espèces de colonnes* (Paris 1683), entitled *Ordonnance for the Five kinds of Columns*, with an introduction by A. Pérez-Gómez (Getty Center 1993). She currently teaches architectural history at the National Theatre School of Canada in Montreal and is engaged in work on Vitruvius.

Helmut Klassen

Helmut Klassen is a graduate of Carleton University (B.Arch.) and McGill University (M.Arch. History and Theory of Architecture). He is engaged in architectural practice and has taught both design and history/theory courses, most recently as visiting professor at Middle East Technical University in Ankara, Turkey.

Donald Kunze

Donald Kunze is currently associate professor of architecture at Pennsylvania State University. He was born in North Carolina in 1947 and received his bachelor of architecture degree from North Carolina State University in 1970 and a Ph.D. from Pennsylvania State University in 1983. Dr Kunze is the author of a book on Giambattista Vico and has lectured at Harvard University, the University of the Arts in Philadelphia, the University of Minnesota, the State University of New York at Buffalo, and the Rhode Island School of Design. He is currently working on projects about kynicism (dog architecture) and architecture as cuisine.

Graham Livesey

Graham Livesey is currently assistant professor of architecture at the University of Calgary, teaching architectural design and history. Born in Vancouver, he received a bachelor of architecture degree in 1984 from McGill University and a master's degree in architectural history and theory from the same institution in 1991. He has worked for a number of years in private practice, most notably for Arcop Associates in Montréal and Rick Mather Architects in London, U.K.

Juhani Palasmaa

Juhani Pallasmaa was born in Hämeenlinna, Finland, in 1936. He obtained a master of science degree in architecture from the Helsinki University of Technology in 1966. He has been the principal of Juhani Pallasmaa Architects since 1983 and professor of architecture at the Helsinki University of Technology since 1991. He was "State Artist Professor" from 1983 to 1988, director of the Museum of Finnish Architecture from 1978 to 1983, associate professor at the Haile Selassie I University (Addis Abeba) from 1972 to 1974, director of the exhibitions department of the Museum of Finnish Architecture from 1968 to 1972 and from 1974 to 1983, and rector of the College of Crafts and Design (Helsinki) from 1970 to 1972.

Professor Pallasmaa has been involved in architecture, graphic design, and town planning since 1963. He has designed exhibitions of Finnish architecture, planning, and fine arts that have been shown in more than thirty countries. His design works have been published in numerous exhibition catalogues and publications in Finland and abroad. He has written many articles and lectured in various countries on cultural philosophy and the essence of architecture and fine arts.

Juhani Pallasmaa is member of the Finnish Architects Association, honorary fellow of the AIA, invited member of the International Committee of Architectural Critics, invited full member of the International Academy of Architecture in Moscow, and was the Eero Saarinen Visiting Professor at Yale University in 1993.

Stephen Parcell

Stephen Parcell was born in Toronto in 1954. He is currently associate professor of architecture at the Technical University of Nova Scotia and an external advisor for the graduate program in architectural history and theory at McGill University. He previously taught at Carleton University, after receiving a bachelor of architecture degree from the University of Toronto and a master of architecture degree from the Cranbrook Academy of Art. His research on panoramas is part of a series of representational studies involving other perspectival institutions – natural-history dioramas, stereographic images, and a late Renaissance perspective treatise.

Louise Pelletier

Louise Pelletier graduated from the Laval University School of Architecture in 1987. She completed a master of architecture degree with honours in the history and theory of architecture at McGill University in 1990 and is currently teaching a design studio in the graduate program at that institution. She is also working as a research associate at McGill and has coordinated several public events for the Institut de recherche en histoire de l'architecture (IRHA), which is sponsored by CCA, the Université de Montréal, and McGill University. Recent projects for the Institut include *Architecture, Ethics, and Technology* (McGill-Queen's University Press); an "Architecture and Film" lecture series; and an annotated bibliography on "Anamorphosis and Architectural Representation," to be published in the Fontanus Monograph Series by McGill University Libraries.

Alberto Pérez-Gómez

Alberto Pérez-Gómez was born in Mexico City in 1949. He obtained his undergraduate degree in architecture and engineering in his native city, did postgraduate work at Cornell University, and was awarded a master of arts degree and a Ph.D. by the University of Essex in England. His numerous articles have been published in various architectural magazines. His book *Architecture and the Crisis of Modern Science* (MIT Press, 1983) won the Alice Davis Hitchcock Award in 1984. His latest book, *Polyphilo or the Dark Forest Revisited*, which deals with *Hypnerotomachia Poliphili* (1499), was also published by MIT Press in 1992.

Dr Pérez-Gómez lectures extensively in Europe and North America. He has taught at universities in Mexico City, Houston, Syracuse, and Toronto and at the Architectural Association in London; he was director of the Carleton University School of Architecture from 1983 to 1986. In January 1987, he was appointed Saidye Rosner Bronfman Professor of the History of Architecture at McGill University, where he is currently director of the graduate program in the history and theory of architecture.

Natalija Subotincic

Natalija Subotincic was born in Alliston, Ontario, in 1959. She began her university studies in science, transferring to architecture in 1980. She completerd her undergraduate degree in architecture at Carleton University in 1985 and obtained a master's degree in architectural history and theory from McGill University in 1989. After graduating, she worked as a visiting professor at the College of the Atlantic in Bar Harbour, Maine, in 1989–90, and at the Illinois Institute of Technology in Chicago in 1990–91. She is presently employed as an assistant professor of architecture at the Carleton University School of Architecture, where she teaches technology workshops and history and theory courses and is the coordinator of the first-year design studio. Much of her research over the years has involved both photography and architecture – in particular, the Canadian Industrial Heritage Project, a Canada Council–funded photo documentation of industrial installations across Canada; and a 168-page continuous collage of photographs for Alberto Pérez-Gómez's book *Polyphilo or the Dark Forest Revisited: An Erotic Epiphany of Architecture*, published by MIT Press in 1992. Her most recent project investigates the architecture of the kitchen/dining rooms within the suburban home. She is currently developing this project and preparing an exhibition catalogue entitled *Incarnate Tendencies: An Architecture of Culinary Refuse*.